主编简介

桑百川 对外经济贸易大学国际经济研究院院长、教授、博士生导师，中国商务部国际投资专家委员会特聘专家，国家社科基金重大项目首席专家，全国社科规划办决策咨询点首席专家，国家社科基金评审委员会委员。曾出版《统筹国内发展和对外开放：依据、内容与路径》《开放视角下的中国经济》《外商直接投资下的经济制度变迁》等专著20余部，发表学术论文300余篇，主持30多项国家和省部级课题。十多次获省部级以上学术奖励，获首都劳动奖章，入选教育部新世纪优秀人才，享受国务院特殊津贴。

李计广 对外经济贸易大学国际经济研究院院长助理，经济学博士、研究员、博士生导师，主要研究领域是全球经济治理。曾出版学术专著2部，在CSSCI期刊发表学术论文30余篇，主持国家社科基金项目2项、教育部人文社科项目2项，学术成果获得省部级奖项6项。

国际经济学科前沿研究报告

桑百川　李计广◎主编

人民日报学术文库

人民日报出版社

图书在版编目（CIP）数据

国际经济学科前沿研究报告／桑百川，李计广主编
. —北京：人民日报出版社，2018.5
ISBN 978－7－5115－5400－0

Ⅰ.①国… Ⅱ.①桑… ②李… Ⅲ.①国际经济学—学科
发展—研究报告 Ⅳ.①F11－0

中国版本图书馆 CIP 数据核字（2018）第 072258 号

书　　名：国际经济学科前沿研究报告
作　　者：桑百川　李计广

出 版 人：董　伟
责任编辑：蒋菊平　钱慧春
封面设计：中联学林

出版发行：人民日报出版社
社　　址：北京金台西路 2 号
邮政编码：100733
发行热线：（010）65369509　65369846　65363528　65369512
邮购热线：（010）65369530　65363527
编辑热线：（010）65363486
网　　址：www.peopledailypress.com
经　　销：新华书店
印　　刷：三河市华东印刷有限公司

开　　本：710mm×1000mm　1/16
字　　数：260 千字
印　　张：15
印　　次：2018 年 6 月第 1 版　　2018 年 6 月第 1 次印刷

书　　号：ISBN 978－7－5115－5400－0
定　　价：68.00 元

前　言

《国际经济学科前沿报告》梳理了国际经济学科2014—2015年的权威研究文献,总结了世界经济学科的重要学术成果,为世界经济领域的研究人员提供了一份概要式的参考资料,希望能够以此促进我国国际经济学科的交流与发展。

笔者们收集了2014—2015年发表在国内外重要期刊上的大量文献,并进行了系统回顾、总结和评述,以期能够反映国内外国际经济学科的最新研究进展和研究成果。从2014—2015年出版的顶级期刊和专著中精选了50篇英文文献、30篇中文文献,以及30本英文专著和30本中文专著,并对这些文献进行了简要介绍。本书还整理了2014—2015年国际经济领域的英文文献索引和中文文献索引,相关文献均来自于中英文核心期刊。中英文文献和索引较大程度上反映了世界经济领域的研究热点和研究主题,以期为相关研究人员提供参考。

本书的编写完成离不开报告组成员的积极参与和辛苦劳动。其中,韩翠茹、毛伟杰、林欣、陈寒搜集和整理了大量的中文文献资料,黄漓江、邓寅、王园园收集并翻译了全部的英文文献资料,张彩云撰写了国内外研究综述,李计广、林欣、陈寒完成了编辑和校对工作。在此对报告组成员付出的努力表示衷心的感谢!通过《国际经济学科前沿报告》的编写工作,报告组成员对国际经济领域的最新发展进行了较为系统的梳理,希望凝聚着笔者们共同努力的这本书能够为我国世界经济领域的研究贡献绵薄之力。

由于书稿编写要求和编写者水平的限制,本书只是介绍了国内外国际经济研究动态的部分文献,所选文献难以覆盖该学科的全部内容,书中的观点和评述有待世界经济领域各位同仁的批评。

桑百川

2017 年 10 月 25 日

目　录
CONTENTS

第一章

世界经济学科 2014—2015 年国内外研究综述

第一节　国内研究综述

2014 年至 2015 年世界经济领域国内研究文献的重点主题有九个:利用外资和对外投资、"一带一路"倡议、服务贸易、全球价值链、货物进出口、区域经济一体化、贸易自由化、环境问题、异质性企业理论。

一、货物贸易

货物贸易领域的国内研究主要集中于影响贸易进出口的因素,货物进出口对就业、收入、环境等的影响,出口品国内技术复杂度测算等。戴翔,金碚(2014)从分工演进视角提出了制度质量、融入产品内国际分工程度及其二者交互作用,促进出口技术复杂度提升作用机制的理论假说。[①] 杜运苏(2014)采用 Hausmann 等(2007)的方法,从整体上、不同贸易方式、不同企业性质等方面测算了 2000—2010 年我国出口技术复杂度的发展变化,并构建经济模型分析了出口技术复杂度对我国经济增长的影响。[②] 鲁晓东(2014)通过一个包含技术含量的异质企业贸易模型在理论上廓清了技术升级与企业出口行为间的关系,利用中国工业企业和高度细分的产品数据,将中国出口竞争力这一宏观概念与中国出口企业的微观特征相

---

① 戴翔,金碚. 产品内分工、制度质量与出口技术复杂度.《经济研究》. 2014 年第 7 期。
② 杜运苏. 出口技术复杂度影响我国经济增长的实证研究——基于不同贸易方式和企业性质.《国际贸易问题》. 2014 年第 9 期。

联系,从企业角度研究中国出口竞争力的变迁。[①] 施炳展,邵文波(2014)从质量视角分析了中国企业出口行为及其决定因素。[②] 张川川(2015)使用微观人口数据和贸易数据,估计了中国出口对就业、工资和收入不平等的影响。发现2000—2005年出口增长显著提高了制造业和服务业就业,并且对年轻人、低学历人口、农村户籍人口和女性的就业影响更显著。[③] 吕延方等(2015)基于1992—2010年我国省际面板数据,构建单一或双重门限模型,对进出口贸易影响生产率、收入和环境的基于人均GDP门限特征进行检验。[④] 余淼杰,李晋(2015)基于2002—2006年中国制造业企业面板数据、高度细化的海关数据和行业差异化程度数据,讨论了进口对于差异化行业的企业生产率的促进作用。[⑤] 齐俊妍,王岚(2015)在新贸易理论框架下,从贸易转型和技术升级两个维度对出口国内技术含量演变路径进行了分解,刻画了"生产率门槛"效应对出口国内技术含量的影响机制。[⑥] 魏浩,李晓庆(2015)在对国际贸易商品技术含量进行具体测度的基础上,利用有序样本聚类分析的最优分割法对国际贸易商品进行分类,构建国际贸易商品技术结构的分析框架,测算了2001—2012年中国进口技术结构的变化趋势。[⑦]

二、全球价值链

罗长远,张军(2014)利用OECD/WTO的TiVA数据库对1995年以来中国出口本地附加值比重的走势,以及它与代表性国家的差异进行了深入考察。发现了中国出口的三个特征:从时间维度看,本地附加值比重呈先下行再回升走势,从国际比较看本地附加值比重处于中下游水平,在本地附加值的组成中直接附加值所

---

① 鲁晓东. 技术升级与中国出口竞争力变迁:从微观向宏观的弥合.《世界经济》.2014年第8期。

② 施炳展,邵文波. 中国企业出口产品质量测算及其决定因素——培育出口竞争新优势的微观视角.《管理世界》(月刊).2014年第9期。

③ 张川川. 出口对就业、工资和收入不平等的影响——基于微观数据的证据.《经济学》(季刊).2015年7月第4期。

④ 吕延方,王冬,陈树文. 进出口贸易对生产率、收入、环境的门限效应——基于1992—2010年我国省际人均GDP的非线性面板模型.《经济学》(季刊).2015年1月第2期。

⑤ 余淼杰,李晋. 进口类型、行业差异化程度与企业生产率提升.《经济研究》.2015年第8期。

⑥ 齐俊妍,王岚. 贸易转型、技术升级和中国出口品国内完全技术含量演进.《世界经济》.2015年第3期。

⑦ 魏浩,李晓庆. 中国进口贸易的技术结构及其影响因素研究.《世界经济》.2015年第8期。

占的比重偏低。① 余娟娟(2014)从理论和实证的双重层面检验了全球价值链分工模式下中国出口技术结构的演进机理及路径。② 刘维林等(2014)提出了基于产品与功能双重嵌入结构的全球价值链嵌入水平测算框架,并从理论上论证了全球价值链嵌入程度、嵌入结构与价值来源对出口技术复杂度的影响及其两面性,进而采用二次优化算法对区分加工贸易与一般贸易的非竞争型投入产出表进行估算,得出用以反映全球价值链嵌入程度的各项国外附加值率指标。③ 程大中(2014)在双边 HOV 基本框架下同时引入要素生产率(TFP)与综合贸易成本(CTC)的跨国差异,并基于"世界投入—产出数据"(WIOD),多角度评估了在全球价值链(GVCs)分工背景下中国增加值贸易(TiVA)隐含的净要素含量流向扭曲程度。④ 夏明,张红霞(2015)剖析了贸易增加值度量中存在的问题以及概念之间的关系,指出增加值贸易和贸易增加值分析路径的差异。⑤ 刘仕国(2015)提出要利用全球价值链来促进中国的产业升级。⑥ 刘琳(2015)提出了参与全球价值链、制度质量以及二者的相互作用对出口品技术含量影响的内在理论机制。⑦ 卫瑞等(2015)基于世界投入产出数据库,采用 MRIO 模型测算了 1995—2009 年中国增加值出口的变动趋势,并采用结构分析方法分析了九种因素对中国增加值出口变化的影响。⑧ 张明之,梁洪基(2015)认为后危机时代全球生产体系下产业链结构出现了新的发展趋势,第三次工业革命、发达国家的"再工业化"与中国经济发展方式转变有可能导致全球要素市场配置方式与生产体系的革命性变化,引发全球财富的流动。作为"世界工厂",中国民族资本可以积极参与先进制造业等现代产业体系的全球分工,深度融入代表先进技术水平的全球生产体系,争取在一

---

① 罗长远,张军. 附加值贸易:基于中国的实证分析.《经济研究》.2014 年第 6 期。

② 余娟娟. 全球价值链分工下中国出口技术结构的演进机理与路径.《产业经济研究》.2014 年第 6 期。

③ 刘维林,李兰冰,刘玉海. 全球价值链嵌入对中国出口技术复杂度的影响.《中国工业经济》.2014 年 6 月第 6 期。

④ 程大中. 中国增加值贸易隐含的要素流向扭曲程度分析.《经济研究》.2014 年第 9 期。

⑤ 夏明,张红霞. 跨国生产、贸易增加值与增加值率的变化——基于投入产出框架对增加值率的理论解析.《管理世界》(月刊).2015 年第 2 期。

⑥ 刘仕国,吴海英,马涛,张磊,彭莉,于建勋. 利用全球价值链促进产业升级.《国际经济评论》.2015 年第 1 期。

⑦ 刘琳. 全球价值链、制度质量与出口品技术含量——基于跨国层面的实证分析.《国际贸易问题》.2015 年第 10 期。

⑧ 卫瑞,张文城,张少军. 全球价值链视角下中国增加值出口及其影响因素.《数量经济技术经济研究》.2015 年第 7 期。

些重要产业领域,实现由一般加工制造环节的竞争优势升级为对关键制造环节和研发等高端环节的控制。[1] 程大中(2015)通过跨国投入—产出分析从中间品关联、增加值关联、投入—产出关联三个角度综合评估了中国参与全球价值链分工的程度及演变趋势,发现中国以外国增加值比重衡量与世界的关联程度趋于上升,且高于以进口中间品比重衡量的程度。[2]

三、异质性企业贸易的研究

席艳乐,胡强(2014)在企业异质性理论的框架下,采用中国海关数据库2000—2006年高度细分的进出口数据,从不同维度出发,全面分析了中间品进口对企业出口绩效的影响。[3] 蒋灵多,陈勇兵(2015)采用2000—2006年中国企业出口数据,构建离散时间生存分析模型探讨了多产品出口企业内异质产品的出口持续时间问题。发现中国多产品出口企业普遍存在,且其企业—产品的出口持续时间较短。[4] 吕越等(2015)采用四种方法测算了企业在全球价值链中嵌入程度,考察效率和融资约束对企业参与全球价值链的影响。[5] 张军,陈磊(2015)通过引入马氏距离法测度了文化的异质性。[6]

四、服务贸易

屠新泉,莫慧萍(2014)研究了 TISA 谈判的现状以及 TISA 谈判与中国的关系。[7] 陈景华(2014)将异质性企业贸易理论的研究对象扩展到服务领域,利用服务业行业面板数据对异质性企业贸易理论对服务企业的适用性进行验证,结果表明无论是全要素生产率还是劳动生产率都显示出与服务贸易出口规模的正相关

---

① 张明之,梁洪基.全球价值链重构中的产业控制力——基于世界财富分配权控制方式变迁的视角.《世界经济与政治论坛》.2015 年 1 月第 1 期。

② 程大中.中国参与全球价值链分工的程度及演变趋势——基于跨国投入—产出分析.《经济研究》.2015 年第 9 期。

③ 席艳乐,胡强.企业异质性、中间品进口与出口绩效——基于中国企业微观数据的实证研究.《产业经济研究》.2014 年第 5 期。

④ 蒋灵多,陈勇兵.出口企业的产品异质性与出口持续时间.《世界经济》.2015 年第 7 期。

⑤ 吕越,罗伟,刘斌.异质性企业与全球价值链嵌入:基于效率和融资的视角.《世界经济》.2015 年第 8 期。

⑥ 张军,陈磊.中国出口贸易文化异质性效应研究——来自主要贸易伙伴国的经验证据.《财贸经济》.2015 年第 7 期。

⑦ 屠新泉,莫慧萍.服务贸易自由化的新选项:TISA 谈判的现状及其与中国的关系.《国际贸易》.2014 年第 4 期。

关系。① 袁志刚,饶璨(2014)运用投入产出模型分析了生产服务业对我国各产业部门生产的投入变迁,采用结构分析剖析了中国生产服务业发展的主要动因,进而考察了全球化对中国生产服务业发展的塑造。② 姚占琪等(2014)分析了全球价值链背景下中国服务业的发展战略及重点领域。③ 阚大学,吕连菊(2014)利用1992—2011 年中国与 31 个国家(地区)的双边服务贸易的面板数据实证研究了中国服务贸易的本地市场效应。④ 李晓峰,姚传高(2014)运用对称显示性比较优势指数(SRCA)对中国、印度服务贸易国际竞争优势进行比较研究,发现中国服务贸易总量大,但服务贸易呈现逆差,具有逐年增大的趋势。印度服务贸易总量虽不及中国,但服务贸易却呈现顺差逐年增大的趋势。⑤ 张宏等(2015)在"JK 模型"的基础上,从需求、比较优势、规模经济和技术进步等角度,对提升生产性服务贸易竞争力的路径进行了系统分析,提出了我国参与国际分工,提升生产性服务贸易竞争力可行性的建议。⑥ 周大鹏(2015)定量测算了进口服务中间投入对制造业全球价值链分工地位的影响,发现进口服务中间投入确实对我国出口复杂度具有积极影响,而且知识与技术需求量高的制造业所受的影响最为显著。⑦ 黄建忠,占芬(2015)系统梳理和分析了区域服务贸易安排的"GATS－"条款的主要特点、存在原因以及潜在的危害,为区域服务贸易合作的发展提供了参考视角。⑧ 王厚双等(2015)采用 WTO 和 OECD 联合发布的 TiVA 统计数据,选定 2009 年服务贸易前六名的国家和金砖四国,测算了这些国家 1995—2009 年的服务业整体和分行业的"全球价值链地位(GVC-Position)"和"全球价值链参与度(GVC-Participa-

---

① 陈景华. 企业异质性视角下中国服务贸易出口的影响因素——基于服务业行业面板数据的实证检验.《世界经济研究》. 2014 年第 11 期。

② 袁志刚,饶璨. 全球化与中国生产服务业发展——基于全球投入产出模型的研究.《管理世界》(双月刊). 2014 年第 3 期。

③ 姚占琪. 全球价值链背景下中国服务业的发展战略及重点领域.《国际贸易》. 2014 年第 7 期。

④ 阚大学,吕连菊. 中国服务贸易的本地市场效应研究——基于中国与 31 个国家(地区)的双边贸易面板数据.《财经研究》. 2014 年第 10 期。

⑤ 李晓峰,姚传高. 中印服务贸易竞争优势比较及影响因素的实证研究.《学术研究》. 2014 年第 9 期。

⑥ 张宏,叶丽,杜学知. 国际分工演变对提升中国生产性服务贸易竞争力的影响.《亚太经济》. 2015 年第 5 期。

⑦ 周大鹏. 进口服务中间投入对我国制造业全球价值链分工地位的影响研究.《世界经济研究》. 2015 年第 8 期。

⑧ 黄建忠,占芬. 区域服务贸易协定中的"GATS－"条款研究.《国际商务研究》. 2015 年 1 月. 总第 36 卷第 201 期。

tion)"指数,来分析对比中国与其他九国的服务业在全球价值链分工中的地位和参与程度。[1] 王恕立等(2015)将环境因素纳入生产率研究体系,引入考虑"坏"产出的 Malmquist-Luenberger 指数法分别测算了中国 2000—2012 年 31 个省市和2004—2012 年服务业细分行业的服务业全要素生产率(TFP)变动情况,同时与未考虑环境因素的服务业 TFP 区域和行业差异进行了比较分析。[2]

五、FDI 和 OFDI

国内对外直接投资领域的文献主要集中于研究我国 OFDI 的影响因素、区位选择,我国 OFDI 对企业创新能力和出口的影响等。董有德,孟醒(2014)利用我国各省分价值链统计的 OFDI 存量数据检验了我国对外直接投资对国内企业创新能力的影响。[3] 杜江,宋跃刚(2014)通过运用动态面板数据的系统 GMM 方法,实证分析了制度距离对我国 OFDI 区位选择的非对称效应以及要素禀赋对我国 OFDI 区位选择影响的差异性。结果发现对于全样本国家,制度距离对我国 OFDI 是负效应。[4] 陈景华(2014)根据中国 2003—2011 年对外直接投资业绩指南的省际数据,采用 Daguma(1997)的方法测算了中国 OFDI 来源的地区差异及演变态势,并利用中国省际面板数据实证检验影响 OFDI 的因素。[5] 毛其淋,许家云(2014)利用高度细化的工业企业数据库和海关贸易数据从微观层面研究了对外直接投资对企业出口的影响,发现对外直接投资不仅显著提高了企业出口占销售的比例,还提高了企业出口的概率。[6] 王永钦等(2014)以中国 2002—2011 年在全球范围内进行的 842 笔对外直接投资作为样本,研究了东道国的话语权与问责制、政治稳定与杜绝暴力/恐怖主义、政府效率、监管质量、法治水平、腐败控制这六类制度

---

① 王厚双,李艳秀,朱奕绮. 我国服务业在全球价值链分工中的地位研究.《世界经济研究》.2015 年第 8 期。
② 王恕立,藤泽伟,刘军. 中国服务业生产率变动的差异分析——基于区域及行业视角.《经济研究》.2015 年第 8 期。
③ 董有德,孟醒. OFDI、逆向技术溢出与国内企业创新能力——基于我国分价值链数据的检验.《国际贸易问题》.2014 年第 9 期。
④ 杜江,宋跃刚. 制度距离、要素禀赋与我国 OFDI 区位选择偏好——基于动态面板数据模型的实证研究.《世界经济研究》.2014 年第 12 期。
⑤ 陈景华. 中国 OFDI 来源的区域差异分解与影响因素——基于 2003—2011 年省际面板数据的实证研究.《数量经济技术经济研究》.2014 年第 7 期。
⑥ 毛其淋,许家云. 中国对外直接投资促进抑或抑制了企业出口.《数量经济技术经济研究》.2014 年第 9 期。

性因素对中国 ODI 区位选择的影响。[①] 蒋冠宏,蒋殿春(2014)利用数据匹配法为 2005—2007 年 1498 家有对外直接投资的工业企业找到可供比较的对照组,运用倍差法实证检验了企业对外直接投资的"出口效应",证实了中国企业对外直接投资总体上是促进了出口。[②] 王碧珺等(2015)通过采用浙江省制造业生产和对外直接投资的企业层面数据,构造了包括内源资金约束、外援资金约束、投资机会等在内的融资约束综合指标,考察了融资约束对中国民营企业海外直接投资决策的影响。发现融资约束一方面抑制了中国民营企业对外直接投资的可能性,另一方面对民营企业海外直接投资规模的扩张也有不利影响。[③]潘镇,金中坤(2015)将政治因素纳入制度分析框架,考察了双边政治关系和东道国制度风险影响中国对外直接投资的机制和效应。[④]

外商直接投资领域,杨振兵(2014)通过对中国工业 22 个行业 FDI 根植性及其影响因素的研究,发现 FDI 的行业根植性相对稳定,并不会迅速迁移。国家政策是使得一些 FDI 根植性在 2007 年出现拐点的最大原因。[⑤] 随洪光,刘廷华(2014)利用 PCA 方法测算主要发展中引资国的经济增长质量,采用静态面板和系统 GMM 方法考察了 FDI 的作用及政府的影响。研究发现亚太、非洲和拉美地区的增长质量基本呈上升趋势,FDI 显著提升了东道国的经济增长质量。[⑥] 计志英,毛杰,赖小峰(2015)通过在 Cobb-Douglas 生产函数基础上发展关于环境污染与外商直接投资、环境规制和产出水平之间关系的理论模型,并利用我国 1999—2012 年 30 个省级面板数据证明了 FDI 规模对我国环境污染的影响效应,结果表明外商直接投资与我国环境污染呈"倒 U"形关系,符合环境库兹涅茨曲线。[⑦] 蔡洪波等(2015)将服务业细分行业的外资数据匹配至中国城乡移民调查数据中的

---

① 王永钦,杜巨澜,王凯. 中国对外直接投资区位选择的决定因素:制度、税负和资源禀赋.《经济研究》. 2014 年第 12 期。

② 蒋冠宏,蒋殿春. 中国企业对外直接投资的"出口效应".《经济研究》. 2014 年第 5 期。

③ 王碧珺,谭语嫣,余淼杰,黄益平. 融资约束是否抑制了中国民营企业对外直接投资.《世界经济》(季刊). 2015 年第 12 期。

④ 潘镇,金中坤. 双边政治关系、东道国制度风险与中国对外直接投资.《财贸经济》. 2015 年第 6 期。

⑤ 杨振兵. FDI 是否会迅速逃离:基于工业行业根植性的视角.《当代经济科学》. 2014 年第 4 期。

⑥ 随洪光,刘廷华. FDI 是否提升了发展中东道国的经济增长质量——来自亚太、非洲和拉美地区的经验证据.《数量经济技术经济研究》. 2014 年第 11 期。

⑦ 计志英,毛杰,赖小峰. FDI 规模对我国环境污染的影响效应研究——基于 30 个省级面板数据模型的实证检验.《世界经济研究》. 2015 年第 3 期。

城镇个人,利用 OLS 和工具变量实证分析了外资进入对服务业工资的影响。[1]

六、贸易自由化

朱维巍(2014)基于汇改后人民币汇率升值凸显的样本期对人民币汇率与中美两国分行业产品双边贸易之间的关系进行了实证研究,并据此探究和剖析了引起中美贸易失衡的主要根源。[2] 刘志成,刘斌(2014)采用 2003—2007 年中国工业企业数据,分析全要素生产率与贸易自由化对企业就业的影响。[3] 汤毅,尹翔硕(2014)通过使用 1998—2007 年中国制造业企业层面的大型面板数据,研究了贸易自由化对企业要素生产率的影响。[4] 李清如等(2014)使用 1998—2007 年的中国制造业企业数据检验了贸易自由化对 71 个制造业的行业内工资不平等的影响。得出基本结论,产成品进口关税和有效保护率的下降显著地降低了行业内工资不平等程度。[5] 余淼杰,梁中华(2014)采用中国制造业贸易企业 1998—2007 年的微观面板数据,研究贸易自由化对企业层面劳动收入份额的影响。[6] 毛其淋,盛斌(2014)基于异质性企业贸易的理论框架,使用中国工业企业微观数据全面深入地考察了贸易自由化对中国制造业企业出口行为的影响。[7] 周丹(2015)在 Novy(2013)超越对数引力模型的基础上,从贸易四个维度将影响贸易成本的主要因素纳入 Novy(2013)超越对数引力模型对其进行扩展,并利用扩展后的模型对中国与主要亚太国家 21 大类产品的贸易成本弹性分别进行了测度与分析。发现中国与上述国家贸易成本弹性均为正,通过降低贸易成本均可提高双

---

① 蔡洪波,刘杜若,张明志. 外商直接投资与服务业工资差距——基于中国城镇个人与行业匹配数据的实证分析.《南开经济研究》.2015 年第 4 期。

② 朱维巍. 究竟谁才是中美贸易失衡的主因——来自中美分行业产品异质性视角的经验证据.《世界经济研究》.2014 年第 9 期。

③ 刘志成,刘斌. 贸易自由化、全要素生产率与就业——基于 2003—2007 年中国工业企业数据的研究.《南开经济研究》.2014 年第 1 期。

④ 汤毅,尹翔硕. 贸易自由化、异质性企业与全要素生产率——基于我国制造业企业层面的实证研究.《财贸经济》.2014 年第 11 期。

⑤ 李清如,蒋亚恒,董鹏馥. 贸易自由化对行业内工资不平等的影响——来自中国制造业的证据.《财贸经济》.2014 年第 2 期。

⑥ 余淼杰,梁中华. 贸易自由化与中国劳动收入份额——基于制造业贸易企业数据的实证分析.《管理世界》(月刊).2014 年第 7 期。

⑦ 毛其淋,盛斌. 贸易自由化与中国制造企业的出口行为:"入世"是否促进了出口参与?.《经济学》(季刊).2014 年第 1 期。

边贸易量。①

七、区域经济一体化

区域经济一体化是当今世界经济发展的重要潮流,也是我国对外开放和经济发展的战略布局。从研究的现状来看,跨太平洋关系协定(TPP)和区域合作受到我国学者的高度关注。东艳,张琳(2014)采用国际政治经济学理论框架,以美国在区域贸易投资协定中推动竞争中立原则为例,分析了其推动新一代高标准贸易投资规则的动因和收益,探讨了国际经济规则调整和实现的具体路径,将国际规则形成机制的分析由宏观层面向微观层面拓展。② 盛斌,果婷(2014)从传统贸易关系、价值链贸易关系、传统贸易政策与"第二代"贸易政策的视角分析了亚太各国对于"区域全面经济合作伙伴关系"和"跨太平洋伙伴关系协议"的路径与策略选择。③ 胡超(2014)以2006—2012年中国—东盟八个国家的24种时间密集型和31种非时间密集型农产品的4900个贸易数据为对象,实证检验并比较了进口通关时间的贸易效应。结果表明,总体上进口国进口通关时间对农产品产生了负面贸易效应。④ 陈志阳(2014)研究了多边贸易协定中的国际核心劳工标准,认为中国应参照国际标准,结合发展水平和国内改革进展,逐步同意将劳工标准与贸易问题适度挂钩,并在自贸协定谈判中先行先试。⑤ 竺彩华,韩剑夫(2015)梳理了"一带一路"沿线的FTA现状及中国与相关经济体的FTA情况,并分析了中国推进"一带一路"FTA建设进程中面临的机遇与挑战,提出了建设"一带一路"的FTA思想路径。⑥ 蔡松锋,张亚雄(2015)利用改进后的GTAP模型分析了跨大西洋贸易与投资伙伴协议的经济影响。⑦

---

① 周丹. 基于扩展的超越对数引力模型贸易成本弹性测度与分析——以中国与主要亚太国家间贸易为例.《南开经济研究》.2015年第3期。

② 东艳,张琳. 美国区域贸易投资协定框架下的竞争中立原则分析.《当代亚太》.2014年第6期。

③ 盛斌,果婷. 亚太区域经济一体化博弈与中国的战略选择.《世界经济与政治》.2014年第10期。

④ 胡超. 中国—东盟自贸区进口通关时间的贸易效应和比较研究——基于不同时间密集型农产品的实证.《国际贸易问题》.2014年第8期。

⑤ 陈志阳. 多边贸易协定中的国际核心劳工标准分析.《国际贸易问题》.2014年第2期。

⑥ 竺彩华,韩剑夫. "一带一路"沿线FTA现状与中国FTA战略.《亚太经济》.2015年第4期。

⑦ 蔡松锋,张亚雄. 跨大西洋贸易与投资伙伴协议(TTIP)对金砖国家经济影响分析——基于含全球价值链模块的动态GTAP模型.《世界经济研究》.2015年第8期。

八、"一带一路"倡议

申现杰,肖金成(2014)从国际区域经济合作的新形势出发,分析了中国实施"一带一路"建设的重要意义,并从落实"五通"建设、高标准自由贸易区战略、扩大国际合作的重点领域、优化国内区域开放格局等方面对"一带一路"建设重点进行了相关思考。① 李向阳(2014)认为与其他区域贸易协定相比,海上丝绸之路的一个突出特征是合作机制的多元化。② 杜秀红(2015)选取了2002—2014年数据,运用显著性比较优势指数、贸易强度指数,对中印两国贸易结构的竞争性与互补性进行了实证分析,发现中国在劳动密集型轻工产品以及机械与运输设备上具有竞争优势,而印度在农产品、矿产资源类产品、医药化工、轻工产品上具有竞争优势,中印的贸易互补性大于竞争性,在"一带一路"背景下,中印两国贸易空间有待进一步加大。③ 孔庆峰,董虹蔚(2015)通过构建一套完整的贸易便利化指标体系,对"一带一路"沿线69个亚欧国家的贸易便利化水平进行了测算。结果发现"一带一路"沿线亚欧国家之间的贸易潜力巨大,贸易便利化水平的提升可以进一步扩大贸易潜力。④ 朴光姬(2015)从区域增长机制形成与发展的角度,考察了中国的"一带一路"倡议对东亚向亚洲增长机制转型扩容的影响,认为"一带一路"为区域增长机制的发展提供了新的解决方案,并为东亚增长机制向亚洲增长机制的转型扩容提供了相关的公共产品。⑤ 李晓(2015)在分析"印度困局"缘由及其表现的基础上,提出中印两国经济关系的发展尤其是中国企业对印度投资的发展,不仅落后于中国同周边其他国家间的经济交往水平,也与两国的经济总量以及两国在亚洲的地位严重不符。中国应从"三个层面"和"两个维度"增进双边政治互信,努力破解"印度困局",促进中国企业对印度投资的发展。⑥ 谭秀杰,周茂

---

① 申现杰,肖金成. 国际区域经济合作新形势与我国"一带一路"合作战略.《宏观经济研究》.2014年第11期。
② 李向阳. 论海上丝绸之路的多元化合作机制.《世界经济与政治》.2014年第11期。
③ 杜秀红."一带一路"背景下的中印货物贸易结构分析:2002—2014年.《审计与经济研究》.2015年第6期。
④ 孔庆峰,董虹蔚."一带一路"国家的贸易便利化水平测算与贸易潜力研究.《国际贸易问题》.2015年第12期。
⑤ 朴光姬."一带一路"与东亚"西扩"——从亚洲区域经济增长机制构建的视角分析.《当代亚太》.2015年第6期。
⑥ 李晓."一带一路"战略实施中的"印度困局"——中国企业投资印度的困境与对策.《国际经济评论》.2015年第5期。

荣(2015)利用随机前沿引力模型研究了"海上丝绸之路"主要沿线国家间的贸易潜力,并采用一步法分析了影响因素,发现"海上丝绸之路"的贸易效率在不断提升,中国对"海上丝绸之路"的出口仍有很大潜力。① 李向阳(2015)认为基于对外开放新举措与经济外交新平台的基本定位,"一带一路"将成为能够体现"亲诚惠容"理念的一种新型区域合作机制。为构建"一带一路",作为倡导者,中国需要处理一系列全新的问题。如政府与企业的关系,中央政府与地方政府的关系,历史与现实的关系,利用现有比较优势与开发新优势的关系等。② 贺艳(2015)认为在明确建设"丝绸之路经济带"自由贸易协定必要性的同时,应充分考虑其所面临的困难和长期性,在此基础上务实创新,探索实现这一长远目标的现实可行路径。③ 黄卫平(2015)认为新丝绸之路经济带建设必将推动国际区域合作,改变中欧经贸格局,跨亚欧高铁是新丝绸之路经济带建设的主要交通载体,新丝绸之路经济带战略与高铁外交需要与相关国家展开合作,通过国际合作在发展中解决问题,实现中欧与新丝绸之路经济带周边国家与地区的共赢。④ 韩永辉等(2015)基于联合国UN Comtrade数据库,依次测算了中国与西亚的出口相似度指数、贸易结合度指数、格鲁贝尔—劳埃德产业内贸易指数、布雷哈特边际产业内贸易指数以及显示性比较优势指数,分析了中国与西亚双边贸易的竞争性与互补性。⑤

九、环境问题

李丽(2014)认为全球应对气候变化和低碳发展正在对国际贸易规则产生影响,而国际贸易规则的制定将极大影响国际贸易的发展。我国应了解低碳规则竞争现状,积极参与WTO多哈回合谈判,特别是环境产品清单的谈判,并关注区域及双边贸易协定中低碳规则的发展趋势,积极参与低碳领域国际标准及非官方标

---

① 谭秀杰,周茂荣.21世纪"海上丝绸之路"贸易潜力及其影响因素——基于随机前沿引力模型的实证研究.《国际贸易问题》.2015年第2期。
② 李向阳.构建"一带一路"需要优先处理的关系.《国际经济评论》.2015年第1期。
③ 贺艳.建设"丝绸之路经济带"自由贸易协定问题研究.《国际经贸探索》.2015年6月,第31卷第6期。
④ 黄卫平.新丝绸之路经济带与中欧经贸格局新发展——兼论跨亚欧高铁的战略价值.《中国流通经济》.2015年第1期。
⑤ 韩永辉,罗晓斐,邹建华.中国与西亚地区贸易合作的竞争性和互补性研究——以"一带一路"战略为背景.《世界经济研究》.2015年第3期。

准的制定。[①] 宋文飞等(2014)采用中国工业 33 个细分行业 2004—2011 年的面板数据,运用门槛回归科技,实证研究了环境规制对 R&D 双环节效率的门槛效应,发现环境规制对 R&D 转换效率的影响呈"U"形特征。[②] 郭晴等(2014)采用 GTAP8.0 模拟欧盟、美国、日本分别和同时征收碳关税时对世界经济和产品贸易的影响。[③] 李小平(2014)采用 1992—2009 年的跨国面板数据,在测算出各国出口复杂度的基础上,实证分析了碳生产率等因素对出口复杂度演进的影响。[④] 周力,李静(2015)基于美国宇航局社会经济数据与应用中心提供的 2001—2013 年中国 30 个省的 PM2.5 面板数据,研究了外商直接投资对中国 PM2.5 空气污染的影响。[⑤] 王敏,黄滢(2015)利用 112 座城市在 2003—2010 年间的大气污染浓度数据,考察了我国经济增长和环境污染之间的关系。[⑥]

第二节　国外研究综述

　　纵观 2014—2015 年国际贸易领域研究文献,重点研究主题有八个:异质性企业理论,贸易自由化效应,贸易谈判与协定,贸易成本与贸易壁垒,全球价值链与生产分割、外国直接投资、对外开放和其他领域。其中,从微观视角分析贸易议题的异质性企业贸易是学术的最前沿,引领国际贸易研究和理论发展的方向,积聚了大量的研究文献。贸易成本与贸易壁垒,福利效应与贸易自由化效应,贸易谈判与协定也是 2014 年和 2015 年国际贸易研究的重点和热点,存在较多的研究文献。

---

① 李丽. 低碳经济对国际贸易规则的影响及中国的对策.《财贸经济》.2014 年第 9 期。

② 宋文飞,李国平,韩先锋. 价值链视角下环境规制对 R&D 创新效率的异质门槛效应——基于工业 33 个行业 2004—2011 年的面板数据分析.《财经研究》.2014 年 1 月第 1 期。

③ 郭晴,帅传敏,帅竞. 碳关税对世界经济和农产品贸易的影响研究.《数量经济技术经济研究》.2014 年第 10 期。

④ 李小平,王树柏,周记顺. 碳生产率变动与出口复杂度演进:1992—2009 年.《数量经济技术经济研究》.2014 年第 9 期。

⑤ 周力,李静. 外商直接投资与 PM2.5 空气污染——基于中国数据的"污染避难所"假说再检验.《国际经贸探索》.2015 年第 12 期。

⑥ 王敏,黄滢. 中国环境污染与经济增长.《经济学》(季刊).2015 年 1 月第 2 期。

一、异质性企业贸易的研究

从微观企业异质性角度探寻企业的一系列贸易行为选择及其影响是国际贸易研究的最新方向与前沿,这一理论被称为异质性企业贸易理论。近年来,国际贸易领域的理论和经验研究大多集中在微观异质性企业的范畴内,传统的贸易问题都被引入微观企业的层面进行研究,呈现了全面扩展的趋势。异质性企业贸易论文可以分为四个方向,以下逐一进行梳理。

(一)异质性企业的贸易行为选择

异质性企业贸易行为选择方面的文献,主要集中于出口和进口行为的选择、出口产品价格和质量的选择、出口目的地的选择、出口产品种类的选择、出口企业生产区位的选择以及贸易的网络结构选择等。Colantone 和 Crinò(2014)选取 25 个欧洲国家数据,分析了新进口投入与采用国产新产品之间的关系,发现新进口投入品对欧洲本地产品创造产生了积极影响,各国从更广泛的中间品中获益,新的进口投入还推动了制造业产量增长。[1] Kropf 和 Saure(2014)从理论上分析了出口企业的出口频率选择,多次出口运输会提高单次出口的固定成本,但降低货物的仓储成本,故而存在一个最优出口频率选择。[2] Silva 等(2014)提出了一个不同的被解释变量双边界测量方法,重新实证计算了企业出口扩展的集约边界,发现新方法下的核算结果和与标准方法下的核算结果之间存在显著差异。[3] Aw 和 Lee(2014)构建一个理论模型分析企业需求和生产率对于出口和跨国生产选择的影响,得出生产技术、消费者偏好、产品质量、固定投资成本、运输成本和相对工资水平影响异质性企业的选择,企业层面数据的实证分析支持理论发现。[4] Chaney(2014)从理论上分析了企业贸易的网络结构,指出企业的关联网络会影响出口行为选择。[5] Wagner 和 Zahler(2014)利用智利新出口数据,分析了追随者是否从先

① Colantone,Italo,Crinò,Rosario,"New imported inputs,new domestic products",Journal of International Economics,92(1),2014,pp. 147 – 165.

② Krishna,P,M. Z. Senses,"International Trade and Labor Income Risk in the U. S. "[J],Review of Economic Studies,81,2014,pp. 186 – 218.

③ Silva,J. M. C. S. ,S. Tenreyro,K. Wei,"Estimating the Extensive Margin of Trade"[J],Journal of International Economics,93(1),2014,pp. 67 – 75.

④ Aw,B. Y,Y. Lee,"A Model of Demand,Productivity and Foreign Location Decision among Taiwanese Firms"[J],Journal of International Economics,92(2),2014,pp. 304 – 316.

⑤ Chaney. T,"The Network Structure of International Trade"[J],American Economic Review,104(11),2014,pp. 3600 – 3634.

驱者中获益。研究发现相同新产品,先驱者的出口水平将低于追随者,证实了先驱者对追随者的溢出效应。[1] Berman 等(2015)实证分析了企业的出口动态和国内销售的变化,发现企业层面出口的外生变动会影响国内销售。[2] Rhodes(2015)关注多产品企业的定价行为,发现企业的产品种类越多则越会定低价,在某一产品上定低价会引起其他产品同样定低价。[3] Harrigan 和 Shlychkov(2015)等分析了美国企业的出口价格,实证研究发现高生产率和技能密集型企业的出口定价较高,而资本密集型企业定价较低。[4]

(二)贸易和贸易自由化的效应

主要包括贸易和贸易自由化对企业生产率、福利、生产规模、资源配置、要素价格、进出口等的影响。Miaojie Yu(2014)探讨了进口投入品和最终商品关税的降低对中国大型贸易公司生产率的影响。发现两种类型的关税削减对生产率的积极影响随着公司加工进口份额的增长而减弱。进口关税削减对生产率提高的影响总体上低于出口关税削减的影响。[5] Breinlich(2014)使用美国和加拿大 1989年关税同盟前后的上市公司企业数据实证分析了贸易自由化的效应,发现加拿大企业对于美国出口关税下降的反应与理论预期一致,但对于加拿大进口关税下降的反应与理论结果存在差异。[6] Blonigen(2014)使用 BEA 企业级数据,发现双边税收协定对外商直接投资的积极影响,其中对使用差异化投入的企业来说影响更大。[7] Melitz 和 Redding(2015)揭示了内生企业选择会为异质性企业贸易模型带来新的福利边际,进而在新的异质性企业型框架下分析了贸易的福利效应。[8] Halpern 等(2015)估计了面向匈牙利微观数据的进口商模型,进行反事实分析,以

---

① Rodrigo Wagner, Andrés Zahler, "New exports from emerging markets: Do followers benefit from pioneers?"[J], Journal of Development Economics, 2015(114), pp. 203 – 223.

② N. Berman, A. Berthou, J. Hericourt, "Export Dynamics & Sales at Home", Journal of International Economics, 96, 2015, pp. 298 – 310.

③ A. Rhodes, "Multiproduct Retailing, Review of Economic Studies", 82, 2015, pp. 360 – 390.

④ Harrigan, James & Ma, Xiangjun & Shlychkov, Victor, "Export prices of U. S. firms", Journal of International Economics, Elsevier, 97(1), 2015, pp. 100 – 111.

⑤ Miaojie Yu, "Processing Trade, Tariff Reductions and Firm Productivity: Evidence from Chinese Firms", The Economic Journal, 125(585), 2014, pp. 943 – 988.

⑥ Breinlich, H, "Heterogeneous Firm-Level Responses to Trade Liberalization: A Test Using Stock Price Reactions"[J], Journal of International Economics, 93, 2014, pp. 270 – 285.

⑦ Bruce A. Blonigen, Lindsay Oldenski, Nicholas Sly, "The Differential Effects of Bilateral Tax Treaties", American Economic Journal: Economic Policy, 6(6), 2014, pp. 1 – 18.

⑧ M. J. Melitz, S. J. Redding, "New Trade Models, New Welfare Implications", American Economic Review, 105, 2015, pp. 1105 – 1146.

调查进口投入对生产率的影响。发现进口所有投入品种将使公司的受益生产力提高 22%。[1] Fan 等(2015)从理论和实证两方面分析了贸易自由化对异质性企业出口质量和价格的影响,并使用细分的中国数据证明了进口关税减让会引起企业提高出口质量和出口价格。[2]

（三）其他政策或者外生冲击的影响效应

其他政策和冲击的影响效应主要在异质性企业贸易框架下分析外在政策变动或者外生冲击对于企业的影响,例如,政策的不确定性、信贷约束的变动、研发投入、经济危机等对于企业进出口、生产率、技术进步等的影响。Handley(2014)从理论和实证两方面分析了贸易政策不确定对出口企业的影响,发现贸易政策的不确定性会延迟出口商进入新市场,并降低其对减免关税的反应。[3] Amiti 等(2014)分析了异质性企业的汇率传递效应,发现出口份额高和市场份额大的企业具有更小的汇率传递效应,即较少受到汇率变动的影响。[4] Gopinath 和 Neiman(2014)使用 2000—2002 年阿根廷危机实证分析了经济危机时企业的贸易调整和生产率变化,发现进口下降中企业内的贸易下降更多,而进口价格下降会显著引起生产率下降。[5] Fracasso 和 Marzetti(2015)研究了国际贸易与研发溢出效应的关系。发现贸易模式会对国际知识传播产生积极影响。[6] Boler 等(2015)在异质性企业框架下分析了研发对进口投入,以及企业生产率的影响,发现研发成本的下降会刺激研发投入和中间品进口,进而促进技术进步。[7] Muuls 等(2015)分析了信贷约束对企业贸易行为的影响,发现没有信贷约束的企业更容易进口和

---

[1] L. Halpern, M. Koren, A. Szeidl, "Imported Inputs & Productivity", American Economic Review, 105, 2015, pp. 3660 – 3703.

[2] H. Fan & Y. A. Li & S. R. Yeaple, Trade Liberalization, Quality, & Export Prices, The Review of Economics & Statistics, 97, 2015, pp. 1033 – 1051.

[3] Kyle Handley, "Exporting under trade policy uncertainty: Theory and evidence", Journal of International Economics, 94(1), 2014, pp. 50 – 66.

[4] Amiti, M., O. Itskhoki, A. J. Lonings, "Importers, Exporters, and Exchange Rate Disconnect" [J], American Economic Review, 104(7), 2014, pp. 1942 – 1978.

[5] Gita Gopinath, Brent Neiman, "Trade Adjustment and Productivity in Large Crises", American Economic Review, 104(3), 2014, pp. 793 – 831.

[6] Andrea Fracasso, Giuseppe Vittucci Marzetti, "International trade and R&D spillovers", Journal of International Economics, 96(1), 2015, pp. 138 – 149.

[7] E. A. Boler, A. Moxnes, K. H. U. Moe, "R&D, International Sourcing, and the Joint Impact on Firm Performance", American Economic Review, 105, 2015, pp. 3704 – 3739.

出口。①

(四)其他有关异质性企业贸易的现象及其解释

主要包括异质性的多元化、异质性企业理论对贸易新现象的解释,以及使用异质性框架扩展传统的贸易理论。Jaef 和 lopez(2014)在异质性企业贸易理论框架下分析了商业周期理论,推导了传统商业周期理论的所有结论。② Atkin 等(2015)分析了企业的利润和成本分布,进而分析利润和成本的异质性。③ Simo-novska(2015)分析了贸易品的价格和人均收入的关系。④

二、全球价值链与生产分割

全球价值链与生产分割的研究内容主要包括全球价值链的度量、价值链的分工、国际生产组织、垂直专业化贸易、生产分割、中间品贸易的模式与效应、企业的外包和一体化选择等。2014—2015 年这一领域的文献主要集中在以下几方面:

一是垂直专业化以及附加值贸易的分解和核算。Koopman 等(2014)构建了一个综合的数理分解方程,将总贸易逐项分解成附加值数据,这一方程可以将以前的 VS、VSI、VAX 等各指标融入统一的框架,同时基于附加值贸易数据,可以对显性比较优势、多阶段生产的贸易成本等问题给出新的解释。⑤

二是全球价值链涉及的中间品贸易的模式与效应以及外包的决策与效应等的研究。Biesebroeck 和 Zhang(2014)采用理论模型研究了企业全球外包中对生产过程复杂性的决策机制。⑥ Schwarz 和 Suedekum(2014)研究了不同中间品外包决策的相互作用机制。Diez(2014)研究了关税对最优生产组织模式的影响,认为北

---

① M. Muuls," Exporters,Importers & Credit Constraints",Journal of International Economics,95, 2015,pp. 333 – 343.

② Jaef,R. N. F. ,J. I. Lopez,"Entry,Trade Costs,and International Business Cycles"[J],Journal of International Economics,94,2014,pp. 224 – 238.

③ D. A. Atkin,A. Chaudhry,S. Chaudry,A. K. Khelwal,"Markup & Cost Dispersion across Firms: Direct Evidence from Producer Surveys in Pakistan",American Economic Review:Papers & Proceedings,105,2015,pp. 537 – 544.

④ I. Simonovska," Income Differences & Prices of Tradable:Insights from an Online Retailer", Review of Economic Studies,82,2015,pp. 1612 – 1656.

⑤ Koopman,R. ,Z. Wang,S. Wei,"Tracing Value-Added and Double Counting in Gross Exports" [J],American Economic Review,104(2),2014,pp. 459 – 494.

⑥ Biesebroeck,J. V. ,l. Zhang," Interdependent Product Cycles for Globally Sourced Intermediates"[J],Journal of International Economics,94,2014,pp. 143 – 156.

方国家的最优关税对外包有阻碍作用,而南方国家的关税则相反。[①]

三是引入附加值贸易时对传统贸易问题重新解读。Baldwin 和 Nicoud(2014)研究了要素禀赋理论的扩展问题,他们将体现全球价值链生产的工序贸易模型与传统贸易模型进行结合,提供了一个简洁但可以进行扩展的,能够同时考虑两种贸易模式的 HO 模型。他们采用这一模型对贸易的收益、要素禀赋理论等传统贸易问题进行了分析。[②]

四是全球价值链问题涉及的生产分割和跨国生产问题。Bernard 和 Fort(2015)分析了零售部门企业的设计和生产的选择,以及分工和生产分割等问题。[③] Ramondo 等(2015)使用数据分析了为什么企业要选择跨国生产,跨国生产如何影响效率,跨国生产如何影响本国和东道国的福利。[④] Bogmans(2015)研究发现跨国公司具有更高的股票市场收益和回报。[⑤]

三、贸易自由化效应

贸易自由化是国际贸易文献中的一个重要组成部分,主要研究包括福利效应对收入、生产率、制度变迁等的影响。其中,针对福利效应影响的研究较为广泛。Jouini 和 Rebei(2014)利用两部门小型开放经济动态和随机一般均衡模型的综合方法,评估了非关税壁垒,量化了服务贸易自由化的影响。研究发现服务贸易自由化有助于提升发展中国家的福利待遇。[⑥] Naranpanawa,和 Arora(2014)发展了第一个一国范围内多区域可计算一般均衡模型,来验证贸易自由化是否会促进区域分化。作者通过对印度经济调查研究,发现短期来看贸易自由化对富裕国家和

① Diez,F. J,"The Asymmetric Effects of Tariffs on Intra-Firm Trade and Offshoring Decisions"[J],Journal of International Economics,93,2014,pp. 76 – 91.

② Baldwin,R.,F. R. Nicoud,"Trade-in-goods and Trade-in-tasks:An Integrating Framework"[J],Journal of International Economics,92,2014,pp. 51 – 62.

③ A. B. Bernard,T. C. Fort,"Factorless Goods Producing Firms,American Economic Review",105,2015,pp. 518 – 523.

④ N. Ramondo,A. R. Clare,F. Tintelnot,"Multinational Production:Data & Stylized Facts",American Economic Review,105,2015,pp. 530 – 536.

⑤ C. Bogmans,"Can the Terms of Trade Externality Outweigh Free-riding The Role of Vertical Linkages",Journal of International Economics,95,2015,pp. 115 – 128.

⑥ Nizar Jouini,Nooman Rebei,"The welfare Implications of Services Liberalization in A Developing Country",Journal of Development Economics,106(106),2014,pp. 1 – 14.

快速增长的中等收入国家有利,但对贫穷国家有边际或负面的影响。[1] Caliendo 和 Parro(2014)通过建立中间产品贸易和生产部门异质性为特征的李嘉图模型,来量化关税变化对贸易和福利的影响。研究发现当生产结构不考虑中间商品或投入产出关联时,减免关税削减的福利效应会减少。[2] Giovanni 等(2014)在一个多国数量化的李嘉图—赫克歇尔—俄林模型中评估了中国贸易一体化与技术进步对全球福利的影响,发现当中国的生产率增长偏向本国的比较劣势部门时,大部分国家经历了显著的、更大的福利收益。Behrens(2014)建立了一般均衡垄断竞争模型分析贸易自由化对工资、生产率、消费多样性以及收益的影响。[3] Puga 和 Trefler(2014)以中世纪威尼斯为研究对象,以历史数据为基础,实证分析了国际贸易对于制度变迁的影响机制。[4] Beverelli 等(2015)估计了贸易便利化对出口多元化的影响。发现贸易便利化对贸易广泛边界具有积极影响,在撒哈拉以南的非洲以及拉丁美洲和加勒比地区,大量的广泛边界从贸易便利化改革中获利。[5]

四、贸易谈判与协定

贸易谈判与协定是国际贸易的一个重要议题,也是未来国际贸易研究的主要方向之一。近年来,伴随区域一体化的推进和多边贸易体系格局的发展,贸易谈判与协定的研究更具现实价值。2014 年和 2015 年贸易谈判与协定领域的研究主要集中于贸易协定的设计和对各国家的影响,合作均衡和非合作均衡的条件,经济一体化的影响效应等。

Gil-Pareja 等(2014)研究发现非互惠优惠贸易协定(NRPTAs)和普遍优惠制

[1] Athula Naranpanawa, Rashmi Arora, " Does Trade Liberalization Promote Regional Disparities Evidence From A Multiregional CGE Model of India", World Development, 64 (C), 2014, pp. 339 – 349.

[2] Lorenzo Caliendo, Fernando Parro, "Estimates of the trade and welfare effects of NAFTA", Review of Economic Studies, 82, 2015, pp. 1 – 44.

[3] Behrens, K. , G. Mion, Y. Murata, J. S. Dekum, "Trade, Wages and Productivity", International Economic Review, 5(4), pp. 1305 – 1438.

[4] Puga, D. , D. Trefler, "International Trade and Institutional Change: Medieval Venice's Response to Globalization", The Quarterly Journal of Economics, 93, 2014, pp. 108 – 122.

[5] Cosimo Beverelli, Simon Neumueller, Robert Teh, "Export Diversification Effects of The WTO Trade Facilitation Agreement", World Development, 76, 2015, pp. 293 – 310.

对发展中国家的出口有着显著影响。[1] Ossa(2014)在垄断竞争和规模经济的新贸易理论模型下测度了最优关税、贸易合作均衡以及贸易非合作均衡结果,发现世界最优关税约为 62% ,贸易战的非合作均衡关税约为 63% ,国际贸易政策合作崩溃的政府福利损失平均为 2.9% ,未来的多边贸易合作约能提高政府福利 0.5% 。[2] Cheong 等(2014)考察了贸易伙伴国家特征的不同对优惠贸易协定(PTA)下贸易流动变化的影响,发现贸易伙伴国家的相似度越高,集团内部贸易的增长越多。其中,发展中国家间的贸易收益是发展中国家与发达国家间贸易收益的 2.5 倍。[3] Baier 等(2014)分析了经济一体化对贸易集约边际和扩展边际的影响,发现经济一体化会同时影响集约边际和扩展边际,不同类型的经济一体化会带来不同的影响,集约边际的反应早于扩展边际。[4] Maggi(2015)研究了政府间补偿效益低下的情况下贸易协定的最优化设计。文章对贸易协定的最佳形式,协议在均衡状况下被重新谈判时所处的条件,以及重新谈判将采取的形式等问题进行了预测。[5]

五、贸易成本与贸易壁垒

贸易成本与贸易壁垒也是国际贸易理论研究的重要方面,研究内容主要包括贸易成本测度、贸易成本和贸易壁垒的影响、贸易保护和贸易壁垒等。Anderson 等(2014)使用加拿大数据实证分析了地理贸易壁垒与服务贸易增长的关系,发现地理壁垒对服务贸易的影响是对货物贸易影响的七倍,服务贸易更加容易受到地理壁垒的影响。[6] Melitz 和 Toubal(2014)实证分析了语言贸易壁垒与贸易的关

---

[1] Salvador Gil-Pareja, Rafael Llorca-Vivero, José Antonio Martínez-Serrano, "Do nonreciprocal preferential trade agreements increase beneficiaries' exports?", Journal of Development Economics, 107, 2014, pp. 291 – 304.

[2] Ralph Ossa, "Trade wars and trade talks with data", American Economic Review, 104(12), 2014, pp. 4104 – 46.

[3] Juyoung Cheong, Do Won Kwak, Kam Ki Tang, "Heterogeneous effects of preferential trade agreements: how does partner similarity matter?", World Development, 66(C), 2015, pp. 222 – 236.

[4] Baier, S. L, J. H. Bergstrand, M. Feng, "Economic Integration Agreements and the Margins of International Trade", Journal of International Economics, 93, pp. 339 – 350.

[5] Giovanni Maggi, Robert W. Staiger, "Optimal design of trade agreements in the presence of renegotiation", American Economic Journal: Microeconomics, 7(1), 2015, pp. 109 – 43.

[6] James E. Anderson, Catherine A. Milot, Yoto V. Yotov, "How Much Does Geography Deflect Services Trade? Canadian Answers", International Economic Review, 55(3), 2014, pp. 791 – 818.

系,发现语言的相通容易形成相互信任,对于贸易的影响非常显著和突出。[1] Faber(2014)使用中国运输基础设施投资数据分析了贸易成本下降对于贸易和产业布局的影响,发现高速运输系统对于 GDP 增长具有显著影响,那些拥有高速运输系统的地区增长速度高于没有高速运输系统的地区。[2] Bown 和 Crowley(2014)估计了总量经济波动对 1989—2010 年 13 个主要新兴经济体的贸易政策的影响。通过构建产品进口管制的双边度量指标并考察指标决定因素,发现宏观经济冲击和新的进口管制之间存在着反周期关系。[3] Irarrazabal 等(2015)创建了一个新的实证框架,即用企业层面贸易数据估计贸易成本,发现贸易成本通常在 14% 左右。[4] Hornok 和 Koren(2015)使用美国和西班牙的出口数据计算分析贸易成本。[5] Sposi(2015)分析了贸易壁垒和可贸易品的相对价格,解释了为什么服务相对于可贸易品的价格与国家之间的发展情况正相关。[6]

六、外国直接投资

针对外国直接投资,主要从产业政策、技术溢出、国民福利等方面进行研究。Luosha Du 等(2014)考察了产业政策,尤其是关税自由化和税收补贴对外商直接投资溢出大小和方向的影响。发现 1998—2007 年的关键时期自由化政策总体上促进了中国的行业生产率增长。[7] Amighini 和 Sanfilippo(2014)探讨了外商直接投资和进出对非洲出口升级的影响。发现南—南一体化对加速陆地国家的结构转型具有强大的潜力。[8] Cheryl Long 等(2015)研究了中国外商直接投资对制度

---

[1] Melitz. J, F. Toubal, "Native Language, Spoken Language, Translation and Trade, Journal of International Economics", 93, pp. 351 – 363.

[2] Benjamin Faber, "Trade Integration, Market Size, and Industrialization: Evidence from China's National Trunk Highway System", Review of Economic Studies, 81, 2014, pp. 1046 – 1070.

[3] Bown, C. P, Crowley, M. A, "Emerging Economies, Trade Policy, and Macroeconomic Shocks, Journal of Development Economics", 111, 2014, pp. 261 – 273.

[4] A. Irarrazabal, A. Moxnes, L. D. Opromolla, "The Tip of The Iceberg: A Quantitative Framework for Estimating Trade Costs", The Review of Economics & Statistics, 97, 2015, pp. 777 – 792.

[5] C. Hornok, M. Koren, "Administrative Barriers to Trade, Journal of International Economics", 96, 2015, pp. s110 – s122.

[6] M. Sposi, "Trade Barriers & the Relative Price of Tradable", Journal of International Economics, 96, 2015, pp. 398 – 411.

[7] Luosha Du, Ann Harrison, Gary Jefferson, "FDI Spillovers and Industrial Policy: The Role of Tariffs and Tax Holidays", World Development, 64, 2014, pp. 366 – 383.

[8] Alessia Amighini, Marco Sanfilippo, "Impact of South – South FDI and Trade on the Export Upgrading of African Economies", World Development, 64, 2014, pp. 1 – 17.

的影响,发现位于外商直接投资水平较高地区的中国国内企业往往享受了较低的税费负担。[1] Jian Wang 和 Xiao Wang(2015)通过比较中国外资收购企业和内资收购企业收购后的绩效变化来考察外商直接投资的影响。结果发现,相对内资收购企业,外资所有制显著提高了目标企业的融资状况和出口,也增加了目标企业的产出、就业和工资。[2] Chunlai Chen(2015)使用省级层面的面板数据和采用固定效应工具变量回归方法,考察了沿海地区的外商直接投资对内陆省份的跨区域溢出效应。研究发现,平均而言,沿海地区的外商直接投资对内陆省份的经济增长具有负向影响。[3] Cezar 和 Escobar(2015)使用异质性企业的框架理论研究解释了制度距离对外商直接投资的影响,发现外商直接投资活动随着制度距离增加而下降,发达国家的企业比发展中国家的企业更容易适应制度距离。[4] Holmes 等(2015)使用模型量化中国以市场换技术政策的影响,研究发现以市场换技术的政策对全球创新和福利产生了显著的影响。[5] Cozza 等(2015)考察了中国企业进入欧洲发达国家的对外直接投资(OFDI)的影响。研究发现中国的对外直接投资对提高国内企业的生产率和经营规模(以销售和就业衡量)具有正向影响。[6]

七、对外开放

Brautigam 和 Tang(2014)分析了中国企业海外投资经济特区对促进非洲经济结构转型的潜力。[7] Mitchener 和 Yan(2014)指出中国贸易开放后,出口产品的技能密集度下降而进口产品的技能密集度在提高,实证研究发现第一次世界大战对

---

[1]　Cheryl Long,Jin Yang,Jing Zhang,"Institutional Impact of Foreign Direct Investment in China",World Development,66,2015,pp. 31 – 48.

[2]　Jian Wang,Xiao Wang,"Benefits of Foreign Ownership:Evidence from Foreign Direct Investment in China",Journal of International Economics,97(2),2015,pp. 325 – 338.

[3]　Chunlai Chen,"Do Inland Provinces Benefit from Coastal Foreign Direct Investment in China?",China & World Economy,23(3),2015,pp. 22 – 41.

[4]　Rafael Cezar,Octavio R. Escobar,"Institutional Distance and Foreign Direct Investment",Review of World Economics,151(4),pp. 713 – 733.

[5]　Thomas J. Holmes,Ellen R. Mcgrattan,Edward C. Prescott,"Quid Pro Quo:Technology Capital Transfers for Market Access in China",Review of Economic Studies,82,2015,pp. 1154 – 1193.

[6]　C. Cozza,R. Rabellotti,M. Sanfilippo,"The Impact of Outward FDI on the Performance of Chinese Firms",China Economic Review,36,2015,pp. 42 – 57.

[7]　Deborah Brautigam,Xiaoyang Tang,"'Going Global in Groups':Structural Transformation and China's Special Economic Zones Overseas",World Development,63(C),2014,pp. 78 – 91.

中国贸易条件的影响减少了技能溢出从而带来贸易进出口技能密集度的变化。[1]
Costinot 等(2015)研究表明在一个标准的李嘉图模型的背景下,最优的进口关税
应该是统一的,然而最优的出口补贴关于比较优势是轻微递减的,这反映了政府
有较大的空间来管制比较优势部门的产品价格。[2] Edmond 等(2015)在一个内生
可变加成的数量化模型中研究了国际贸易的竞争促进效应所产生的收益。结果
发现,如果存在大量资源错配以及贸易开放使国内企业面临更大的国际竞争压
力,国际贸易的竞争促进效应能够显著地减少加成扭曲。[3] Grossman 和 Helpman
(2015)讨论了贸易一体化与激励知识积累和知识使用效率之间联系的机制。研
究发现,贸易一体化促进了跨国界的知识流动,为创新者提供了一个更大的潜在
市场,影响技术扩散的激励机制。[4] Ortega 和 Peri(2014)探讨了跨国的贸易开放、
移民和人均收入之间的关系。发现移民开放对长期人均收入具有稳健的正向影
响,而贸易开放对人均收入的影响无法确定。[5]

八、其他

关于贸易新现象及其解释,主要是对新出现的贸易现象或者现有文献没有涉
及的新贸易现象从理论上给出解释和分析。2014 年的贸易新现象及其解释主要
包括中国对外贸易增长的解释,国际贸易理论的困惑,对贸易的重新核算等。
Klasing 和 Milionis(2014)使用历史进出口数据和购买力平价调整 GDP,采用短截
断(short-cut)方法重新估算了 1870—1949 年的世界贸易数据。2015 年的贸易新
现象及其解释主要是对"出口超级明星"(export superstar)现象的分析、贸易中间
商的作用、世界贸易增长的解释和贸易停滞问题等。[6] Caron 等(2014)发现了贸易

① Kris James Mitchener, Se Yan, "Globalization, Trade, and Wages: What Does History Tell Us A-bout China?", International Economics Review, 55(1), 2014, pp. 131 – 168.

② Arnaud Costinot, Dave Donaldson, Jonathan Vogel, Iván Werning, "Comparative Advantage and Optimal Trade Policy", Quarterly Journal of Economics, 130, 2015, pp. 659 – 702.

③ Chris Edmond, Virgiliu Midrigan, Daniel Yi Xu, "Competition, Markups, and the Gains from International Trade", American Economic Review, 105, 2015, pp. 3183 – 3221.

④ Gene M. Grossman, Elhanan Helpman, "Globalization and Growth", American Economic Review, 105, 2015.

⑤ Francesc Ortega, Giovanni Peri, "Openness and Income: The Roles of Trade and Migration", Journal of International Economics, 92(2), 2014, pp. 231 – 251.

⑥ Klasing, M. J., P. Milionis, "Quantifying the Evolution of World Trade, 1897 – 1949"[J], Journal of International Economics, 92, 2014, pp. 185 – 197.

产品的劳动技能密集性和收入弹性的强相关性,并通过实证进行解释。[1] Freund 和 Pierola(2015)分析了"出口超级明星"如何影响一国的贸易行为。[2] Zymek (2015)从要素比重解释了世界贸易的增长。[3] Etkes 和 Zimring 分析了贸易停滞现象及其福利影响效应。[4]

关于贸易不平衡。Barattieri(2014)指出全球不平衡中,美国是由于较大的货物贸易逆差和较少的服务贸易顺差,而日本、德国和中国是较大的货物贸易顺差和较小的服务贸易逆差。论文从服务贸易视角解释了不平衡的原因,由于服务贸易的开放远滞后于货物贸易,导致主要不平衡国家难以通过货物和服务贸易平衡贸易。[5] Crino 和 Epifani(2014)研究了贸易不平衡对不同半球国家的出口结构和工资不平等性的影响。发现过去 30 年来,南北贸易不平衡的大幅增长可能会加剧全球的工资不平等。[6]

关于贸易与金融市场。Cho 和 Madrid(2014)分析了贸易密度和汇率动态联系,给出了两者负相关的证据。[7] Basu 和 Stiglitz(2015)认为欧元区危机的部分原因在于债务结构及其在欧元区以及在欧洲联盟范围内的负债,提出修改里斯本条约,构建欧盟内各个国家主权债务跨国赔偿责任框架,可以很大程度上缓解问题的观点。[8]

关于贸易与劳动力市场。Autor 等(2014)通过研究由于中国作为制造业出口商的壮大崛起后的进口竞争,加之近 20 年来雇主个人收入的时序数据而引发的

---

[1] Justin Caron, Thibault Fally, James R. Markusen, "International Trade Puzzles: A Solution Linking Production and Preferences"[J], Quarterly Journal of Economics, 129(3), 2014, pp. 1501 – 1552.

[2] C. Freund, M. D. Pierola, "Export Superstars, The Review of Economics & Statistics", 97, 2015, pp. 1023 – 1032.

[3] R. Zymek, "Factor Proportions & the Growth of World Trade", Journal of International Economics, 95, 2015, pp. 42 – 53.

[4] H. Etkes & A. Zimring, "When Trade Stops: Lessons from the Gaza Blockade 2007 – 2010", Journal of International Economics, 95, 2015, pp. 16 – 27.

[5] Alessandro Barattieri, "Comparative Advantage, Service Trade, and Global Imbalances", Journal of International Economics, 92(1), 2014, pp. 1 – 13.

[6] Rosario Crino, Paolo Epifani, "Trade Imbalances, Export Structure and Wage Inequality", The Economic Journal, 124(576), 2014, pp. 507 – 539.

[7] Cho, D, A. D. Madrid, "Trade Intensity and Purchasing Power Parity"[J], Journal of International Economics, 93, 2014, pp. 194 – 209.

[8] Kaushik Basu, Joseph E. Stiglitz, "International Lending, Sovereign Debt and Joint Liability", The Economic Journal, 125(586), 2015, pp. F115 – F130.

行业冲击,分析了 1992—2007 年国际贸易的深化对美国员工收入和就业的影响。[①] Carluccio 和 Bas(2015)从理论和实证两方面分析了贸易对技能劳动收入的影响,发现贸易会更多地增加高技能劳动力的收入,而低技能劳动力的收入增长有限。[②]

① David H. Autor,David Dorn,Gordon H. Hanson,Jae Song,"Trade Adjustment:Worker-Level Evidence",The Quarterly Journal of Economics,2014,pp. 1799 – 1860.

② Carluccio, M. Bas, "The Impact of Worker Bargaining Power in the Organization of Global Firms",Journal of International Economics,96,2015,pp. 162 – 181.

第二章

世界经济学科 2014—2015 年期刊论文精选

第一节　中文期刊论文精选

出口企业的产品异质性与出口持续时间

蒋灵多　陈勇兵

《世界经济》2015 年第 7 期

摘要：提要本文首次采用2000—2006 年中国企业出口数据,构建离散时间生存分析模型探讨了多产品出口企业内异质产品的出口持续时间问题。研究发现,中国多产品出口企业普遍存在,且其企业—产品的出口持续时间较短。多产品出口企业异质产品的出口行为存在差异,企业核心产品的出口持续时间显著长于其边缘产品。因此,企业可通过调整出口产品组合来应对外生环境变动以实现企业资源的更优配置,政府应合理制定贸易政策以促进企业内"可持续"贸易关系的持续发展。

关键词：多产品出口　企业产品异质性　出口持续时间

Product heterogeneity and export duration of export enterprises

Abstract：For the first time, this paper adopts the export data of Chinese enterprises from 2000 to 2006, and analyzes the export duration of heterogeneous products in multi-product export enterprises. The study found that China's multi-product export enterprises are ubiquitous, and the export of its products is relatively short.

The export behavior of heterogeneous products of multi-product export enterprises is different, and the export duration of core products of enterprises is significantly longer than that of its peripheral products. Therefore, the enterprise can be combined by adjusting the export products in response to exogenous environment change in order to realize the enterprise resources more optimal configuration, the government should be reasonable trade policy to promote the sustainable development of enterprises "sustainable" in trade relations.

Key words: multi-product; export enterprise product heterogeneity; export duration;

异质性企业与全球价值链嵌入:基于效率和融资的视角

吕越　罗伟　刘斌

《世界经济》2015 年第 8 期

摘要:本文采用 4 种方法测算了企业在全球价值链(GVC)中的嵌入程度,考察效率和融资约束对企业参与全球价值链的影响。研究发现:高效率企业更倾向嵌入全球价值链,而融资约束会形成阻碍;动态研究发现,融资约束对企业参与 GVC 的消极影响仅体现在企业是否参与 GVC 的决策上,而效率对企业的 GVC 参与程度也存在显著影响。此外,本文还发现效率与 GVC 嵌入呈现 U 形关系。这些发现对深入理解"走出去"战略的合理性和必要性以及突破"价值链低端锁定"困局提供了有益的理论探索。

关键词:全球价值链　企业异质性　生产效率 融资约束

Heterogeneity enterprise and global value chain embed: Efficiency and financing perspective

Abstract: This paper USES four methods to measure the degree of embedding of enterprises in GVC, and the impact of efficiency and financing constraints on enterprises' participation in GVC. The study found that high-efficiency enterprises are more inclined to embed global value chains, while financing constraints can form obstacles. Dynamic research has found that the negative impact of financing constraints on enterprises participating in GVC is only reflected in whether enterprises participate in the decision-making of GVC, while efficiency has significant influence on the degree of GVC participation of enterprises. In addition, this paper also found that the efficiency and GVC embed the U-type relationship. These findings provide a useful theoretical exploration of the rationality and necessity of "going out" strategy and the breakthrough of "low-end locking in the value chain".

Key words: global value chain; enterprise heterogeneity; production efficiency; financing constraint

贸易自由化与中国劳动收入份额——基于
制造业贸易企业数据的实证分析

余淼杰　　梁中华

《管理世界》2014 年第 7 期

摘要：我国的劳动收入占国民总收入的份额自 1995 年不断下降，深入而广泛的贸易自由化也发生在这一时期。本文采用中国制造业贸易企业 1998—2007 年的微观面板数据，研究贸易自由化对企业层面劳动收入份额的影响。我们将 2002 年中国加入 WTO 后关税的迅速下调视为一次自然实验，用倍差法进行实证回归。实证结果显示，在劳动力成本不断上升的背景下，中国的贸易自由化过程通过降低资本品成本、中间投入品价格和技术引进的成本，显著降低了企业层面的劳动收入份额。企业面临的关税水平下降幅度越大，其劳动收入份额减少越多。在考虑了序列相关性、同趋势假设和非关税贸易壁垒的稳健性检验后，实证结果依然显著。

关键词：贸易自由化　劳动收入份额　劳动替代　中间产品

Trade liberalization and China's labor income share
——empirical analysis based on data of manufacturing trade enterprises

Abstract: China's labor income has been declining since 1995, and extensive trade liberalization has occurred during this period.

This paper adopts the micro panel data of China's manufacturing trade enterprises from 1998 to 2007 to study the impact of trade liberalization on the share of labor income at the enterprise level.

We regard the rapid reduction of tariff after China's accession to WTO in 2002 as a natural experiment and return with the double difference method.

The empirical results show that under the background of rising labor costs, China's trade liberalization process by reducing the cost of capital goods, intermediate inputs into the price and the cost of the technology import, significantly reduced the labor income share of the enterprise level.

The greater the decline in tariff levels, the more the reduction in the share of labor income.

The empirical results are still significant after considering the sequential correlation, the same trend hypothesis and the robustness test of non-tariff trade barriers.

Key words: trade liberalization; labor income share; labor substitute; intermediate product

贸易自由化与中国制造业企业出口行为："入世"是否促进了出口参与?

毛其淋　盛斌

《经济学(季刊)》2014 年第 2 期

摘要:基于异质性企业贸易的理论框架,本文使用中国工业企业微观数据全面深入地考察了贸易自由化对中国制造业企业出口行为的影响。研究表明:(1)贸易自由化显著地促进了制造业企业的出口参与,本研究选取合适的工具变量克服内生性问题,并进行多角度的稳健性分析,结果均支持了这一结论;(2)贸易自由化通过竞争效应与成本效应两个不同渠道促进了企业出口参与,其中成本效应对企业出口参与的影响程度相对更大;(3)中国加入世界贸易组织显著地推动了企业的出口参与,其中对本土企业的推动作用更大,并且入世主要是通过集约边际的途径影响企业的出口行为。

关键词:贸易自由化　出口参与　企业生产率

Trade Liberalization and Chinese Firms' Export Behavior:Dose WTO Entry Facilitate Export Participation

Abstract:Based on the theoretical framework of heterogeneity-firms trade,this paper

comprehensively investigates the impact of trade liberalization on firms' export behavior by using the micro data of Chinese manufacturing firms. 丁he results show that:(ⅰ)trade liberalization significantly facilitates Chinese firms' export participation. We use suitable instrumental variable to overcome the endogen city problem and the multiple perspectives of robust analysis to support this conclusion. (ⅱ)trade liberalization facilitates firms' export participation through pro-competitive effect and cost effect,of which,the cost effect is larger. (ⅲ)China's WTO entry has significantly boosted firms' export decision,but has a larger effect on local firms,and WTO entry is also mainly through the way of intensive margin to affect firms' export behavior.

Key words:trade liberalization;export participation in;enterprise productivity

中国—东盟自贸区进口通关时间的贸易效应及比较研究

——基于不同时间密集型农产品的实证

胡 超

《国际贸易问题》2014 年第 8 期

摘要:本文以 2006—2012 年中国—东盟 8 个国家的 24 种时间密集型和 31 种非时间密集型农产品的 4900 个贸易数据为对象,实证检验并比较了进口通关时间的贸易效应。总体上,进口国进口通关时间对农产品产生了显著的负面贸易效应。进口通关时间每延长 10% 可导致自贸区内农产品贸易额下降 5.68%,即使剔除新加坡贸易数据的稳健性检验显示这一负面影响仍达到 4.25%,且进口通关时间对时间密集型农产品负面贸易效应显著高于非时间密集型农产品 4.5% ~ 6.2%,同时进口通关时间接近的国家农产品年贸易额亦更大。论文的政策蕴意在于,后自贸区时代,在互利共赢的基础上,以降低通关时间作为贸易便利化的突破口,通关时间的降低和同步化可以实现对中国—东盟关税削减的制度红利式微的有效替代。

关键词:贸易通关时间　农产品贸易　时间密集型　非时间密集型

Comparison of Trade Effects of China-ASEAN Import Customs Clearance Time:An Empirical Analysis Based on Different Time-intensive Agricultural Products

Abstract:Using trade data of 24 time-intensive and 31 non time-intensive agricultural products in China and ASEAN countries during 2006 – 2012,the empirical analysis tests and compares trade effects of different import customs clearance time,finding that import customs clearance time has a negative effect on agricultural products trade. Every 10% delay in import customs clearance time can result in a 5.68% fall in the trade volume of agricultural products;the adverse effects are still significant at 4.25% even by dropping the robustness test with Singapore data. This paper also finds that the adverse effect of import customs clearance time on the time-intensive products is about 4.5% – 6.2% higher than that on the time-intensive agricultural products and the trade volume is larger between countries with similar import customs time. The paper also suggests that,in the post free trade era,driven by mutual interest,reducing customs clearance time to facilitate trade is an effective alternative of the less incentive tariff reduction measure in China-ASEAN trade.

Key words:Trade customs clearance time;Agricultural trade;Time-intensive;Non time intensive

亚太区域经济一体化博弈与中国的战略选择

盛斌　果婷

《世界经济与政治》2014 年第 10 期

摘要:随着亚太区域新型生产与服务网络的日益深化,近年来该地区的自由贸易协定迅猛。其中,"区域全面经济伙伴关系"和"跨太平洋伙伴关系协议"这两个巨型自由贸易协定是当前由东亚国家和美国分别主导的推进亚太经济一体化的不同轨道,对亚太各国都产生了深刻的影响。作者从传统贸易关系、价值链贸易关系、传统贸易政策与"第二代"贸易政策的视角分析了亚太各国对于"区域全面经济伙伴关系"和"跨太平洋伙伴关系协议"的路径与策略选择。未来亚太经济一体化有四种方式,即自由贸易协定网络、区域全面经济伙伴关系、跨太平洋伙伴关系协议和亚太自由贸易区。它们之间具有整合、趋同、互补和竞争的相互关系与发展路径。中国应灵活利用亚太地区的多重合作机制,统筹兼顾,重点以"区域全面经济伙伴关系"谈判推进亚太区域一体化建设,并积极倡导与推进亚太自贸区,同时应逐步接纳与试行基于全球价值链的现代高标准与高质量的贸易规则,提高自身自由贸易协定网络的质量水平。

关键词:亚太经济一体化　跨太平洋伙伴关系协议　区域全面经济伙伴关系亚太自由贸易区亚太区域合作

The integration game of the city of Asia is a slightly different choice for China

Abstract:With the fast growing new regional production and servicer network in the Asia-Pacific region,free trade agreements(FTAs)have been proliferating rapidly in recent years. Among others,RCEP and TTP,two mega FTAs,have become main different tracks led by the East Asian countries and the United States respectively to promote the Asia-pacific economic integration,which has a profound impact on each country in the region. The paper attempts to analyze the Asia-pacific economies ' option between RCEP and TPP from the perspective of traditional trade relation,value-added trade relation,traditional trade policy and the "second generation" of trade policy. The results indicate that RCEP members more rely on traditional trade relation focusing on trade volume,traditional trade policy focusing on market access,and comprehensive economic and technological cooperation aiming members,while TPP members endeavor to establish a brand-new FTA agreement focusing on value-added trade relation regulatory coherence and "second generation" of trade policy.

Key words:Asia-pacific economic integration;Trans-Pacific Partnership Agreement;Regional Comprehensive Economic Partnership;Free Trade Area of the Asia-Pacific;Asia-pacific regional cooperation

中国增加值贸易隐含的要素流扭曲程度分析

程大中

《经济研究》2014 年第 9 期

摘要：本文在双边基本框架下同时引入要素生产率（TFP）与综合贸易成本（CTC）的跨国差异，并基于"世界投入—产出数据（WIOD）"，多角度评估了在全球价值链（GVCs）分工背景下中国增加值贸易（TiVo）隐含的净要素含量流向扭曲程度。研究发现，资本与劳动力流向扭曲程度总体上趋于下降；相对于进口，出口隐含的资本流向扭曲程度较高、劳动力流向扭曲程度则较低；相对于高技能劳动力，中低技能尤其是低技能劳动力的流向扭曲程度较低；相对于跟俄罗斯、印度和巴西等"金砖"国家的双边贸易，中国与美国、日本、韩国、德国和中国台湾等五个最重要贸易伙伴的双边贸易隐含的资本和劳动力要素流向扭曲程度较轻；受到中低技能特别是低技能劳动力要素流向扭曲影响的行业较少，贸易量较大的行业受到要素流向扭曲的影响较轻。本文初步表明，要素禀赋结构仍是反映一国增加值贸易是否以及在多大程度受到要素流向扭曲影响的基础。因此，中国要促进增加值贸易（及其产业链基础）转型升级，同时减轻贸易所含要素流向的扭曲程度，应首先着眼于国内（相对于国外）的要素禀赋结构优化升级。

关键词：增加值贸易　世界投入—产出表　HOV 模型　贸易的要素含量　要素流向

Factor Flow Distortions Embodied in China's Trade in Value-Added

Abstract：This paper introduces transnational differences in both total factor productivity（TFP）and comprehensive trade costs（CTC）into the basic bilateral dimensional evaluation of distortions in both capital net factor HOV framework, and uses the World Input-Output Database（WIOD）, m make a multi-flow distortions embodied in China's trade in value-added（TiVo）. On the whole, the import, but it skilled labor is converse and labor flows are declining. The distortions in capital flows are more profound in export than in for labor flows. Compared with high-skilled labor, low and medium-skilled and especially low-less distorted in the cross-border trade. Compared with

China's bilateral trade with the so-called BRICS economies such as Brazil, India, and Russia, China's bilateral trade with the major partners like LISA, Japan, South Korea, Germany and Taiwan is characterized by less distorted capital and labor cross-border movements. There are fewer sectors that are affected by distortions in low-and medium-skilled and especially low-skilled labor flows. Sectors with more trade are less affected by factor flow distortions. The study shows that factor endowment structures are still the basis determining whether and how much an economy's TiVo is influenced by the distortions in factor cross-border flows.

Therefore, in order to upgrade the TiVo and related industrial basis, and meanwhile to reduce factor flow distortions embodied in TiVo, China should prioritize the optimization and upgrading of domestic factor endowment structures relative to foreign economies.

Key words: value added trade; world input-output table; HOV model; trade element content; element flow direction

附加值贸易:基于中国的实证分析

罗长远 张军

《经济研究》2014 年第 6 期

摘要:结合对现有文献的拓展和应用,本文给出了一个理解中国附加值贸易发展的框架。在此基础上,本文运用 OECE/WTO 的 TiVA 数据库进行实证研究,结果表明,在中国的出口中,本地附加值所占比重从 1995 年的 88% 降至 2005 年的 64%。此后,这一比重缓慢回升,至 2009 年达到 67%。从产业角度所做的分解显示,出口本地附加值比重走低(回升),主要是产业内本地附加值比重下降(提高)造成的,而出口行业构成的变化则是第二位的因素。从国际比较来看,行业内出口本地附加值比重偏低是中国整个出口本地附加值比重低于美国、德国和日本的主要因素,而出口行业构成偏重于本地附加值比重低的制造业则是中国整个出口本地附加值比重低于印度的主要因素。另外,直接附加值比重偏低,也即出口行业自身创造附加值的能力有限,是中国出口本地附加值比重总体水平较低的一个重要原因。

关键词:本地附加值 直接附加值 产业内效应 产业间效应

Urban-Rural Income Disparity, Labor Quality and Economic Growth in China

Abstract: As demographic dividend disappeared gradually, improving labor quality will have a significant impact on economic growth. Based on the OLG model, this paper builds a theoretical model of developing country to explain the interacted relationship among urban-rural income disparity, labor quality and economic growth. By empirically analyzing Chinese provincial panel data from 1995 to 2012, we find the estimation result of our model is well consistent with the conclusions from theoretical study: Urban-rural income disparity has significantly negative relationships with the economic growth.

Key words: urban-rural income disparity; labor quality; economic growth

跨国生产、贸易增加值与增加值率的变化

——基于投入产出框架对增加值率的理论解析

夏明　张红霞

《管理世界》2015 年第 2 期

摘要：本文剖析了贸易增加值度量中存在的问题以及概念之间的关系，指出增加值贸易和贸易增加值分析路径的差异。然而在贸易增加值的计算中，增加值率作为对生产与收入关系的一种关键度量，只是作为一个外生变量来处理，这样就无法全面解释为什么我国的增加值率明显偏低。为此，本文基于投入产出框架，对增加值率的内涵及其比较静态性质进行了分析，指出增加值率的高低不只反映技术，也受到各种分配因素的影响。一国增加值率的高低不仅取决于自身的技术努力，也同样与现有的国际分配体系及制度等诸多因素密切相关。我国增加值率远低于发达国家，且持续降低在一定程度上正是国际分工背景下技术与分配诸多因素共同影响的结果。

关键词：贸易增加值　增加值率　投入产出分析

The change of transnational production, added value of trade and value of added value——theoretical analysis of the value added value based on input output framework

Abstract: This paper analyzes the problems in the measurement of trade value added value and the relationship among concepts, points out the difference between the value added value trade and the analysis path of the value added value.

In the calculation of the added value of trade, however, the value added rate as a key measure for the relationship between production and income, is treated as an exogenous variable, which makes it impossible to fully explain why China's value added rate is significantly lower.

Based on input-output framework, this paper, the connotation of value rate and its comparative static properties are analyzed, and points out that the value rate of high and low not only reflect the technology, also under the influence of various factors allocation.

The value added of a country depends not only on its own technical efforts, but also on many factors such as the existing international distribution system and system.

China's added value is much lower than that of developed countries, and the continuous decrease is partly the result of the combination of technology and distribution in the background of international division of labor.

Key words: added value of trade; value added rate; input-output analysis

全球价值链视角下中国增加值出口及其影响因素

卫瑞　张文城　张少军

《数量经济技术经济研究》2015 年第 7 期

摘要：基于世界投入产出数据库，采用 MRIO 模型测算 1995～2009 年中国增加值出口的变动趋势，并采用结构分解方法分析了 9 种因素对中国增加值出口变化的影响。结果显示，1995～2009 年外需引致的中国增加值出口由 1425 亿美元增加到 10396 亿美元，增幅高达 629. 36%，增加值出口对于国内增加值创造的重要性在不断提高;外国最终需求的来源地结构变动、中国前向国际产业关联变动和外国最终需求规模变动是影响中国增加值出口变化的 3 个最主要因素,分别使中国增加值出口增长 278.81%、262.02% 和 122.28%;中国国内生产部门增加值系数变动和外国最终需求的产品结构变动不利于中国增加值出口增长或影响很小。

关键词:增加值出口　投入产出　结构分析　全球价值链

China's Value-added Export and Its Determinants
under Global Value Chain

Abstract:Under the background of Global Value Chain, a country's ability to export domestic value added reflects its international division status. Based on Multi-Region Input-Output tables from World Input-Output Database, we analyze China's value-added export and use Structural Decomposition Analysis to decompose 1995-2009 value-ue-added export of China. The results reveal that:during the research period there is a huge increase for China's value-added export, from 142.5 billion to 1039.6 billion. Value-added export is becoming more and more important for China's GDP. The change of the source structure of foreign final demand, the strengthening of the forward international industry linkage, the foreign final demand expansion are three factors to increase China's value-added export, contributing 278.81%、262.02% and 122.02% to the change of China's value-added export respectively. The decrease of value-added coefficient in China goes against the increase of China's value-added export, while the effect of the composition of final demand is indistinctive. Therefore, in the instance of China's high participation of Global Value Chain but low domestic value added creation, in order to improve China's international division status ¦ we should increase China's value-added export by speeding up the opening up progress of producer services and encouraging producer services export.

Key words: value-added export; input output; structural analysis; global value chain

全球价值链嵌入对中国出口技术复杂度的影响

刘维林　李兰冰　刘玉海

《中国工业经济》2014 年第 6 期

摘要：本文提出了基于产品与功能双重嵌入结构的全球价值链嵌入水平测算框架,并从理论上论证了全球价值链嵌入程度、嵌入结构与价值来源对出口技术复杂度的影响及其两面性,进而采用二次优化算法对区分加工贸易与一般贸易的非竞争型投入产出表进行估算,得出用以反映全球价值链嵌入程度的各项国外附加值率指标。在此基础上利用 2001—2010 年中国 27 个制造部门的面板计量模型检验了国外附加值率对制造业出口技术复杂度的影响。研究表明,中国制造业通过参与全球价值链分工所获取的国外中间投入推动了出口技术复杂度的提升,而相对于原材料、零部件等产品投入服务投入对技术提升的贡献更大;在控制了国外附加值的直接贡献情况下,来自发达国家的国外附加值对出口制造业的 R&D 活动具有抑制作用,更容易形成对链主企业的单向技术依赖和低端锁定",而利用其他国家国外附加值所形成的嵌入方式对出口企业自身 R&D 能力的依赖程度更强,更有利于出技术复杂度的提升。

关键词：全球价值链　国外附加值　出口技术复杂度

The impact of global value chain embeddedness on China's export technology complexity

Abstract：This paper presents the global value chain framework and function level of embedded products based on double embedded structure, and demonstrates the embedding degree, the global value chain and value source embedded structure affects the sophistication of export and its two sides, and then using the two optimization algorithm to distinguish between processing trade and general trade of non competitive table to estimate the input and output, that used to reflect the degree of foreign embedded in global value chain index value added rate. On the basis of the 2001 panel econometric model 27 manufacturing sector in 2010 China inspection of foreign influence on the rate of value-added manufacturing export technical complexity. Research shows that China manufacturing through participation in global value chain division acquired foreign intermediate inputs promote the technology level, compared to the raw materials, parts and other products put into service of technology to promote greater contribution; in the control of the direct contribution of foreign value-added, from the developed countries abroad added the value of export manufacturing R&D activity has an inhibitory effect on the formation of the main chain, more enterprises and one-way technology relies on the low-end locked ", and the use of other foreign countries added value depends on the formation of stronger embedding export enterprises R&D capability, more conducive to the increasing complexity of technology.

Key words: global value chain; foreign value-added export; technology complexity

21世纪"海上丝绸之路"贸易潜力及其影响因素

——基于随机前沿引力模型的实证研究

谭秀杰　周茂荣

《国际贸易问题》2015年第2期

摘要：共同建设21世纪"海上丝绸之路"是推动我国新一轮对外开放、促进沿线国家共同发展的重大战略，国际贸易是该战略的基础和纽带。本文利用随机前沿引力模型研究了"海上丝绸之路"主要沿线国家间的贸易潜力，并采用一步法分析了影响因素。研究表明，"海上丝绸之路"的贸易效率在不断提升，中国对"海上丝绸之路"的出口仍有很大潜力。为进一步提高"海上丝绸之路"贸易效率，应加快推进自贸区谈判，降低关税和非关税壁垒，提高贸易便利化，加强海运互联互通，改善交通基础设施，并注重金融风险防范的合作。

关键词：海上丝绸之路　贸易潜力　随机前沿　引力模型

The Impact of Global Value Chain Embeddedness on Technological Sophistication of China's Export

Abstract: This paper constructs a measuring framework for the embeddedness of global value chain(GVC) based on the dual perspective of product and function architecture. The influence and two-side effect from the embeddedness level, structure and value sources to the export technological sophistication are demonstrated theoretically. Then a quadratic programming model is used to estimate the non-competitive input-output table with processing trade and normal trade separated, in order to calculate the foreign value added ratio(FVAR) indexes to reflect the embeddedness. We use the panel data model of 27 manufacturing sectors in 2001 – 2010 to testify the influence of FVAR on export sophistication. The results suggest that the foreign input of Chinese manufacturing enterprises participating in the GVC promoted the export sophistication and the contribution of service inputs is larger than the product inputs such as the materials and accessories. Controlling the direct contributions of FVAR, the FVAR from developed countries has an inhibitory effect on the R&D activities of export manufacturing and more easily lead to a one-way technical dependence to the dominant firms and low-locked. The embeddedness of export enterprises by utilizing the FVAR from other countries rely more on own R&D abilities and is more beneficial to the export sophistication.

Key words: global value chain; foreign value added; export technological sophistication

构建"一带一路"需要优先处理的关系

李向阳

《国际经济评论》2015 年第 1 期

摘要: 基于对外开放新举措与经济外交新平台的基本定位,"一带一路"将成为能够体现"亲诚惠容"理念的一种新型区域合作机制。为构建"一带一路",作为倡导者,中国需要处理一系列全新的问题。其中包括政府与企业的关系,中央政府与地方政府的关系,历史与现实的关系,利用现有比较优势与开发新优势的关系,经济合作与非经济合作的关系,以及机制化合作与非机制化合作的关系等。

关键词: 丝绸之路经济带 海上丝绸之路 一带一路 经济外交

Relations to Be Prioritized in China's
"Belt and Road Initiative"

Abstract: The Silk Road Economic Belt and the 21st Century Maritime Silk Road plans, or the "Belt and Road Initiative", which serves as a new step of opening up and a new platform for economic diplomacy, is a new-type regional cooperative mechanism that reflects the China's diplomatic philosophy of "friendliness, credibility, mutual benefit and tolerance". As the advocate of the Belt and Road Initiative, China needs to properly handle a series of issues, including government-enterprise relations, relations between central and local authorities, between history and current conditions; between utilization of existing comparative advantages and exploration of new edges, between economic cooperation and non-economic cooperation and between mechanism-based cooperation and non-systematic cooperation.

Key words: the silk road economic belt; the maritime silk road; the belt and road initiative; economic diplomacy

碳生产率变动与出口复杂度演进:1992~2009 年

李小平　王树柏　周记顺

《数量经济技术经济研究》2014 年第 9 期

摘要:采用1992~2009 年的跨国面板数据,在测算出各国出口复杂度的基础上,实证分析碳生产率等因素对出口复杂度演进的影响。研究发现,碳生产率作为一种新的比较优势决定因素,对提高各国出口复杂度至关重要;不论是高收入国家还是低收入国家,碳生产率的提高都能够显著促进出口复杂度的提升;各类资本禀赋与出口复杂度之间存在倒"U"形关系,并且这种关系在高收入国家和低收入国家中存在差异;自然资源禀赋不利于出口复杂度提升的"资源诅咒"现象更容易在低收入国家出现;经济开放度的扩大更有利于低收入国家出口复杂度的提升。

关键词:碳生产率　出口复杂度　产品异质性

Changes of Carbon Productivity and the Evolution
of Export Sophistication:1992 – 2009

Abstract: Adopting multinational panel data from 1992 to 2009, based on the computed export sophistication index with considering heterogeneity of export products and the empirical analysis of the effects of carbon productivity and other factors on the evolution of export sophistication, we find that; as a new determinant of comparative advantage, carbon productivity plays an extremely important role; whether high-income or low-income countries, carbon productivity improvement can significantly promote export sophistication; there exists a kind of inverted "U" shaped relationship between every capital factor and export sophistication var-ying from high-income to low-income countries; the "resource curse" phenomenon, that is to say, natural resource is not conducive to the improvement of export sophistication, is much more likely to occur in low-income countries.

Key words: carbon productivity; export sophistication; product heterogeneity

中国的环境污染与经济增长

王敏　黄滢

《经济学(季刊)》2015 年第 1 期

摘要：中国经济经历三十多年高速增长，但环境质量也日趋恶化。本文利用 112 座城市在 2003—2010 年间的大气污染浓度数据，考察我国经济增长和环境污染之间的关系。与以往研究不同的是，基于传统的环境库兹涅茨曲线模型，我们发现所有的大气污染浓度指标都呈现出"U 形"曲线关系。但是在考虑了每个城市特定的时间趋势变量后，高增长并不一定会导致高污染。最后，通过对同一污染物的排放数据和大气浓度数据进行对比分析，发现两者的回归结果截然相反。

关键词：环境污染　环境库兹涅茨曲线　经济增长

China's Environmental Pollution and Economic Growth

Abstract: China has experienced more than three decades of rapid growth, but suffers from severe environmental degradation. This paper uses latest panel dataset covering 112 critics from 2003 to 2010 to test the relationship between growth and air pollution. Using traditional environmental Kuznets model, we find that all pollutants exhibit shaped "curve", which are radically different from the results found by previous studies. By controlling individual time trend, we show that growth does not have to deteriorate the environment. Finally, we also show that regression results could be completely opposite if we use different data source for the same pollutant.

Key words: environmental pollution; environment Kuznets curve; economic growth

中国服务业生产率变动的差异分析

——基于区域及行业视角

王恕立　滕泽伟　刘军

《经济研究》2015 年第 8 期

摘要:本文将环境因素纳入生产率研究体系,引入考虑"坏"产出的 malmquist-luenberger 指数法分别测算了中国 2000—2012 年 31 个省市和 2004—2012 年服务业细分行业的服务业全要素生产率(TFP)变动情况,同时与未考虑环境因素的服务业 TFP 区域和行业差异进行了比较分析。研究表明:中国服务业 TFP 增长表现出了较大的区域和行业异质性,未考虑环境因素的传统测算方法显著高估了服务业 TFP 的增长率及其对服务业增长的贡献,环境因素对服务业增长绩效存在影响,服务业发展过程中出现了浪费资源和破坏生态环境的粗放型增长。服务业 TFP 增长的源泉主要是技术进步,通过提升技术效率来促进服务业增长还有很大的余地。

关键词:服务业生产率　环境约束　"坏"产出　异质性

The Disparity and Convergence of TFP Change in China's Service Industry
——Based on Regional and Industry Perspectives

Abstract: This paper introduces Malmquist-Luenberger productivity index, taking into account of the growth of "good" output and the reduction of "bad" output at the same time. We apply the index to measure the TFP growth of service industry for China's 31 provinces and services sub-sector industry based on the provincial panel data from 2000 – 2012 and industry panel data from 2004 – 2012, and conduct a comparative analysis to the regional and industry disparity of TFP change that was not taken into account of environmental factors. The result shows that the TFP growth of China's service industry possessed greater heterogeneity of the regional and industry. We also find that the growth of service total factor productivity is mainly caused by technical progress, not to consider environmental factors overestimates total factor productivity and its contribution to service growth. The services economic rapid growth is at the expense of natural resource destruction and service environmental pollution in China. There is still a lot technical efficiency to improve the service growth.

Key words: productivity of service Industry; environmental constraint; "bad" output; Heterogeneity

全球化与中国生产服务业发展

——基于全球投入产出模型的研究

袁志刚　饶璨

《管理世界》2014 年第 3 期

摘要：本文运用全球投入产出模型分析生产服务业对我国各产业部门生产的投入变迁，同时采用结构分解剖析中国生产服务业发展的主要动因，进而考察全球化对中国生产服务业发展的塑造。我们的研究发现，全球化趋势造成生产服务业对主要产业部门投入的停滞和下滑。同时出现国外生产服务业投入对国内投入产生替代，并且这一替代集中在中、高技术含量产业部门。与此同时，虽然全球化造成国内技术变动抑制本国主要生产服务业发展，但国外技术变动和国内及国外最终需求变动都有力拉动了中国生产服务业发展。中国未来生产服务业发展必须坚持服务业进一步对外开放，并在鼓励货物贸易出口和国内最终需求增长的同时，破除服务业领域国有企业垄断和加快人力资本积累。

关键词：全球化　生产服务业　投入产出　结构分解分析

Globalization and the development of China's service industry
Research on the global input-output model

Abstract: This paper USES global input-output model to analyze production services for the change of each industrial sector production input, at the same time, the decomposition analysis is adopted the main motivations of production service industry development in China, and then examine globalization shape of production service industry development in China.

Our research shows that the trend of globalization leads to the stagnation and decline of major industrial sectors in the production services sector.

At the same time, there is an alternative to domestic investment in foreign production services, and this alternative is concentrated in the middle and high-tech industries.

Although domestic technology due to the change of globalization, meanwhile, inhibit its main production service industry development, but the foreign technology changes and changes in final demand domestic and abroad are strong pull production service industry development in China.

Production services for China's future development must adhere to the service industry to further opening to the outside world, and to encourage trade in goods exports and domestic final demand growth at the same time, break service sector monopoly of state-owned enterprises and speeding up human capital accumulation.

Key words: globalization; production service; input and output; structure decomposition analysis

进口服务中间投入对我国制造业全球价值链分工地位的影响研究

周大鹏

《世界经济研究》2015 年第 8 期

摘要:文章选取 48 个国家和地区 1997—2007 年的出口、人均 GDP 数据计算了各国(地区)出口复杂度 排名,并以此为依据对我国制造业在全球价值链中的地位进行了定量评估。结合中国投入产出表数据,文章构建了一个包含四类产业截面的面板数据误差修正模型,定量测算了进口服务中间投入对制造业全 球价值链分工地位的影响。实证分析表明:中国供应商主导型、规模经济型、专业制造型和科技主导型等 四类制造业出口复杂度的国际排名总体上较为靠后;从长期效应看,进口服务中间投入确实对我国出口 复杂度具有积极影响,而且知识与技术需求量高的制造业所受的影响最为显著。

关键词:服务中间投入 出口复杂度 全球价值链 制造业

Influence of Imported Services Intermediate Input on Manufacturing Industry's Export Sophistication in China

Abstract：Based on the export data and per capita GDP data of 48 countries and regions between 1997 and 2007, this article calculates the export sophistication ranking. It then examines the long run relationship between manufacturing industry sophistication and imported services intermediate inputs by using China's input, output table data. By constructing an error correction model, it finds that：China's SDOM, SCALE, SPEC and SCIB sectors are all in the bottom of the ranking list. China still has a long way to go to become a leading manufacturing power. In the long run the imported services intermediate inputs do have a positive impact on China's export sophistication, and the impact on knowledge-and technology intensive manufacturing sector is most significant. Finally this article puts forward several recommendations on the services intermediate input trade policy.

Key words：service input；export complexity；global value chain；manufacturing industry

中国服务贸易的本地市场效应研究

——基于中国与 31 个国家(地区)的双边贸易面板数据

阚大学　吕连菊

《财经研究》2014 年第 10 期

摘要：文章利用 1992—2011 年中国与 31 个国家(地区)的双边服务贸易的面板数据实证研究了中国服务贸易的本地市场效应,发现相对需求结构、需求规模作用的本地市场效应和以劳动力要素禀赋为传统的比较优势均促进了中国服务出口,并且后者促进作用大于前者;还发现需求规模作用的本地市场效应促进了中国的传统服务、新兴服务、生产性服务和非生产性服务的出口,其中对新兴服务和生产性服务出口的促进作用更为明显;需求结构作用的本地市场效应也促进了中国新兴服务和生产性服务出口,但促进作用较小,同时需求结构弱化了本地市场效应对传统服务和非生产性服务出口;最后发现中国的运输服务、旅游服务、建筑服务、通信服务、金融服务和保险服务都存在显著的需求规模作用的本地市场效应,而旅游服务、金融服务和保险服务则都存在显著的需求结构作用的本地市场效应,计算机和信息服务、专有权利及许可费、个人、文化和娱乐服务、其他商业服务的本地市场效应都不显著。

关键词:服务贸易 比较优势 本地市场效应 引力模型

On Home Market Effects of Chinese Services Trade Based on Panel Data of Bilateral Trade between China and 31 Countries

Abstract: By using the panel data of bilateral trade in services between China and 31 countries from 1992 to 2011, this paper empirically studies the home market effect of Chinese services trade and shows that as follows: firstly, compared to demand structure, the home market effect resulting from demand scale and traditional comparative advantages with labor force factor endowment promote Chinese services export, but the promotion role of the later is bigger than the one of home market effect resulting from demand scale; secondly, the home market effect resulting from demand scale promotes traditional, emerging, productive and non-productive services export and the promotion role in emerging and productive services export is more significant; thirdly, the home market effect resulting from demand structure promotes emerging and productive services trade, but the promotion role is small; demand structure weakens the promotion role of home market effect in traditional and non-productive services export; fourthly, the home market effect resulting from demand scale obviously exists in transportation, tourism, construction, communication, finance and insurance services and the home market effect resulting from demand structure exists in tourism, finance and insurance services. The home market effects of computer and information services, copyright and license fees, personal, cultural and recreational services, and other business services are not significant.

Key words: services trade; comparative advantage; home market effect; gravity model

产品内分工、制度质量与出口技术复杂度

戴翔 金碚

《经济研究》2014 年第 7 期

摘要：本文从分工演进视角，提出了制度质量、融入产品内国际分工程度及其二者交互作用，促进出口技术复杂度提升作用机制的理论假说。借鉴 hausmanaet-al. (2005) 的方法，利用 1996—2010 年 HS92 六位数分类贸易统计数据，本文测算了个国家（地区）的出口技术复杂度，并分别运用 OLS 法和系统 GMM 法进行了实证研究。计量结果表明，制度质量的完善对提升出口技术复杂度具有显著正向作用，与此同时，融入产品内国际分工程度及其与制度质量的交互作用，同样也对出口技术复杂度提升具有显著促进作用。理论假说通过了较好的逻辑一致性计量检验。据此，伴随中国人口红利等传统低成本国际竞争优势逐步丧失，新一轮开放应注重释放制度红利，从而在进一步深度融入产品内国际分工体系中提升中国出口技术复杂度，谋求全球分工新地位。

关键词：产品内分工 制度质量 出口技术复杂度

Intra-product Specialization, Institution Quality and Export technology complexity

Abstract：From point of international labor division, we put forward the theoretical hypothesis that institution quality, integration into intra-product specialization and the two items interaction can improve export sophistication. Base on the method given by Haussmann et al. (2005), we calculate 62 countries' export sophistication by using HS92 6-digit trade data covering from 1996 to 2010. On the basis of which, we carry out empirical analysis by using OLS and System GMM and results indicate that, better institution quality as well as integration into infra-product specialization can help improve export sophistication, at the same time, interaction of the above two items also can help improve export sophistication. Therefore, with Chinese demographic dividend diminishing, in a new round development of open economy, we should create new competitive advantage by releasing institution dividend, so that we can improve export sophistication by integrating into intra-product specialization further.

Key words: infra-product specialization; institution quality; export sophistication

进口类型、行业差异化程度与企业生产率提升

余淼杰　李晋

《经济研究》2015 年第 8 期

摘要:本文基于 2002—2006 年间中国制造业企业面板数据、高度细化的海关数据和行业差异化程度数据,讨论进口对于差异化行业的企业生产率的促进作用。考虑到进口与企业生产率可能存在反向因果关系影响估计结果的一致性,本文通过使用关税指数构建工具变量来解决内生性问题。本文发现了中间投入品进口与最终产品进口对于企业生产率的促进作用。进一步考虑行业差异化问题,研究发现进口仅对于同质性行业的企业生产率提升有显著的促进作用。通过引入市场集中度,实证回归结果表明进口竞争效应对于同质性行业更为重要,而进口技术外溢效应对于差异化程度较大的行业更为重要。数据显示的差异化较大的行业从技术外溢中获益数值较小的原因可能源于阶段性企业科技研发投入的不足。

关键词:进口竞争效应　进口技术外溢效应　企业生产率　差异化行业　市场集中度

Imports, Heterogeneous Industry and Improvement of Firm Productivity

Abstract: This paper studies the impact of imported intermediate inputs and imports of final goads on firm by taking product complexity into account, based on highly disaggregated Chinese transaction-level trade data and firm-level production data from 2002 to 2006. After controlling for the endogeneity of imported intermediate inputs, we confirm that firms could benefit from imports. Further, we find import could improve firm productivity which produce homogeneous goods, but has little effect on those produce complex goods. To explain this heterogeneous effect, market concentration is introduced, and the result reveals that import competition effect weighs in homogeneous industry while import spillover effect is more important to heterogeneous industry. The little impact of imports on firm productivity in heterogeneous industry could be explained by weak import spillover effect due to low R&D efficiency.

Key words：import competition effect；import spillover effect；firm productivity；product complexity；market concentration

中国企业出口产品质量测算及其决定因素

——培育出口竞争新优势的微观视角

施炳展　　邵文波

《管理世界》2014 年第 9 期

摘要：本文从质量（quality）视角入手分析中国企业出口行为及其决定因素。借鉴新新贸易理论最新进展，我们首先放弃单位价值（unitvalue）等同于质量的假设，采用 2485 个产品层面回归反推方法，测算中国企业出口产品质量；然后匹配海关数据和工业企业数据，分析企业出口产品质量的决定因素。结论发现，中国企业出口产品质量总体呈上升趋势，但本土企业与外资企业产品质量差距扩大；生产效率、研发效率、广告效率、政府补贴、融资约束缓解、市场竞争均会提升产品质量，但研发投入、广告投入并没有明显效果；企业出口空间分布特征也会反作用于产品质量；外资对本土企业产品质量影响不利，但提升了外资企业出口产品质量。从政策层面看，提升企业效率、促进金融市场发展、增强市场竞争均有益于出口产品质量提升，但对外资作用应审慎对待。

关键词：企业质量　决定因素　效率

The quality of export products of Chinese enterprises and their determinants
——cultivate the micro perspective of the new advantages
of export competition

Abstract：This paper analyzes the export behavior and determinants of Chinese enterprises from the perspective of quality（quality）. Reference to the latest progress in new trade theory，we first give up unit value（unit value）is equal to the quality of assumptions，using 2485 product level regression back stepping method，measuring the

Chinese enterprises to export products quality. Then match the data of the customs data and industrial enterprises to analyze the determinants of the quality of export products.

The conclusion is that the quality of Chinese enterprises' export products is increasing.

However, the gap between local enterprises and foreign-funded enterprises has widened.

Production efficiency, research and development efficiency, advertising efficiency, government subsidies, financing constraints, and market competition will improve product quality. However, red investment and advertising investment have no obvious effect.

The distribution characteristics of enterprises' export space will also adversely affect product quality. Foreign capital has an unfavorable influence on the quality of domestic enterprises, but it has promoted the quality of export products of foreign enterprises. At the policy level, improving the efficiency of enterprises, promoting the development of financial market and enhancing market competition are beneficial to the improvement of the quality of export products, but should be treated with caution.

Key words: enterprise quality; determine factor; efficiency

出口对就业、工资和收入不平等的影响

——基于微观数据的证据

张川川

《经济学(季刊)》2015 年第 3 期

摘要:使用微观人口数据和贸易数据,本文重点估计了中国出口对就业、工资和收入不平等的影响。结果显示,2000－2005 年间的出口增长显著提高了制造业和服务业就业,并且出口增长对年轻人、低学历人口、农村户籍人口和女性的就业影响更显著,效果更大。进一步研究显示,出口显著提高了在业者的收入水平,降低了城市内部的收入不平等。最后,本文补充考察了进口的影响,没有发现显著的就业和工资效应。但是,进口显著增加了城市内部的收入不平等。

关键词:出口　就业　收入不平等

Effects of Exporting on Employment，Wage and Income Inequality： Evidence from Micro Data

Abstract：Using micro population data and trade data，this paper estimates the effects of China's exporting on employment，wage and income inequality. Results show that exporting growth during 2000 to 2005 significantly promoted employment in manufacturing sector and service sector，and the effects of exporting growth on younger，less-educated，rural and women labor force arc stronger. Further studies show that exporting significantly promoted income of current workers and lowered income inequality within cities. Finally，the paper takes into account the impacts of importing，but finds no significant effects on employment and wage. However，importing significantly increases income inequality within cities.

Key words：exporting；employment；income inequality

中国进口贸易的技术结构及其影响因素研究

魏浩 李晓庆

《世界经济》2015 年第 8 期

摘要：本文在对国际贸易商品技术含量进行具体测度的基础上，利用有序样本聚类分析的最优分割法对国际贸易商品进行分类，构建国际贸易商品技术结构的分析框架，测算了 2001—2012 年中国进口商品技术结构的变化趋势。此外，还利用中国与 57 个贸易伙伴国的双边数据，分析了影响中国不同类型技术商品进口的因素及其差异性。研究结果表明：自 2001 年以来，中高技术商品一直是中国第一大进口商品，中低技术商品所占份额大幅上升，各类产品的进口占世界各类产品总进口的份额整体呈日益增加态势；双边贸易成本、出口国在中国的直接投资规模、出口国技术水平、中国知识产权保护度等因素是影响中国高技术、中高技术进口的重要因素。

关键词：技术复杂度指数 最优分割法 进口技术结构

The technical structure of China's import trade and its influence are studied

Abstract:This article in the international trade goods on the basis of the specific measures of technical content, using the optimal partition of ordered sample cluster analysis method to categorize international trade goods, international technology trade goods structure analysis framework, calculate the years 2001 – 2012 imports the change trend of technical structure.

In addition, the factors affecting the import of different types of technical commodities in China and their differences are analyzed using bilateral data from China and 57 trading partners.

The results show that since 2001, the high technology products has always been China's largest imports, low technology products share rise sharply, the import of all kinds of products of total imports of all kinds of products in the world as a whole was increasingly increase;

Bilateral trade cost and exporter in China exporters of direct investment scale, technical level, degree of China's intellectual property rights protection factor is an important factor of China's high technology, high technology import.

Key words:technology of technology; optimal segmentation import; technology structure

技术升级与中国出口竞争力变迁:从微观向宏观的弥合

鲁晓东

《世界经济》2014 年第 8 期

摘要:本文首先通过一个包含产品技术含量的异质企业贸易模型在理论上廓清了技术升级与企业出口行为间的关系,然后利用中国工业企业和高度细分的产品数据将中国出口竞争力这一宏观概念与中国出口企业的微观特征相联系,从企业角度研究中国出口竞争力的变迁。研究结果表明:在中国出口规模激增的同时其出口技术含量仅有微弱提升,中国出口技术水平仍较低,出口增长存在系统性风险。出口企业的生产率提高有效地促成了中国出口技术复杂度的变化,这说明提高企业生产率是实现产品升级以及保持中国出口竞争力可持续性的关键。此外,企业技术升级对中国出口技术含量提升的积极作用总是倾向于发生在那些经济规模较大、经济发展水平较高的贸易伙伴国。

关键词:技术升级　出口竞争力　技术复杂度　全要素生产率

Technological upgrading and changes in China's export competitiveness:from micro to macro

Abstract:This paper through a contains the product technology content of heterogeneous enterprise trade model in theory,clear the relationship between the technology upgrading and enterprise export behavior,and then take advantage of China's industrial enterprises and height niche product data will China export competitiveness the macro concept and the microscopic characteristics of the Chinese export enterprises,from the perspective of enterprise research the changes of China's export competitiveness.

The results show that while the export volume of China is surging and its export technology is only slightly improved,the level of Chinese export technology is still low, and there is a systemic risk to export growth.

Export enterprises to improve the productivity of effectively contributed to China's export technical complexity change suggesting that raise the productivity of enterprises is to implement product upgrade,and maintain the key to China's export competitiveness of sustainability.

In addition,the positive role of technological upgrading in China's export technology is always in favor of those trading partners with larger economies and higher levels of economic development.

Key words:technology upgrade;export competitiveness,export competitiveness; total factor productivity

中国企业对外直接投资的"出口效应"

蒋冠宏　　蒋殿春

《经济研究》2014 年第 5 期

摘要:中国企业对外直接投资是替代还是促进了出口？针对该问题,本文利用数据匹配法为 2005—2007 年 1498 家有对外直接投资的工业企业找到可供比较的对照组,运用倍差法(different-in-different,DID)实证检验了企业对外直接投资的"出口效应"。经过检验本文有如下发现:第一,中国企业对外直接投资总体促进了企业出口;第二,与其他投资动机相比,商贸服务类投资显著促进了企业出口;第三,与其他东道国相比,投资高收入国家的"出口效应"最为明显;第四,企业对外直接投资的"出口效应"先上升后下降,呈现倒"U"型;第五,企业对外直接投资不仅增加了出口的深度边际,也扩展了出口的广度边际。因此通过本文的微观数据检验,深化了对该问题的认识。

关键词:对外直接投资　出口　马氏距离匹配　倍差法

Outward Direct Investment and Export

Abstract:ODI substitutes the export or complement? We use firm-level data to examine the relations between ODI of Chinese firms and their export. The results of our examination present some evidences. Firstly, ODI of firms complete the export of firms. Secondly, the investment of business has the most export effect. Thirdly, if the host countries are rich, the effect of export is obvious. Forth, the effect of export is invert U. At last, ODI not only adds the intensive of export but also enlarges the extensive of export.

Key words:outward direct investment;export;mahalanobis matching;different-in-different

中国对外直接投资区位选择的决定因素：制度、税负和资源禀赋

王永钦 杜巨澜 王凯

《经济研究》2014 年第 12 期

摘要：中国目前已经成为世界第三大对外直接投资 ODI 输出国。东道国（或地区）的不同制度维度是如何影响中国的 ODI 区位选择的？本文以中国 2002—2011 年间在全球范围内进行的 842 笔对外直接投资作为样本，研究了东道国的话语权与问责制、政治稳定与杜绝暴力恐怖主义、政府效率、监管质量、法治水平、腐败控制这六类制度性因素对中国 ODI 区位选择的影响。本文还讨论了税收（避税）因素和自然资源因素的作用，以及它们与制度因素的交互作用。本文的研究发现，总体而言，与大部分跨国公司不同的是：中国的 ODI 不太关心对方国家（或地区）的政治制度（话语权与问责制）和政治稳定度，而更关心政府效率、监管质量和腐败控制，并倾向于避开法律体系严格的国家；同时，中国的 ODI 存在明显的避税和获取资源的动机；东道国的制度质量与避税功能之间存在替代关系。本文的研究有助于理解中国和新兴市场经济体的决定因素和国际间资本流动的规律。

关键词：中国 ODI 制度 税收 资源

The Determinants of Location Choices of China's ODI：
Institutions, Taxations and Resources

Abstract：China has become the third largest source of outward direct investment (ODI). This paper studies how institutions in the host countries affect the location choices of China's ODI. Based on a deal-level sample from 2002 – 2011, this paper empirically tests how political institutions, political stability, government effectiveness, regulatory quality, rule of law and corruption control in the host countries affect the location choices of China's ODI. On top of these institutional factors, we study the effects of tax evasion and natural resources in host countries, and their interactions with the institutional factors. We find that political institutions in the host countries are not major concerns of the ODI, while government effectiveness, regulatory quality, and corruption control have significant effects on the locations of ODI. And China's ODI tend to avoid countries with strict legal system. Tax evasion and resources are also major motives of China's ODI. General institutional quality and tax evasion are substitutes in China's ODI location decisions.

Key words：China；ODI；institutions；tax；resources

中国对外直接投资促进抑或抑制了企业出口？

毛其淋　许家云

《数量经济技术经济研究》2014 年第 9 期

摘要：2001 年以来中国对外直接投资实现了持续快速的增长，本文旨在考察对外直接投资究竟对企业出口产生了怎样的影响。利用高度细化的工业企业数据库和海关贸易数据库首次从微观层面进行系统的研究，结果表明，对外直接投资不仅显著地提高了企业出口占销售的比例，而且提高了企业出口的概率。此外，通过引入生存分析模型的研究表明，对外直接投资显著降低了企业退出出口市场的风险，即倾向于延长企业出口持续期。本文从微观层面证实了中国对外直接投资具有显著的出口创造效应，这一核心结论在剔除贸易中间商、排除加工贸易、剔除投资于避税港的企业以及采用最近邻匹配样本进行估计时都非常稳健。

关键词：对外直接投资　出口倍差法　生存分析模型

Does Chinese Outward FDI Promote or Suppress Firms' Export？
Evidence from Manufacturing Firms

Abstract：This paper aims to analyze how does outward FDI affect firms' export. Using highly disaggregated Chinese firm level production data and product level trade data, this paper explores such an important question systematically from the microcosmic aspect. The results show that, outward FDI not only significantly raises firms' export intensity, but it also raises the probability of firms' export. Furthermore, the survival analysis model indicates that outward FDI significantly decreases the hazard rate of firm exits from export market, which means it helps to raise the duration of firm's export. This paper confirms that there exists a significant export-creating effect for Chinese outward FDI firms from the microcosmic aspect. Such conclusion remains the same for various robustness tests, like eliminating intermediary firms, eliminating processing trade, eliminating the firms which invest in tax havens, and using another matching technique such as nearest neighbor matching.

Key words: qutward foreign direct investment; export; difference-in-difference; survival analysis model

融资约束是否抑制了中国民营企业对外直接投资

王碧珺　谭语嫣　余淼杰　黄益平

《世界经济》2015 年第 12 期

摘要:本文采用浙江省制造业生产和对外直接投资的企业层面数据,构造包括内源资金约束、外源资金约束、投资机会等在内的融资约束综合指标,考察了融资约束对中国民营企业海外直接投资决策的影响。基于 Heckman 两阶段选择模型的研究表明,融资约束一方面抑制了中国民营企业对外直接投资的可能性,另一方面对民营企业海外直接投资规模的扩张也有不利影响。本文进一步研究发现,融资约束对于不同类型的对外直接投资具有差异性影响。

关键词:民营企业　对外直接投资　融资约束

Whether the financing constraint inhibits the foreign direct investment of Chinese private enterprises

Abstract: this paper USES the manufacturing production and foreign direct investment enterprises in Zhejiang province level data, structure including internal financing constraints, external funding constraints, investment opportunities, such as financing constraints, the comprehensive index, examines the financing constraints on China's private enterprises the influence of foreign direct investment decisions. Based on two phase Heckman selection model of research shows that the financing constraints on the one hand, inhibits the possibility of China's private enterprise of foreign direct investment, on the other hand also to the expansion of the scale of foreign direct investment of private enterprises have an adverse effect. Further research in this paper finds that the financing constraints have different impacts on different types of foreign direct investment.

Key words: private enterprises; Outward Foreign Direct Investment; Financing constraints

双边政治关系、东道国制度风险与中国对外直接投资

潘镇 金中坤

《财贸经济》2015 年第 6 期

摘要:本文将政治因素纳入制度分析框架,考察了双边政治关系和东道国制度风险影响中国对外直接投资的机制和效应。在理论分析的基础上,通过对 2003—2013 年在 117 个国家直接投资数据的分析,本文发现:(1)从总体上看,中国的对外直接投资趋于流向政治关系好和制度风险高的东道国;(2)政治关系和制度风险的效应在发达国家和发展中国家有着明显的差异;(3)在制度风险大的东道国,良好的政治关系作为一种替代性的制度安排,减弱了在东道国经营的不确定性,有效地促进了对外直接投资,而在制度风险小的东道国,良好的政治关系没有带来对外直接投资的明显增加,更多地起到了对东道国环境的补充作用。

关键词:中国对外直接投资 双边政治关系 制度风险 制度距离

Bilateral Political Relationship, Host Country Institutional Risk and China's Outward FDI

Abstract: Incorporating political factors into the framework of institutional analysis, the paper investigates the impact mechanisms and effects of bilateral political relationship and host country institutional risk on China's outward FDI simultaneously. Based on theoretical analysis, using outward investment flow data in 117 host countries from 2003 to 2013, the empirical results show that Chinese Outward FDIs tend to invest in those countries with good political relationship and high institutional risk, and the effects of political relationship and institutional risk differ between developed countries and developing countries significantly. In addition, good political relationship is served as alternative arrangement of lessening uncertainty to encourage outward FDI in the context of high host country's institutional risk, and in the context of low host country's institutional risk, good institutional quality is a complementary rather than promoting FDI obviously. The findings are still robust after controlling sample selection bias.

Key words：China's outward FDI；bilateral political relationship；institutional risk；institutional distance

第二节　英文期刊论文精选

Title：Going Global in Groups Structural Transformation and China's Special Economic Zones Overseas

Author：Deborah Brautigam，Xiaoyang Tang

Periodical：World Development

Date：2014，v. 63，iss. 11

Abstract：China's special economic zones helped the country industrialize by attracting foreign investment. In 2006，Beijing initiated an overseas trade and cooperation zone program，assisting Chinese companies to invest abroad while also building China's soft power through the transfer of a key component of China's development success. Little is known about the 19 zones approved so far under this program，or the impact they are likely to have on structural transformation and industrial development in their host countries. This paper identifies the 19 zones and their proposed locations，the process of selection，developers，implementation，and the Chinese incentive regime. It then focuses on the African zones. Using a typology of factors that have proven critical for zone development in the past，the paper evaluates the potential of these zones for fostering structural transformation in Africa.

题目："组团式走出去"：结构转型与中国海外的经济特区

作者：黛博拉·布劳提根，唐晓阳

期刊：世界发展

日期：2014 年；第 63 卷，第 11 期

摘要：中国的经济特区通过吸收外国投资推动了国家工业化的发展。在 2006 年，北京政府启动了一项海外贸易合作区计划，旨在援助中国企业海外投资，同时

通过传播中国经济发展的主要成功经验来构建中国的软实力。迄今该计划批准的 19 个经济特区及其对东道国的结构转型和工业发展所产生的可能影响都鲜为人知。本文先确定了 19 个经济特区以及这些特区的拟建布局,选择开发实施的过程和中国的激励体制,然后集中讨论非洲的经济特区。使用已被证明对经济特区发展具有关键作用的同类因素,本文评估了这些经济特区对促进非洲经济结构转型的潜力。

Title:Emerging economies,trade policy,and macroeconomic shocks

Author:Chad P. Bown, Meredith A. Crowley

Periodical:Journal of Development Economics

Date:2014,v. 111,iss. 11

Abstract:This paper estimates the impact of aggregate fluctuations on the time-varying trade policies of thirteen major emerging economies over 1989 – 2010;by 2010, these WTO member countries collectively accounted for 21% of world merchandise imports and 22% of world GDP. We examine determinants of carefully constructed,bilateral measures of new import restrictions on products arising through the temporary trade barrier(TTB)policies of antidumping,safeguards,and countervailing duties. We find evidence of a counter-cyclical relationship between macroeconomic shocks and new TTB import restrictions as well as an important role for fluctuations in bilateral real exchange rates. Furthermore,the trade policy responsiveness coinciding with WTO establishment in 1995 suggests a significant change relative to the pre-WTO period;i. e. ,new import restrictions became more counter-cyclical and sensitive to real exchange rate shocks over time. Finally,we also present results that explicitly address changes to the institutional environment facing these emerging economies as they joined the WTO and adopted disciplines to restrain their application of other trade policies such as applied import tariffs.

题目:新兴经济体、贸易政策与宏观经济冲击

作者:查德·鲍恩,梅雷迪思·克劳利

期刊:发展经济学杂志

日期:2014 年;第 111 卷,第 11 期

摘要:本文估计了总量经济波动对 1989—2010 年 13 个主要新兴经济体的贸

易政策的影响;截至 2010 年,这些 WTO 成员国总共占据了 21% 的世界商品进口和 22% 的世界 GDP。根据由反倾销、保障措施、反补贴税组成的临时贸易壁垒(TTB)政策所产生的新的产品进口管制,我们精心构造了产品进口管制的双边度量指标并考察了该度量指标的决定因素。结果发现宏观经济冲击和新的 TTB 进口管制之间存在反周期关系并且反周期关系对双边实际汇率波动具有重要影响。另外,与 1995 年 WTO 建立同步的贸易政策响应表明相对 WTO 以前的一个显著变化,新的进口管制随时间变化表现得更为反周期以及对实际汇率冲击更为敏感。最后,由于这些新兴经济体加入 WTO 并且调整规则以限制诸如采用进口关税的其他贸易政策的使用,因此我们也给出了控制其所面对的制度环境的变化的结果。

Title:Globalization,Trade,and Wages:What Does History Tell Us About China?

Author:Kris James Mitchener,Se Yan

Periodical:International Economics Review

Date:2014,v. 55,iss. 1

Abstract:Newly assembled data show that,as China opened up to global trade during the early 20th century,its exports became more unskilled-intensive and its imports more skill-intensive. Difference-in-differences estimates show that World War I dramatically increased Chinese exports,raising the relative demand for the unskilled workers producing them. When the war ended,trade costs declined and China's terms of trade increased,further stimulating exports. A simulation of a dynamic general equilibrium model demonstrates that the effects of the war on China's terms of trade produces a decline in the skill premium similar to what China experienced in the 1920s.

题目:全球化、贸易与工资:关于中国,历史告诉了我们什么?

作者:克里斯·詹姆斯·米契纳,颜色

期刊:国际经济评论

日期:2014 年;第 55 卷,第 1 期

摘要:新近收集的数据显示,尽管 20 世纪早期中国开始了全球化贸易,但是出口了更多的非技能密集型产品而进口了更多的技能密集型产品。双重差分估计显示,第一次世界大战大幅增加了中国的出口,提高了生产出口产品所需要的非技能工人的相对需求。当一战结束后,贸易成本下降且中国的贸易条件上升,

进一步刺激了出口。动态一般均衡模型的模拟分析表明,第一次世界大战对中国的贸易条件的影响产生了一个类似于 20 世纪 20 年代中国所经历了的技能溢价的下降。

Title: The Global Welfare Impact of China: Trade Integration and Technological Change

Author: Julian di Giovanni, Andrei Levchenko, Jing Zhang

Periodical: American Economic Journal: Macroeconomics

Date: 2014, v. 6, iss. 3

Abstract: This paper evaluates the global welfare impact of China's trade integration and technological change in a multi-country quantitative Ricardian-Heckscher-Ohlin model. We simulate two alternative growth scenarios: a "balanced" one in which China's productivity grows at the same rate in each sector, and an "unbalanced" one in which China's comparative disadvantage sectors catch up disproportionately faster to the world productivity frontier. Contrary to a well-known conjecture (Samuelson 2004), the large majority of countries experience significantly larger welfare gains when China's productivity growth is biased toward its comparative disadvantage sectors. This finding is driven by the inherently multilateral nature of world trade.

题目:中国对全球福利的影响:贸易一体化与技术进步

作者:朱利安·乔凡尼,安德列·列夫琴科,张婧

期刊:美国经济杂志:宏观经济学

日期:2014 年;第 6 卷,第 3 期

摘要:本文在一个多国数量化的李嘉图—赫克歇尔—俄林模型中评估了中国的贸易一体化与技术进步对全球福利的影响。模拟了两个替代的增长状况:一个是平衡增长状况,其中中国的每个部门的生产率以同样的速度增长;一个是非平衡增长状况,即中国的比较劣势部门以不相同的速度赶超世界生产率前沿。与萨缪尔森(2004)著名的猜想相反,当中国的生产率增长偏向本国的比较劣势部门时,大部分国家经历了显著的更大的福利收益。这一发现是由世界贸易内在的多边属性驱动的。

Title: Comparative Advantage and Optimal Trade Policy

Author：Arnaud Costinot，Dave Donaldson，Jonathan Vogel，Iván Werning

Periodical：Quarterly Journal of Economics

Date：2015，v. 130，iss. 2

Abstract：The theory of comparative advantage is at the core of neoclassical trade theory. Yet we know little about its implications for how nations should conduct their trade policy. For example，should import sectors with weaker comparative advantage be protected more? Conversely，should export sectors with stronger comparative advantage be subsidized less? In this article we take a first stab at exploring these issues. Our main results imply that in the context of a canonical Ricardian model，optimal import tariffs should be uniform，whereas optimal export subsidies should be weakly decreasing with respect to comparative advantage，reflecting the fact that countries have more room to manipulate prices in their comparative-advantage sectors. Quantitative exercises suggest substantial gains from such policies relative to simpler tax schedules.

题目：比较优势与最优贸易政策

作者：阿尔诺·科斯提诺，戴夫·唐纳森，乔纳森·福格尔，埃尔·韦宁

期刊：经济学季刊

日期：2015 年；第 130 卷，第 2 期

摘要：比较优势理论是新古典贸易理论的核心理论。然而关于国家应该如何实施贸易政策的含义却知之甚少。例如，比较优势较小的进口部门是否应该得到更多的保护? 反之，比较优势较大的出口部门是否应该给予更少的补贴? 在这篇文章中，本文第一次尝试探讨这些问题。本文的主要结果意味着，在一个标准的李嘉图模型的背景下，最优的进口关税应该是统一的，然而最优的出口补贴关于比较优势是轻微递减的，这反映了政府有较大的空间来管制比较优势部门的产品价格。数量分析表明相对简单的税收计划，这些政策获得了可观的收益。

Title：Competition，Markups，and the Gains from International Trade

Author：Chris Edmond，Virgiliu Midrigan，Daniel Yi Xu

Periodical：American Economic Review

Date：2015，v. 105，iss. 10

Abstract：We study the procompetitive gains from international trade in a quantitative model with endogenously variable markups. We find that trade can significantly reduce markup distortions if two conditions are satisfied: (i) there is extensive misallocation, and (ii) opening to trade exposes hitherto dominant producers to greater competitive pressure. We measure the extent to which these two conditions are satisfied in Taiwanese producer-level data. Versions of our model consistent with the Taiwanese data predict that opening up to trade strongly increases competition and reduces markup distortions by up to one-half, thus significantly reducing productivity losses due to misallocation.

题目:竞争、加成与国际贸易收益

作者:克里斯·爱德蒙,默尔吉努·马迪根,丹尼尔·徐一

期刊:美国经济评论

日期:2015 年;第 105 卷,第 10 期

摘要:本文在一个内生可变加成的数量化模型中研究了国际贸易的竞争促进效应所产生的收益。结果发现,如果满足这两个条件,即存在大量资源错配以及贸易开放使国内企业面临更大的国际竞争压力,国际贸易的竞争促进效应能够显著地减少加成扭曲。本文使用中国台湾的企业数据估计了这两个条件的实施状况。结合中国台湾的数据本文的模型预测贸易开放强有力地增加了竞争且减少了一半的加成扭曲,因此显著降低了资源错配导致的生产率损失。

Title: Globalization and Growth

Author: Gene M. Grossman, Elhanan Helpman

Periodical: American Economic Review

Date: 2015, v. 105, iss. 5

Abstract: How does globalization affect economic growth? We discuss mechanisms that link international integration to the incentives for knowledge accumulation and the efficacy of that process. First, integration facilitates the flow of knowledge across national borders. Second, integration affords innovators a larger potential market even as it subjects them to additional competition from foreign rivals. Third, integration encourages specialization according to comparative advantage. Finally, integration affects the incentives for technological diffusion. Taken together, the literature offers many theoretical insights. Some progress has also been made on the empirical side, although data and methodological impediments have left assessment and measurement lagging behind.

题目:全球化与经济增长

作者:吉恩·格罗斯曼,埃尔赫南·赫尔普曼

期刊:美国经济评论

日期:2015 年;第 105 卷,第 5 期

摘要:全球化如何影响经济增长? 本文讨论了贸易一体化与激励知识积累和知识使用效率之间联系的机制。首先,贸易一体化促进了跨国界的知识流动;其次,贸易一体化为创新者提供了一个更大的潜在市场,即使创新者面临来自外国竞争对手的额外竞争;再次,贸易一体化激励基于比较优势的专业化;最后,贸易一体化影响技术扩散的激励机制。总之,文献提供了许多理论洞见。尽管数据和方法上的障碍使评估和计量有所滞后,但是实证方面还是取得了一些进展。

Title: Input-trade Liberalization, Export Prices and Quality Upgrading

Author: Maria Bas, Vanessa Strauss-Kahn

Periodical: Journal of International Economics, 2015, v. 95, iss. 2

Abstract: This paper explores the impact of input trade liberalization on imported input and exported product prices. Using Chinese transaction data for 2000 – 2006, we capture causal effects between exogenous input tariff reductions and within firm changes in HS6-traded product prices. For identification, we make use of a natural control group of firms that are exempted from paying tariffs. Both imported input and export prices rise. The effect on export prices is specific to firms sourcing inputs from developed economies and exporting output to high-income countries. Results are consistent with a scenario within which firms exploit the input tariff cuts to access high-quality inputs in order to quality-upgrade their exports.

题目:输入贸易自由化、出口价格和质量升级

作者:玛丽亚·巴斯,瓦内萨·特劳斯－卡恩

期刊:国际经济学杂志

日期:2015 年;第 95 卷,第 2 期

摘要:本文探讨了投入品贸易自由化对进口投入品和出口产品价格的影响。使用2000—2006 年中国海关的数据,本文探讨了外生的投入品关税下降与6 位码HS 贸易产品价格的企业内变化之间的因果效应。为了进行识别,本文将豁免支付关税的企业作为控制组。进口投入品和出口产品的价格都提高,对出口产品价

格的影响只是进口发达国家投入品和向高收入国家出口的企业。分析结果与企业利用投入品关税削减获得高质量的投入来提升出口产品质量的情况是一致的。

Title: International Trade and Institutional Change: Medieval Venice's Response to Globalization

Author: Diego Puga, Daniel Trefler

Periodical: Quarterly Journal of Economics, 2014; v. 129, iss. 2

Abstract: International trade can have profound effects on domestic institutions. We examine this proposition in the context of medieval Venice circa 800 – 1600. Early on, the growth of long-distance trade enriched a broad group of merchants who used their newfound economic muscle to push for constraints on the executive, that is, for the end of a de facto hereditary Doge in 1032 and the establishment of a parliament in 1172. The merchants also pushed for remarkably modern innovations in contracting institutions that facilitated long-distance trade, for example, the colleganza. However, starting in 1297, a small group of particularly wealthy merchants blocked political and economic competition: they made parliamentary participation hereditary and erected barriers to participation in the most lucrative aspects of long-distance trade. Over the next two centuries this led to a fundamental societal shift away from political openness, economic competition, and social mobility and toward political closure, extreme inequality, and social stratification. We document this oligarchization using a unique database on the names of 8,178 parliamentarians and their families' use of the colleganza in the periods immediately before and after 1297. We then link these families to 6,959 marriages during 1400 – 1599 to document the use of marriage alliances to monopolize the galley trade. Monopolization led to the rise of extreme inequality, with those who were powerful before 1297 emerging as the undisputed winners.

题目:国际贸易与制度变迁:中世纪威尼斯对全球化的回应

作者:迭戈·普加,丹尼尔·特雷夫莱

期刊:经济学季刊

日期:2014 年;第 129 卷,第 2 期

摘要:国际贸易对国内制度产生了深远的影响。本文在中世纪威尼斯约800—1600 年的背景下检验了这个命题。早期,长距离的贸易增长使一大批商人

富有起来,这些商人利用其新成立的经济组织来奋力抗争行政限制,也就是说,在 1032 年结束了事实上的世袭总督和在 1172 年建立了议会。商人们也推动了便利长距离贸易的承包制度的非凡的近代创新,如合伙制。然而,从 1297 年开始,一小群特别富裕的商人阻挡了政治和经济竞争,他们使议会参与世袭并且阻碍长距离贸易的最有利可图的参与机会。在接下来的两个世纪,这导致了一个基本的社会转变,即从政治开放、经济竞争和社会流动转变为政治封闭、极端不平等和社会分层。使用在 1297 年之前和之后时期的关于 8178 名议员的名字及其家族使用的合伙制的一个独特的数据库,本文记录了这种组织寡头化。然后将 1400—1599 年的这些家庭与 6959 个婚姻联系起来,以记录利用婚姻联盟垄断船运贸易。垄断导致了极端不平等的增加,1297 年之前的强者成为了无可后议的赢家。

Title:International Trade Puzzles:A Solution Linking Production and Preferences

Author:Justin Caron,Thibault Fally,James. R. Markusen.

Periodical:Quarterly Journal of Economics

Date:2014,v. 129,iss. 3

Abstract:International trade literature tends to focus heavily on the production side of general equilibrium,leaving us with a number of empirical puzzles. There is,for example, considerably less world trade than predicted by Heckscher-Ohlin-Vanek (HOV)models. Trade among rich countries is higher and trade between rich and poor countries lower than suggested by HOV and other supply-driven theories,and trade-to-GDP ratios are higher in rich countries. Our approach focuses on the relationship between characteristics of goods and services in production and characteristics of preferences. In particular,we find a strong and significant positive correlation of more than 45% between a good's skilledlabor intensity and its income elasticity,even when accounting for trade costs and cross-country price differences. Exploring the implications of this correlation for empirical trade puzzles,we find that it can reduce HOV's overprediction of the variance of the net factor content of trade relative to that in the data by about 60%. Since rich countries are relatively skilled-labor abundant,they are relatively specialized in consuming the same goods and services that they are specialized in producing,and so trade more with one another than with poor countries. We also find a positive sector-level correlation between income elasticity and a sector's tradability,which helps explain the higher trade-to-GDP ratios in high-income relative to low-income countries.

题目:国际贸易谜题:链接生产和偏好的解决方案

作者:贾斯廷·卡伦,蒂博·法利,詹姆斯·马库森

期刊:经济学季刊

日期:2014 年;第 129 卷,第 3 期

摘要:国际贸易文献往往把重点放在一般均衡的生产方面,这给我们留下了大量的谜题。例如,世界贸易远低于赫克歇尔—俄林—凡涅克(HOV)模型的理论预测。与 HOV 理论和其他供给面理论的预测相比,富国间的贸易更高,富国与穷国之间的贸易更低,而且富国的贸易产出比更高。本文主要分析了商品和服务在生产方面的特征与偏好的特征之间的关系。特别地,即使控制了贸易成本和国家间的价格差异之后,本文发现超过 45% 的产品的技能劳动密集度及其收入弹性之间具有显著的正相关关系,在探索了实证贸易谜题的这种相关性的含义后,本文发现相对数据中的高估来看,这种相关性降低了 HOV 理论对贸易产品净要素比例的方差的大约 60% 的高估。由于富国的技能型劳动力相对富余,他们相对专注于消费其专业生产的产品和服务,因此与穷国相比,富国之间的贸易更多。本文也发现收入弹性与产业的可贸易性之间在产业层面具有正相关关系,这有助于解释高收入国家比低收入国家更高的贸易产出比。

Title:Openness and Income:The Roles of Trade and Migration

Author:Francesc Ortega,Giovanni Peri

Periodical:Journal of International Economics

Date:2014;v. 92,iss. 2

Abstract:This paper explores the relationship between openness to trade,immigration,and income per person across countries. To address endogeneity concerns we extend the instrumental-variables strategy introduced by Frankel and Romer(1999). We build predictors of openness to immigration and to trade for each country by using information on bilateral geographical and cultural distance(while controlling for country size). Since geography may affect income through other channels,we also control for climate,disease environment,natural resources,and colonial origins. Most importantly,we also account for the roles of institutions and early development. Our instrumental-variables estimates provide evidence of a robust,positive effect of openness to immigration on long-run income per capita. In contrast, we are unable to establish an effect of trade openness on income. We also show that the effect of migration operates through an increase in total factor productivity, which appears to reflect increased diversity in productive skills and, to some extent, a higher rate of innovation.

题目：对外开放与收入：贸易与移民的作用

作者：弗兰塞斯克·奥尔特加，乔瓦尼·佩里

期刊：国际经济学

日期：2014 年；第 92 卷，第 2 期

摘要：本文探讨了跨国的贸易开放、移民和人均收入之间的关系。为了解决内生性问题，本文扩展了弗兰克尔和罗默（1999）引入的工具变量方法。通过使用双边地理和文化距离（同时控制国家规模）的信息，为每个国家构建移民开放和贸易开放的预测指标。考虑到地理距离可能通过其他渠道影响收入，引入气候、疾病环境改为疾病状况，自然环境以及殖民地起源等控制变量。最重要的是，还考虑了制度和早期经济发展的作用。工具变量估计显示，移民开放对长期人均收入具有稳健的正向影响。与此相反，本文无法确定贸易开放对人均收入的影响。结果还显示移民的影响是通过提高全要素生产率来发挥作用的，这似乎反映了生产技能的多样性增加以及一定程度上较高的创新率。

Title：Processing Trade, Tariff Reductions and Firm Productivity: Evidence from Chinese Firms

Author：Miaojie Yu

Periodical：Economic Journal

Date：2015；v. 125，iss. 6

Abstract：This article explores how reductions in tariffs on imported inputs and final goods affect the productivity of large Chinese trading firms, with the special tariff treatment that processing firms receive on imported inputs. Firm-level input and output tariffs are constructed. Both types of tariff reductions have positive impacts on productivity that are weaker as firms' share of processing imports grows. The impact of input tariff reductions on productivity improvement, overall, is weaker than that of output tariff reductions, although the opposite is true for non-processing firms only. Both tariff reductions are found to contribute at least 14.5% to economy-wide productivity growth.

题目:加工贸易、关税削减与企业生产率:来自中国企业的证据

作者:余淼杰

期刊:经济学杂志

日期:2015 年;第 125 卷,第 6 期

摘要:结合加工贸易企业享受的进口投入品的特殊关税待遇,本文探讨了进口投入品和最终品关税削减如何影响大型的中国贸易企业的生产率。本文构建了企业层面的投入品关税和产品关税。两类关税削减对生产率具有正向影响,由于企业的加工贸易进口份额的增长,这种正向影响较弱。总体来看,投入品关税削减对生产率增长的影响弱于最终品关税削减的影响,而仅对非加工贸易企业,情况却是相反的。两类关税削减至少贡献了 14.5% 的生产率增长。

Title: Estimating the extensive margin of trade

Author: J. M. C. Santos Silva, Silvana Tenreyro, KehaiWei

Periodical: Journal of International Economics

Date: May. 2014

Abstract: Understanding and quantifying the determinants of the number of sectors or firms exporting in a given country is of relevance for the assessment of trade policies. Estimation of models for the number of exporting sectors, however, poses a challenge because the dependent variable has both a lower and an upper bound, implying that the partial effects of the explanatory variables on the conditional mean of the dependent variable cannot be constant. We argue that ignoring these bounds can lead to erroneous conclusions and propose a flexible specification that accounts for the doubly-bounded nature of the dependent variable. We empirically investigate the problem and the proposed solution, finding significant differences between estimates obtained with the proposed estimator and those obtained with standard approaches.

题目:对贸易广泛边界的估计

作者:J. M. C. 桑托斯·席尔瓦,锡尔弗纳·滕雷罗,魏克海

期刊:国际经济学杂志

日期:2014 年 3 月

摘要:本文了解和量化了在某一特定国家内出口行业或企业数量的决定因

素,与贸易政策评估相关。然而,对出口部门数量的模型的估计是一个挑战,因为因变量既具有下限还具有上限,这意味着解释变量对因变量条件均值的偏效应不能保持不变。我们认为,忽略这些界限可能会导致错误的结论,并提出一个灵活的规范,以说明因变量的双边界性质。我们经验性地调查了这个问题和提出的解决方案,发现使用上文中提出的方法获得的估计量的估计值,与使用标准方法获得的估计值之间存在显著差异。

Title: Exporting under trade policy uncertainty: Theory and evidence

Author: Kyle Handley

Periodical: Journal of International Economics

Date: Jun. 2014

Abstract: I provide novel evidence for the impact of trade policy uncertainty on exporters. In a dynamic, heterogeneous firms model, trade policy uncertainty will delay the entry of exporters into new markets and make them less responsive to applied tariff reductions. Policy instruments that reduce or eliminate uncertainty, such as binding trade policy commitments at the WTO, increase entry. The predictions are tested on dis-aggregated, product-level Australian imports with model-consistent measures of uncertainty. The estimates show that growth of exporter-product varieties would have been 7% lower between 1993 and 2001 without the binding commitments implemented after the WTO was formed in 1996. If Australia reduced all its tariffs and bindings to zero, more than half of predicted product growth is accounted by by removing uncertainty. These results illuminate and quantify an important new channel for trade creation.

题目: 贸易政策不确定下的出口

作者: 凯尔·霍德利

期刊: 国际经济学杂志

日期: 2014 年 1 月

摘要: 我(本文)为贸易政策不确定性对出口商的影响提供了新的证据。在一个充满活力,异质性的企业模式中,贸易政策的不确定性将会导致出口商延迟进入新市场,并使其对减免关税的反应较少。减少或消除不确定性的政策手段,如世贸组织对贸易政策的约束力,增加出口商的进入。这些预测通过运用产品层次分类的澳大利亚进口数据,对与模型一致的不确定性措施进行了检验。估计显示,1993—2001 年,出口商品种类多样性的增长率将下降 7%,而在 1996 年成立 WTO 之后,对出口商品种类的约束力就消失了。如果澳大利亚将所有关税和约束力降至零,则预计产品的一半以上增长是通过消除不确定性来解释的。这些结果说明和量化了贸易创造的重要新渠道。

Title:International Trade Puzzles:A Solution Linking Production and Preferences

Author:Justin Caron,Thibault Fally,James R. Markusen

Periodical:Quarterly Journal of Economics

Date:May. 2014

Abstract:International trade literature tends to focus heavily on the production side of general equilibrium,leaving us with a number of empirical puzzles. There is,for example, considerably less world trade than predicted by Heckscher-Ohlin-Vanek (HOV)models. Trade among rich countries is higher and trade between rich and poor countries lower than suggested by HOV and other supply-driven theories,and trade-to-GDP ratios are higher in rich countries. Our approach focuses on the relationship between characteristics of goods and services in production and characteristics of preferences. In particular,we find a strong and significant positive correlation of more than 45% between a good's skilled labor intensity and its income elasticity,even when accounting for trade costs and cross-country price differences. Exploring the implications of this correlation for empirical trade puzzles,we find that it can reduce HOV's over prediction of the variance of the net factor content of trade relative to that in the data by about 60%. Since rich countries are relatively skilled-labor abundant,they are relatively specialized in consuming the same goods and services that they are specialized in producing,and so trade more with one another than with poor countries. We also find a positive sector-level correlation between income elasticity and a sector's tradability,which helps explain the higher trade-to-GDP ratios in high-income relative to low-income countries.

题目:国际贸易谜题:连接生产和偏好的解决方案

作者:贾斯汀·卡龙,蒂博·法利,杰姆斯·R. 马库森

期刊:经济学季刊

日期:2014 年 3 月

摘要:国际贸易文献往往侧重于生产方面的一般均衡,给我们带来了一些经验难题。例如,比起 Heckscher-Ohlin-Vanek(HOV)模型预测的那样,世界贸易量大大减少。富国之间的贸易量较高,富国和穷国之间的贸易低于 HOV 和其他供应驱动理论的建议,而富国的贸易与 GDP 的比率也较高。我们的方法着重于揭示生产中的商品和服务特征与偏好特征之间的关系。特别是,即使在考虑贸易成本和跨国价格差异的情况下,我们也发现,在熟练的劳动强度与收入弹性之间,有 45% 以上的强烈和显著正相关。探索这种相关性对经验上的贸易谜题的影响,我们发现可以将 HOV 的交易净因子内容方差的估计值减少约 60%。富国熟练劳动力的相对丰富,相对专门从事消费与生产相同的商品和服务,所以这种贸易相对贫穷国家而言更多。我们也发现收入弹性与部门的可交易性之间存在积极的部门层面的相关性,这有助于解释高收入国家相对于低收入国家的高贸易—GDP 的比重。

Title:New imported inputs, new domestic products

Author:Italo Colantone, Rosario Crinò

Periodical:Journal of International Economics

Date:January. 2014

Abstract:We study the relationship between new imported inputs and the introduction of new domestic products. To this purpose, we assemble a novel data set covering 25 European countries over 1995 – 2007 and containing information on domestic production and bilateral trade for the universe of goods. We develop a procedure to identify new imported inputs and new domestic products, while dealing with the complications raised by the yearly changes in the commodity classifications. We augment these data with information on prices and novel estimates of quality. We organize the empirical analysis around a version of the endogenous growth model with expanding variety, in which inputs are allowed to be heterogeneous in terms of quality. In line with this framework, we find three main results. First, new imported inputs have a strong positive effect on product creation in Europe. Second, they work through a combination of mechanisms, allowing countries to benefit from both wider and better sets of intermediate products. Finally, new imported inputs give a substantial boost to output growth in manufacturing.

题目:新进口投入品和国内产品

作者:伊塔洛·科兰托内,罗萨里奥·克里诺

期刊:国际经济学杂志

日期:2014 年 1 月

摘要:我们研究新进口投入与引进国产新产品之间的关系。为达到该目的,我们选取在 1995—2007 年间涵盖 25 个欧洲国家的数据集,包含了有关国内生产和物质世界双边贸易的信息。我们制定并发展了一个程序,以确定新的进口投入和新的国内产品,同时处理商品分类年度变化引起的并发难题。我们增加了包含了价格与新产品质量信息的数据进行估算。我们围绕增加的多样性为特征的内生增长模型的一个版本来组织实证分析,其中外国进口输入在质量方面是异构性的。根据这个框架进行工作,我们发现三个主要结果。首先,新进口投入品对欧洲本地产品创造产生了积极影响。其次,上述二者通过机制相结合,让各国从更广泛和更好的中间产品中获益。最后,新的进口投入大大推动了制造业产量的增长。

Title:The Network Structure of International Trade

Author:Thomas Chaney

Periodical:American Economic Review

Date:Nov. 2014

Abstract:Motivated by empirical evidence I uncover on the dynamics of French firms' exports,I offer a novel theory of trade frictions. Firms export only into markets where they have a contact. They search directly for new trading partners,but also use their existing network of contacts to search remotely for new partners. I characterize the dynamic formation of an international network of exporters in this model. Structurally,I estimate this model on French data and confirm its predictions regarding the distribution of the number of foreign markets accessed by exporters and the geographic distribution of exports.

题目:国际贸易网络结构

作者:托马斯·汉尼

期刊:美国经济评论

日期:2014 年 11 月

摘要:在我所发现的法国企业出口动态的实证证据的驱动下,我提出了一种新的贸易摩擦理论。公司只能进入与他们联系的市场而出口。他们直接搜索新的贸易伙伴,还可以使用他们现有的联系人网络,远程搜索新的合作伙伴。在这个模式中,我描述了出口国的国际网络的形成。在结构上,我利用法国数据估计这个模型,并证实了其关于出口商进入外国市场数量和出口地理分布的预测。

Title:Trade Adjustment and Productivity in Large Crises

Author:Gita Gopinath, Brent Neiman

Periodical:American Economic Review

Date:May. 2014

Abstract:We empirically characterize the mechanics of trade adjustment during the Argentine crisis. Though imports collapsed by 70 percent from 2000 to 2002, the entry and exit of firms or products at the country level played a small role. The within-firm churning of imported inputs, however, played a sizeable role. We build a model of trade in intermediate inputs with heterogeneous firms, fixed import costs, and roundabout production. Import demand is non-homothetic and the implications of an import price shock depend on the full distribution of firm-level adjustments. An import price shock generates a significant decline in productivity.

题目:大规模危机中的贸易调整与生产力

作者:吉塔·郭匹纳斯,布伦特·内曼

期刊:美国经济评论

日期:2014 年 3 月

摘要:我们在阿根廷危机中经验性地描述了贸易调整的机制。尽管 2000—2002 年企业进口下降了 70%,但其中国家层面企业或产品的进出口变动占比很少。然而,进口投入的企业内部冲撞或重组起了很大的作用。我们建立了针对异构企业的中间投入品、固定进口成本和迂回生产的贸易模型。进口需求是非同质的,进口价格震荡的影响取决于企业层面调整的充分分配。进口价格冲击导致生产力大幅度下降。

Title:Trade Adjustment:Worker-Level Evidence

Author:David H. Autor, David Dorn, Gordon H. Hanson, Jae Song

Periodical：The Quarterly Journal of Economics

Date：Sep. 2014

Abstract：We analyze the effect of exposure to international trade on earnings and employment of U. S. workers from 1992 through 2007 by exploiting industry shocks to import competition stemming from China's spectacular rise as a manufacturing exporter paired with longitudinal data on individual earnings by employer spanning close to two decades. Individuals who in 1991 worked in manufacturing industries that experienced high subsequent import growth garner lower cumulative earnings, face elevated risk of obtaining public disability benefits, and spend less time working for their initial employers, less time in their initial two-digit manufacturing industries, and more time working elsewhere in manufacturing and outside of manufacturing. Earnings losses are larger for individuals with low initial wages, low initial tenure, and low attachment to the labor force. Low-wage workers churn primarily among manufacturing sectors, where they are repeatedly exposed to subsequent trade shocks. High-wage workers are better able to move across employers with minimal earnings losses and are more likely to move out of manufacturing conditional on separation. These findings reveal that import shocks impose substantial labor adjustment costs that are highly unevenly distributed across workers according to their skill levels and conditions of employment in the pre-shock period.

题目：贸易调整：来自员工层次的证据

作者：大卫·H. 奥特尔, 大卫·多恩, 戈登·H. 汉森, 宋载

期刊：经济学季刊

日期：2014 年 10 月

摘要：中国制造业出口大幅提升导致进口竞争。我们利用行业冲击作为该进口竞争的代理变量, 并考虑雇主所支付的个人工资历时近 20 年的纵向数据, 分析了 1992—2007 年国际贸易的深化对美国工人收入和就业的影响。1991 年从事正处在进口高速增长的制造业的个人只获得较低的累积收益,（由于公共福利系统）获得公共残疾福利的可能性较高, 他们花更少的时间为雇主工作, 减少在初始的两位数（行业编码）制造业中的工作时间, 而将更多的工作时间用在制造业其他部门和制造业之外。起始工资越低, 初始任职期限越低, 对劳动力依赖程度越低的个人收入损失越大。低工资工人主要在制造业部门之间流动, 在那里他们多次遭受随后的贸易冲击。而高薪工人能够更好地找到新雇主以尽可能最小化收入损

失,并更有可能离职以脱离制造业。这些调查结果显示,进口冲击提高了劳动力调整成本,这些成本却根据劳动者在冲击到来之前的技能水平和就业条件,而在工人群体中不均衡分配。

Title: Imported Inputs and Productivity

Author: László Halpern, Miklós Koren, Adam Szeidl

Periodical: American Economic Review

Date: Dec. 2015

Abstract: We estimate a model of importers in Hungarian microdata and conduct counterfactual analysis to investigate the effect of imported inputs on productivity. We find that importing all input varieties would increase a firm's revenue productivity by 22 percent, about one-half of which is due to imperfect substitution between foreign and domestic inputs. Foreign firms use imports more effectively and pay lower fixed import costs. We attribute one-quarter of Hungarian productivity growth during the 1993 – 2002 period to imported inputs. Simulations show that the productivity gain from a tariff cut is larger when the economy has many importers and many foreign firms.

题目:进口投入与生产力

作者:拉斯洛·哈珀恩,米克洛斯·高伦,亚当·塞伊德尔

期刊:美国经济评论

日期:2015 年 12 月

摘要:我们估计了面向匈牙利微观数据的进口商模型,并进行反事实分析,以调查进口投入对生产率的影响。我们发现,进口所有投入品种将使公司的受益生产力提高22%,其中约一半是由于国内外投入不完全替代所致。外国公司使用进口更有效,因其能够支付较低的固定进口成本。我们把1993 —2002 年期间匈牙利生产力增长的四分之一归因于进口投入。模拟结果显示,当一国经济中有许多进口商和许多外国公司时,关税削减引致的生产率增长更大。

Title: International trade and R&D spillovers

Author: Andrea Fracasso, Giuseppe Vittucci Marzetti

Periodical: Journal of International Economics

Date: Feb. 2015

Abstract: Departing from the usual tenets of proportionality between cross-border trade flows and knowledge spillovers, we investigate whether relatively intense trade relationships are associated with particularly large international R&D spillovers. A nonlinear specification nesting the hypothesis of global and trade-unrelated R&D spillovers is estimated on a sample of 24 advanced countries over 1971 – 2004. We find evidence that trade patterns positively affect the international transmission of knowledge, in particular when we consider bilateral trade flows that, thanks to the estimation of an auxiliary gravity model, are normalized for the size and the distance of the trading partners. Finally, we discuss the patterns of the bilateral relationships characterized by both relatively intense trade and large R&D spillovers.

题目: 国际贸易与研发溢出效应

作者: 安德烈·弗拉卡萨, 朱塞佩·维丘奇·马尔泽蒂

期刊: 国际经济学杂志

日期: 2015 年 2 月

摘要: 通过将跨境贸易流动与知识溢出之间的通常原理分离出来, 我们研究相对紧密的贸易关系是否与特别大的国际研发溢出有关。利用 1971— 2004 年间对 24 个先进国家的抽样数据, 本文以非线性规范检验了有关于全球性的和与贸易无关研发溢出效用的假设。我们发现贸易模式对国际知识传播产生了积极影响的证据, 特别是当我们考虑双边贸易流动时情况尤其如此, 这是由于对辅助重力模型的估计, 此几轮与对于贸易伙伴的规模和距离相一致。最后, 我们讨论了以相对激烈的贸易和大型研发溢出为特征的双边关系模式的具体形态。

Title: New exports from emerging markets: Do followers benefit from pioneers?

Author: Rodrigo Wagner, Andrés Zahler

Periodical: Journal of Development Economics

Date: Dec. 2014

Abstract: We study the micro dynamics of new exports from a country. The modern international trade work horse models(e. g. Melitz, 2003) assume heterogeneous productivity and, implicitly, predict that the ex-post largest exporters in a new product would be the pioneers, since they can pay back exploration costs. However, using detailed data on the early dynamics of new exports in Chile(1990 – 2007) we show that, on average, pioneers export less than comparable followers in the same new product. Moreover, followers are 40% more likely to enter a product if a pioneer survives more than one year exporting. These facts are consistent with pioneer-to-follower spillovers, or at least with stories in which the cost of entering early is disproportionally higher for larger exporters. Otherwise they would enter first. Firms better at "exploration" could be worse at "exploitation" (scale-up) in a new export product. This phenomenon is scarce, though, since inmost new products pioneers are not followed, even if they survive.

题目:来自新兴市场的新出口增长:追随者是否从先驱者中获益?

作者:罗德里格·瓦格纳,安德烈斯·扎勒

期刊:发展经济学杂志

日期:2014 年 12 月

摘要:我们研究一个国家新出口的微观动态过程。现代国际贸易驮马模型(例如,Melitz,2003)假定了异质性的生产力,并且隐晦地预测,新产品上市前后,最大出口商将成为先驱者,因为他们可以偿还研发成本。然而,利用智利新出口的早期动态过程的详细数据(1990—2007 年),我们揭示出:就平均而言,相同新产品的先驱者的出口水平将低于同类追随者。此外,如果先驱者出口一年以上,追随者进入产品的可能性就有 40% 。这些事实与先驱者到追随者的溢出效应是一致的,或者至少对于较大出口商而言,早期进入的成本过高,否则他们会首先进入。在"探索新产品"中表现更好的公司,往往在新出口产品的"深入探究"(规模化生产)上可能更糟。尽管如此,这种现象很少,因为最新产品开创先锋几乎没有跟随者,即使他们生存了下去。

Title: Comparative advantage, service trade, and global imbalances

Author: Alessandro Barattieri

Periodical: Journal of International Economics

Date: 2014

Abstract: The large current account deficit of the U. S. is the result of a large deficit in the goods balance and a modest surplus in the service balance. The opposite is true for Japan, Germany, and China. Moreover, I document the emergence from the mid-nineties of a strong negative relation between specialization in the export of services and the current account balances of a large sample of OECD and developing countries. Starting from these new stylized facts, I propose in this paper a service hypothesis for global imbalances, a new explanation based on the interplay between the U. S. comparative advantage in services and the asymmetric trade liberalization process in goods trade versus service trade that took place starting in the mid-nineties. First, I use a structural gravity model to show that service trade liberalization lagged behind goods trade liberalization, and I quantify the extent of this asymmetry. Second, I show that a simple two-period model can rationalize the emergence of current account deficits in the presence of such asymmetric liberalization. The key inter-temporal mechanism is the asymmetric timing of trade policies, which affects saving decisions. Finally, I explore the quantitative relevance of this explanation for global imbalances. I introduce trade costs in an otherwise standard 2-sector 2-country international real business cycle model. When fed with the asymmetric trade liberalization path found in the data, the model generates a trade deficit of about 5% of GDP. I conclude that the service hypothesis for global imbalances is quantitatively relevant.

题目:比较优势、服务贸易和全球失衡

作者:亚历山德罗·巴拉蒂耶

期刊:国际经济学杂志

日期:2014 年

摘要:美国的经常账户赤字是由于货物平衡中的巨额逆差和服务余额的适度盈余造成的。日本、德国和中国是相反的。此外,我记录了经合组织和发展中国家组成的大样本在 20 世纪 90 年代中期的服务出口专业化与经常账户余额之间强烈的负相关关系。从这些新的现象出发,我在本文中提出了一个全球失衡的服务假设:基于美国服务比较优势与 20 世纪 90 年代中期货物贸易和服务贸易不对称的贸易自由化进程之间的相互作用的新解释。首先,我使用结构性重力模型来表明服务贸易自由化滞后于货物贸易自由化,我量化了这种不对称的程度。其次,我表明,一个简单的两期模式可以使经常项目赤字不对称自由化存在的合理化。关键时间间隔机制即不对称时间是影响储蓄决策的贸易政策。最后,我探讨了这一解释对全球失衡的定量相关性。我在另一个标准的两个国家两个部门的国际实体商业周期模型中引入了贸易成本。在数据中发现不对称的贸易自由化道路的情况下,该模型产生的贸易逆差约占国内生产总值的 5%。我得出结论,全球失衡的服务假说是定量相关的。

Title：How much does geography deflect services trade？ Canadian answers

Author：James E. Anderson，Catherine A. Milot，Yoto V. Yotov

Periodical：International Economic Review

Date：Aug. 2014

Abstract：We estimate geographic barriers to trade in nine service categories for Canada's provinces from 1997 to 2007 with novel high-quality bilateral provincial trade data. The border directly reduces average provincial trade with the United States relative to interprovincial trade to 2. 4% of its borderless level. Incorporating multilateral resistance reduces foreign trade relative to interprovincial to 0. 1% of its frictionless potential. Geography reduces services trade some seven times more than goods trade overall. Surprisingly，intraprovincial（local）trade in services and goods is equally deflected upward，implying that the border increases interprovincial trade much more in services than goods.

题目：地理对服务贸易的影响——加拿大的答案

作者：詹姆斯·安德森，凯瑟琳·米洛，雅图·V. 雅图

期刊：国际经济评论

日期：2014 年 8 月

摘要：我们估计 1997—2007 年加拿大各省九个服务类别的地理贸易壁垒，所使用的双边省份贸易数据新颖优质。各省与美国的边境贸易平均水平直接降低到相当于无国界的省际贸易的 2.4%。纳入多边将外贸阻力降低到相当于省际无摩擦贸易潜力的 0.1%。地理位置使服务贸易减少了货物贸易总额的七倍以上。令人惊讶的是，服务业和商品方面的省内（地方）贸易同样向上偏转，这意味着边境地区的服务贸易增加比货物贸易更多。

Title：Rent-seeking at home，capturing market share abroad：The domestic determinants of the transnationalization of China state construction engineering corporation

Author：Chih-Shian Liou

Periodical：World Development

Date：2014

Abstract：How do the Chinese central state and central state-owned construction enterprises interact with one another as China's overseas contracting unfolds in the post-corporatization period? Building upon a neo-institutional analysis of the principal-agent relationship, this article finds that contrary to most of the accusations leveled against the global outreach of Chinese SOEs, state-backed transnationalization is by no means state-dominated. SOE managers' continuous bureaucratic ties enable the firm to navigate through China's gigantic but fragmented bureaucracy in favor of corporate commercial interests, which reflects the negotiated nature of the state-SOE relationship in the course of transnationalization.

题目:国内寻租,获取海外市场份额:中国建筑工程总公司国际化的国内决定因素

作者:刘志先

期刊:世界发展

日期:2014 年

摘要:中国国家和中央国有建筑企业的海外承包事业在后公司化时期如何相互影响? 在对委托代理关系的新制度分析的基础上,本文认为,与大多数对中国国有企业全球扩张的指责不同,国家支持的国际化并不意味着国家主导。国有企业管理人员持续的官僚关系,使企业能够在中国庞大但分散的官僚机构中,以企业的商业利益为导向,这反映了国有企业在跨国化过程中关系谈判的性质。

Title:The welfare implications of services liberalization in a developing country

Author:Nizar Jouini, Nooman Rebei

Periodical:Journal of Development Economics

Date:2014

Abstract:We propose an integrated method based on a two-sector small open economy dynamic and stochastic general equilibrium model to estimate non-tariff barriers and quantify the impact of services liberalization. The major component of trade barriers is explicitly modeled through the introduction of entry-sunk costs. Hence, liberalization is treated assuming a government's policy decision aimed at reducing those costs. Then, we estimate the model using Bayesian techniques for Tunisia and the Euro Area. The paper presents a precise quantitative evaluation of services trade barriers as the difference between entry-sunk costs in Tunisia versus the Euro Area. We find significant welfare benefits in addition to aggregate and sectoral growth gains the Tunisian economy could attain following services liberalization. Surprisingly, the good sector is the one that benefits the most from services liberalization in the short-and long-term horizons.

题目:服务贸易自由化对发展中国家的福利影响

作者:尼萨尔·乔尼,努南·雷贝

期刊:发展经济学杂志

作者:余淼杰

期刊:经济学杂志

日期:2014 年;第 125 卷,第 6 期

摘要:我们提出了一种基于两部门小型开放经济动态和随机一般均衡模型的综合方法,用以估计非关税壁垒和量化服务自由化的影响。贸易壁垒的主要组成部分,通过引入沉没成本来明确建模。因此,在假设政府的政策决定旨在减少这些成本的基础上,对自由化进行处理。然后,我们使用贝叶斯技术进行突尼斯和欧元区的模型估计。本文在考虑到突尼斯与欧元区的入境成本之间存在差异的情况下,对服务贸易壁垒进行了精确的定量评估。我们在突尼斯经济服务开放之后可以实现的总体和部门增长之外,还发现了显著的福利待遇。令人惊讶的是,无论从短期还是长期来看,好的行业都是从服务自由化中受益最多的行业。

Title: FDI Spillovers and Industrial Policy: The Role of Tariffs and Tax Holidays

Author: Luosha Du, Ann Harrison, Gary Jefferson

Periodical: World Development, 2014; v. 64, iss. 12

Abstract: This paper examines how industrial policy-specifically tariff liberalization and tax subsidies-affects the magnitude and direction of FDI spillovers. We examine these spillover effects across the diverse ownership structure of China's manufacturing sector for 1998 through 2007. We find that tariff reforms, particularly tariff reductions associated with China's WTO ascension, increased the productivity impacts of FDI's backward spillovers. Tax policy-both corporate income and VAT subsidies-has seemingly drawn FDI into strategic industries that spawn significant vertical spillovers. We conclude that liberalization measures during the critical 1998 – 2007 period on balance served to enhance productivity growth in Chinese industry.

题目:外商直接投资溢出与产业政策:关税和免税期的作用

作者:杜罗莎,安·哈里森,格雷·杰弗逊

期刊:世界发展

日期:2014 年;第 64 卷,第 12 期

摘要:本文考察了产业政策——尤其是关税自由化和税收补贴——如何影响外商直接投资溢出的大小和方向。分析了 1998—2007 年中国的制造业部门的不同所有制结构间的外商直接投资溢出效应。结果发现,关税改革特别是与中国加入 WTO 相关的关税削减,增加了外商直接投资的后向溢出的生产率效应。税收政策——企业所得税和增值税补贴——似乎吸引了外商直接投资进入能够产生显著的垂直溢出的战略性产业。结论表明,在 1998—2007 年的关键时期,总的来看自由化政策促进了中国的行业生产率增长。

Title:Impact of South-South FDI and Trade on the Export Upgrading of African Economies

Author:Alessia Amighini, Marco Sanfilippo

Periodical:World Development

Date:2014;v. 64, iss. 12

Abstract:We explore the impact of FDI and imports on the upgrading of African exports. We find that South-South flows impact di erently from North-South ones on the ability of recipients to absorb the positive spillovers. Results support the view that South-South integration has a strong potential for accelerating structural transformation in the continent. South-South FDI foster diversification in key low-tech industries such as agro-industry and textiles, and raise the average quality of manufacturing exports, while importing from the South increases the ability to expand the variety of manufactured exports and to introduce more advanced goods in less-diversified economies.

题目:南—南外商直接投资和贸易对非洲国家出口升级的影响

作者:阿莱西亚·埃米赫尼,马尔科·圣菲利波

期刊:世界发展

日期:2014 年;第 64 卷,第 12 期

摘要:本文探讨了外商直接投资和进口对非洲出口升级的影响。结果发现,

南—南之间投资和进口对接受国吸收正向溢出的能力的影响不同于南—北之间投资和进口的影响。结果支持了这样的观点,即南—南一体化对加速陆地国家的结构转型具有强大的潜力。南—南外商直接投资培育了农业和纺织业等重点低技术产业的多样化,提高了制造业出口的平均质量,与此同时,来自南方国家的进口提升了多元化程度较低的国家扩大制造品出口种类和生产更先进产品的能力。

Title: Institutional Impact of Foreign Direct Investment in China

Author: Cheryl Long, Jin Yang, Jing Zhang

Periodical: World Development

Date: 2015; v. 66, iss. 2

Abstract: We provide firm level empirical evidence that the presence of foreign direct investment (FDI) has positively affected the institutional quality of the host regions in China. Specifically, Chinese domestic firms located in regions with a higher level of FDI tend to enjoy a lower level of tax and fee burdens, less arbitrariness in such burdens, as well as better legal protection. To address the potential issue of endogeneity, we adopt the instrumental variable approach. In addition, we explore the specific mechanisms through which the institutional impact is materialized and provide various extensions of the empirical findings that o er further support for the FDI-induced institutional improvement argument.

题目: 中国的外商直接投资对制度的影响

作者: 龙小宁,杨进,张晶

期刊: 世界发展

日期: 2015 年;第 66 卷,第 2 期

摘要: 本文为外商直接投资正向影响了中国地区的制度质量提供了企业层面的证据。具体而言,位于外商直接投资水平较高地区的中国国内企业往往享受了较低的税费负担,税费负担的可预期性以及更好的法律保护。为了处理内生性的潜在问题,本文采用了工具变量方法。此外,本文探讨了制度影响得以发生的具体机制,并展示了各种扩展的实证研究结果,以为外商直接投资诱致性制度变迁理论提供进一步的支持。

Title: Benefits of Foreign Ownership: Evidence from Foreign Direct Investment in China

Author：Jian Wang，Xiao Wang

Periodical：Journal of International Economics

Date：2015；v. 97，iss. 2

Abstract：To examine the effect of foreign direct investment，this paper compares the post-acquisition performance changes of foreign-and domestic-acquired firms in China. Unlike previous studies，we investigate the purified effect of foreign ownership by using domestic-acquired firms as the control group. After controlling for the acquisition effect that exists in domestic acquisitions，we find no evidence that foreign ownership can bring additional productivity gains to target firms，though both foreign and domestic acquisitions bring productivity improvements to target firms. In contrast，a strong and robust finding is that foreign ownership significantly improves target firms' financial conditions and exports relative to domestic-acquired firms. Foreign acquisition is also found to improve output，employment and wages for target firms. These findings conflict with the conventional view of productivity-driven FDI and highlight the financial channel through which FDI benefits the host countries.

题目：外资所有制的利益：来自中国外商直接投资的证据

作者：王健，王潇

期刊：国际经济学

日期：2015 年；第 97 卷，第 2 期

摘要：为了考察外商直接投资的影响，本文比较了中国的外资收购企业和内资收购企业收购后的绩效变化。与以往的研究不同，本文使用内资收购企业作为控制组分析了外资收购的净效应。在控制了内资收购存在的收购效应后，本文并没有发现外资收购能够给目标企业带来额外的生产率收益，尽管外资收购和内资收购都提高了目标企业的生产率。相比而言，一个显著且稳健的发现是相对内资收购企业，外资收购显著提高了目标企业的融资状况和出口。外资收购也增加了目标企业的产出、就业和工资。这些发现与驱动生产率的外商直接投资的传统观点不一致，强调了外商直接投资使东道国受益的金融渠道。

Title：Do Inland Provinces Benefit from Coastal Foreign Direct Investment in China？

Author：Chunlai Chen

Periodical：China & World Economy

Date：2015 年；v. 23，iss. 3

Abstract：Foreign direct investment(FDI) in China is heavily concentrated in the coastal regions. Do inland provinces benefit from coastal FDI? We use a provincial-level panel dataset and employ the fixed-effects instrumental variables regression technique to investigate the interregional spillovers from coastal FDI to inland provinces. The study finds that，on average，coastal FDI has a negative impact on the economic growth of inland provinces. In addition，depending on the different trade activities engaged in (i. e. whether processing trade or ordinary trade)，coastal FDI has different impacts on the economic growth of inland provinces.

题目：中国的内陆省份是否受益于沿海地区的外商直接投资？

作者：陈春来

期刊：中国与世界经济

日期：2015 年；第 23 卷，第 3 期

摘要：中国的外商直接投资(FDI)主要集中在沿海地区。内陆省份是否受益于沿海地区的外商直接投资？本文使用省级层面的面板数据和采用固定效应工具变量回归方法，考察了沿海地区的外商直接投资对内陆省份的跨区域溢出效应。研究发现，平均而言沿海地区的外商直接投资对内陆省份的经济增长具有负向影响。此外，依赖于从事不同的贸易活动(加工贸易或一般贸易)，沿海地区的外商直接投资对内陆省份的经济增长的影响不同。

Title：Institutional Distance and Foreign Direct Investment

Author：Rafael Cezar，Octavio R. Escobar

Periodical：Review of World Economics

Date：2015 年；v. 151，iss. 4

Abstract：This paper studies the link between foreign direct investment(FDI) and institutional distance. Using a heterogeneous firms framework，we develop a the-oretical model to explain how institutional distance influences FDI，and it is shown that institutional distance reduces both the likelihood that a firm will invest in a foreign country and the volume of investment it will undertake. We test our model using inward and outward FDI data on OECD countries. The empirical results confirm the theory and indicate that FDI activity declines with institutional distance. In addition, we find that firms from developed economies adapt more easily to institutional distance than firms from developing economies.

题目:制度距离与外商直接投资

作者:拉斐尔·塞萨尔,奥克塔维奥·埃斯科巴

期刊:世界经济评论

日期:2015 年;第 151 卷,第 4 期

摘要:本文研究了外商直接投资与制度距离之间的关系。使用异质性企业的框架,本文开发了一个理论模型来解释制度距离如何影响外商直接投资,结果显示制度距离降低了企业投资外国的可能性以及企业承诺的投资数量。使用经合组织(OECD)国家的内向和外向外商直接投资数据检验了模型。实证结果证实了理论并且表明外商直接投资活动随着制度距离增加下降了。此外,本文还发现发达国家的企业比发展中国家的企业更容易适应制度距离。

Title:Quid Pro Quo: Technology Capital Transfers for Market Access in China

Author:Thomas J. Holmes, Ellen R. Mcgrattan, Edward C. Prescott

Periodical:Review of Economic Studies

Date:2015 年;v. 82, iss. 3

Abstract:By the 1970s, quid pro quo policy, which requires multinational firms to transfer technology in return for market access, had become a common practice in many developing countries. While many countries have subsequently liberalized quid pro quo requirements, China continues to follow the policy. In this article, we incorporate quid pro quo policy into a multicountry dynamic general equilibrium model, using microevidence from Chinese patents to motivate key assumptions about the terms of the technology transfer deals and macroevidence on China's inward foreign direct investment(FDI) to estimate key model parameters. We then use the model to quantify the impact of China's quid pro quo policy and show that it has had a significant impact on global innovation and welfare.

题目:以市场换技术:进入中国市场的技术资本转让

作者:托马斯·霍姆斯,艾伦·马克格拉顿,爱德华·普雷斯科特

期刊:经济研究评论

日期:2015 年;第 82 卷,第 3 期

摘要:20 世纪 70 年代,以市场换技术的政策要求跨国公司转让技术以获得市场准入的回报,这项政策成为许多发展中国家的普遍做法。虽然许多国家相继放宽了以市场换技术的要求,但是中国继续遵循这项政策。本文将以市场换技术的政策纳入多国动态一般均衡模型,使用中国专利的微观证据做出关于技术转让交易的关键假设,以及使用中国的内向外商直接投资的宏观证据估计模型的关键参数。然后使用模型来量化中国的以市场换技术的政策的影响,结果显示以市场换技术的政策对全球创新和福利产生了显著的影响。

Title: Resource-based FDI and Expropriation in Developing Economies

Author: Christopher Hajzler

Periodical: Journal of International Economics

Date: 2014; v. 92, iss. 1

Abstract: Globally, foreign direct investment (FDI) assets are expropriated more in resource extraction industries com-pared to other sectors. Despite the higher apparent risk of expropriation in resources, countries more likely to ex-propriate also have a larger share of FDI in the resource sector. An incomplete markets model of FDI is developed to account for this puzzle. The type of government regime is stochastic, with low penalty regimes facing a rela-tively low, exogenous cost of expropriating FDI, and country risk is measured by the variation in these costs across different regimes. The key innovation of the model is that the government, before the regime type is known, is able to charge different prices to domestic and foreign investors for mineral rights. Granting cheap access in-creases FDI and reduces the country's share of resource rents, increasing the temptation to expropriate in a rel-atively low penalty regime. In very high-risk countries, subsidizing resource FDI increases the total value of output by raising investment, and the net gains from expropriating in a low penalty regime outweigh the rents foregone under a high penalty one. However, a stochastic resource output price results in relatively low-risk countries restricting FDI inflows to the resource sector instead-"windfall profits" in this sector raise incentives to expropriate when prices are high, yet minimization of the ex ante risk of expropriation is preferred owing to the relatively high penalty for expropriating. These results imply a higher average share of resource-based FDI in countries most likely to expropriate, while resources account for a high share of expropriated assets compared to the sector's global share of FDI. We show that the model is able to reconcile observed patterns of foreign invest-ment and expropriation for a sample of 38 developing and emerging economies.

题目:发展中国家的资源导向型外商直接投资与征用

作者:克里斯托夫·哈吉勒

期刊:国际经济学

日期:2014 年;第 92 卷,第 1 期

摘要:在全球范围内,外商直接投资资产在资源开采行业相比其他行业被征用更多。尽管资源行业存在被征用的更高风险,但是更可能征用的国家在资源开采行业还是具有较高比例的外商直接投资。本文开发了一个外商直接投资的不完全市场模型来解释这个谜题。政府体制的类型是随机的,低惩罚体制面对着征用外商直接投资相对较低的外生的成本,以及使用不同体制间的这些成本的方差测度国家风险。这个模型的关键创新在于在知晓政府体制的类型之前,政府能够为矿业权对国内投资者和外国投资者索要不同的价格。低廉的获取权增加了外商直接投资以及减少了国家的资源租金的份额,同时增加了低惩罚体制的征用诱惑。在高风险国家,补贴资源导向型外商直接投资通过提高投资增加了总产值,以及低惩罚体制下征用的净收益超过了高惩罚体制下的租金。然而,随机的资源产出价格使得相对低风险的国家限制外商直接投资流入资源开采行业,而不是当价格较高时这些行业的"暴利"提高了征用激励,但是由于对征用的相对高惩罚,最小化征用的事前风险是首要的。这些结果意味着在最可能征用的国家资源导向型外商直接投资的平均份额更高,与资源开采行业的外商直接投资的全球份额相比,资源占据了征用资产中的较高份额。本文证明了这个模型能够解释 38 个发展中和新兴经济体的外商投资和征用的可观测的模式。

Title:The Impact of Outward FDI on the Performance of Chinese Firms

Author:C. Cozza, R. Rabellotti, M. Sanfilippo

Periodical:China Economic Review

Date:2015;v. 36,iss. 12

Abstract：Using new firm-level data from the Emerging Multinationals' Events and Networks DATAbase(EMENDATA), this paper investigates the effects on Chinese firms of Outward FDI(OFDI)into advanced European countries. Propensity score matching is combined with a difference-in-difference(DiD)estimator to reduce the problem of self-selection of treated firms in foreign markets, and to eliminate time-invariant and unobservable differences between those firms and the controls. The results provide robust evidence supporting the view that China's OFDI so far have had a positive impact on domestic activities in enhancing firms' productivity and scales of operation, measured by sales and employment. When we distinguish among investments on the basis of entry mode, accounting for endogeneity in the selection process, acquisitions facilitate early access to intangible assets, but are detrimental to financial performance, while greenfield investments have a stronger impact on the scale and productivity of Chinese multinationals investing in Europe.

题目：对外直接投资对中国企业绩效的影响

作者：C. 科扎，热贝罗蒂，圣菲利波

期刊：中国经济评论

日期：2015 年；第 36 卷，第 12 期

摘要：使用来自新兴跨国公司的时间和网络数据库的新的企业层面数据，本文考察了中国企业进入欧洲发达国家的对外直接投资（OFDI）的影响。倾向匹配得分和双重差分相结合的估计结果减少了外国市场中处理组企业的自选择问题，以及消除了处理组企业和控制组企业之间的时序不变和不可观测的差异。分析结果稳健地支持了这一观点，即到目前为止中国的对外直接投资对提高国内企业的生产率和经营规模（以销售和就业衡量）具有正向影响。当区分了基于进入模式的投资后，以及控制了选择过程的内生性，收购便利了早期无形资产的获取，但是不利于金融绩效，与此同时，绿地投资对投资欧洲的中国跨国公司的规模和生产率具有更大的影响。

Title：Do nonreciprocal preferential trade agreements increase beneficiaries' exports?

Author：Salvador Gil-Pareja, Rafael Llorca-Vivero, José Antonio Martínez-Serrano

Periodical：Journal of Development Economics

Date: Jan. 2014

Abstract: This paper investigates whether and to what extent nonreciprocal preferential trade agreements (NRPTAs) have increased developing countries' exports to richer countries. Using recent developments in the econometric analysis of the gravity equation over the period 1960 – 2008, we find robust evidence that, on the whole, NRPTAs and the Generalized System of Preferences have had an economically significant effect on exports from developing countries. However, the estimation of catch-all dummies masks heterogeneous results for the individual programs.

题目: 非互惠贸易协定会增加受益方的出口吗？

作者: 萨尔瓦多·吉尔－帕雷亚,拉斐尔·洛尔卡－比韦罗,何塞·安东尼·马丁内斯－塞拉诺

期刊: 发展经济学杂志

日期: 2014 年 1 月

摘要: 本文调查了非互惠优惠贸易协定(NRPTAs)是否能够以及在多大程度上能够增加发展中国家对更富裕国家的出口。利用引力方程计量分析的最新发展成果分析 1960—2008 年的数据,我们发现有力的证据表明,NRPTA 和普遍优惠制在整体上对发展中国家的出口产生了经济上的显著影响。然而,对所有虚拟变量的估计掩盖了对每个特殊协定的异质性结果。

Title: Does trade liberalization promote regional disparities? Evidence from a multiregional CGE model of India

Author: Athula Naranpanawa, Rashmi Arora

Periodical: World Development

Date: Dec. 2014

Abstract: Over last few decades, there has been a growing interest among researchers in understanding the link between trade liberalization and regional disparities within the context of an individual country. In this study, we develop the first ever single-country multiregional Computable General Equilibrium (CGE) model for the Indian economy to investigate this linkage. Overall our results suggest that, in the short run, trade liberalization has a beneficial impact on the rich and fast-growing middle-income states and a marginal or negative impact on the poor states.

题目:贸易自由化是否会促进区域分化——来自印度多区域可计算一般均衡模型的证据

作者:艾休拉·纳兰帕纳瓦,拉什米·阿拉拉

期刊:世界发展

日期:2014 年 11 月

摘要:在过去几十年中,研究人员对了解贸易自由化与个别国家范围内区域差异之间的联系越来越感兴趣。在本文研究中,我们发展了第一个单一国家的多区域可计算一般均衡(CGE)模型,并用于调查研究印度经济中这一联系。总的来说,我们的结果表明,短期来看,贸易自由化对富裕国家和快速增长的中等收入国家有利,但对贫穷国家有边际或负面的影响。

Title:The Differential Effects of Bilateral Tax Treaties

Author:Bruce A. Blonigen, Lindsay Oldenski, and Nicholas Sly

Periodical:American Economic Journal:Economic Policy

Date:Jun. 2014

Abstract:Bilateral tax treaties(BTTs) are intended to promote foreign direct investment through double-taxation relief. Using BEA firm-level data, we find a positive effect of BTTs on FDI, which is larger for firms that use differentiated inputs. BTTs allow multinational firms to request assistance from treaty partners' governments if they have a grievance about how tax liabilities are determined. These provisions disproportionately benefit firms that use inputs for which an arm's-length price is difficult to observe, since allocation of earnings across countries is more complex. We find differential BTT effects for both sales by existing affiliates and entry of new affiliates.

题目:双边税收协定的差异化影响

作者:布鲁斯·布隆根,林赛·奥尔登斯基,尼古拉斯·斯利

期刊:美国经济杂志:经济政策

日期:2014 年 6 月

摘要:双边税收协定旨在通过双重课税减免促进外商直接投资。使用 BEA 企业级数据,我们发现双边税收协定对外商直接投资的积极影响,其中对使用差异化投入的企业来说影响更大。双边税收协定允许跨国公司如果对如何确定税

收负担抱有不满,可以向税收条约合作方政府要求提供援助。这些规定对那些使用难以了解其公平交易价格的投入的公司来说收益是不成比例的,因为各国间的收益分配比较复杂。我们发现,现有附属公司新进入的附属公司的销售将分别受到不同的税收协定效应。

Title: Trade imbalances, export structure and wage inequality

Author: Rosario Crino and Paolo Epifani

Periodical: The Economic Journal

Date: May. 2014

Abstract: We study, both theoretically and empirically, how trade imbalances affect the structure of countries' exports and wage inequality. We show that, in a Heckscher-Ohlin model with a continuum of goods, a Southern(Northern) trade surplus leads to an increase(reduction) in the average skill intensity of exports, in the relative demand for skills and in the skill premium in both countries. We provide robust support for the mechanism underlying these predictions using a large panel of countries observed over the past 30 years. Our results suggest that the large and growing North-South trade imbalances arisen over the last three decades may have exacerbated wage inequality worldwide.

题目:贸易不平衡、出口结构和工资不平等

作者:罗萨里奥·克里诺,保罗·埃皮法尼

期刊:经济学杂志

日期:2014 年 3 月

摘要:在理论和实证两方面,我们研究了贸易不平衡对不同半球国家的出口结构和工资不平等性的影响。我们的研究显示,在具有连续货物的赫克歇尔—俄林模型中,南部地区国家(或北部地区国家)的贸易顺差会导致出口平均技术强度的增加(或减少),以及两国相对技能需求和技能溢价的增加(或减少)。我们使用过去 30 年来观察到的一大群国家,为这些对该机制的预测提供了有力的支持。我们的研究结果表明,过去 30 年来,南北贸易不平衡的大幅增长可能会加剧全球的工资不平等。

Title: Trade wars and trade talks with data

Author：Ralph Ossa

Periodical：American Economic Review

Date：Dec. 2014

Abstract：How large are optimal tariffs? What tariffs would prevail in a worldwide trade war? How costly would a breakdown of international trade policy cooperation be? And what is the scope for future multilateral trade negotiations? I address these and other questions using a unified framework which nests traditional, new trade, and political economy motives for protection. I find that optimal tariffs average 62 percent, world trade war tariffs average 63 percent, the government welfare losses from a breakdown of international trade policy cooperation average 2. 9 percent, and the possible government welfare gains from future multilateral trade negotiations average 0. 5 percent.

题目：贸易战与基于数据的贸易谈判

作者：拉尔夫·奥萨

期刊：美国经济评论

日期：2014 年 11 月

摘要：最优关税有多大？ 全球贸易战争中关税将会如何制定？ 国际贸易政策合作崩溃的代价是多少？ 未来多边贸易谈判的范围如何？ 在本文中，我使用统一的框架来解决上述这些问题以及若干其他问题，这个框架将传统的与新的贸易和政治经济的保护动机联系了起来。我发现，最优关税平均为 62%，在世界贸易战争中关税平均为 63%，国际贸易政策合作崩溃的政府福利损失平均为 2. 9%，未来政府能从多边贸易谈判获取的可能福利收益平均为 0. 5%。

Title：Anti-dumping, intra-industry trade and quality reversals?

Author：JL. Moraga-González, Jean-Marie Viaene

Periodical：International Economic Review

Date：Aug. 2015

Abstract：We examine an export game where two(home and foreign)firms produce vertically differentiated products. The foreign firm is more R&D efficient and is based in a larger and richer market. The unique(risk-dominant)Nash equilibrium exhibits intra-industry trade, and the foreign producer manufactures a higher-quality product. When transport costs are low, unilateral dumping by the foreign firm arises; otherwise, reciprocal dumping occurs. For some parameters, a domestic antidumping policy leads to a quality reversal in the international market whereby the home firm becomes the quality leader. This policy is desirable for the implementing country, though world welfare decreases.

题目:反倾销、产业内贸易与质量逆转

作者:JL. 莫拉加 – 冈萨雷斯,简 – 玛丽·威尼斯

期刊:国际组织评论

日期:2015 年 8 月

摘要:我们检验了两家(国内外)公司生产垂直差异化产品时的出口博弈。其中外资企业的研发效率更高,其总部位于更大、更丰富的市场。独特的(风险主导的)纳什均衡表现出行业内的贸易,并且外国生产者生产出更高质量的产品。而在运输成本低的时候,出现了外国公司的单边倾销;否则,将会发生相互倾销。对于一些参数,国内反倾销政策将导致国际市场的质量逆转,本国企业成为质量领导者。尽管世界福利将因此减少,但这一政策对执行国来说是可取的。

Title: Export diversification effects of the WTO trade facilitation agreement

Author: Cosimo Beverelli, Simon Neumueller, Robert Teh

Periodical: World Development

Date: Jul. 2015

Abstract: We estimate the effects of trade facilitation on export diversification, as measured by two extensive margins: the number of products exported by destination and the number of export destinations served by product. To address causality we use only exports of new products, or exports to new destinations. We find a positive impact of trade facilitation on the extensive margins of trade. The results are robust to alternative definitions of extensive margins, different sets of controls, and various estimation methods. Simulation results suggest substantial extensive margin gains from trade facilitation reform in Sub-Saharan Africa and in Latin America and the Caribbean.

题目:WTO 贸易附属协定的出口多样性效应

作者:科西莫·贝弗瑞利,西蒙·纽曼勒

期刊:世界发展

日期:2015 年 7 月

摘要:以对两个广泛的边界的测算为依据,以目的地划分的出口产品的数量和以产品划分出口目的地的数量,我们估计了贸易便利化对出口多元化的影响。为了了解这其中的因果关系,我们只使用新产品的出口,或到新的目的地的出口数据。贸易便利化对贸易广泛边界产生了积极的影响。在使用对于广泛边界,不同的控制集合和各种估计方法的替代定义后,估计结果也是稳健的。模拟结果表明,在撒哈拉以南的非洲以及拉丁美洲和加勒比地区,大量的广泛边界从贸易便利化改革中获利。

Title:Heterogeneous effects of preferential trade agreements:how does partner similarity matter?

Author:Juyoung Cheong,Do Won Kwak,Kam Ki Tang

Periodical:World Development

Date:Aug. 2014

Abstract:This paper examines how dissimilarity of partner country characteristics affects the change in trade flows under a preferential trade agreement(PTA). Our results show that the more similar the partner countries are,the larger the increase in intra-bloc trade is under a PTA. Particularly,there is a substantial "development neighborhood premium":the gain for developing countries from a PTA among themselves is about two and a half times that from partnering with industrial countries. Our findings challenge the perception that by becoming more integrated with industrial countries,developing countries could automatically gain access to a much larger and lucrative export market.

题目:优惠贸易协定的异质效应:合作伙伴的相似性如何发挥重要作用?

作者:朱扬·切,郭度沅,金基堂

期刊:世界发展

日期:2014 年 8 月

摘要:本文考察了贸易伙伴国家特征的不同如何影响优惠贸易协议(PTA)下的贸易流动变化。我们的研究结果表明,贸易伙伴国家的相似度越高,集团内部贸易的增长越多。特别地,"邻近地区的发展"是一个实质性的问题:发展中国家间的贸易收益是发展中国家与发达国家贸易收益的 2.5 倍。我们的发现对通过与工业化国家更加一体化的观点造成了挑战,而认为发展中国家之间可以自动获得更大、更有利可图的出口市场。

Title:Economic integration agreements and the margins of international trade

Author:Scott L. Baier,Jeffrey H. Bergstrand,Michael Feng

Periodical:Journal of International Economics

Date:Apr. 2014

Abstract:One of the main policy sources of trade-cost changes is the formation of an economic integration agreement (EIA), which potentially affects an importing country's welfare. This paper:(i)provides the first evidence using gravity equations of both intensive and extensive(goods)margins being affected by EIAs employing a panel data set with a large number of country pairs,product categories,and EIAs from 1962 to 2000;(ii)provides the first evidence of the differential(partial)effects of various "types" of EIAs on these intensive and extensive margins of trade;and(iii)finds a novel differential "timing" of the two margins'(partial)effects with intensive-margin effects occurring sooner than extensive-margin effects,consistent with recent theoretical predictions. The results are robust to correcting for potential sample-selection,firm-heterogeneity,and reverse causality biases.

题目:经济一体化协议和国际贸易边界

作者:斯科特·贝尔,杰夫里·伯格斯特兰德,迈克尔·冯

期刊:国际经济学杂志

日期:2014 年 4 月

摘要:影响贸易成本变化的主要政策来源之一,是可能潜在影响进口国福利的经济一体化协议(EIA)的形成。本文:(i)利用 1962—2000 年的包含大量国家对产品类别和一体化协议的面板数据集,在估计了受一体化协议影响的集约边际和扩展边界的重力方程之后提供了第一个证据;(ii)为各种“类型”的一体化协议对这些贸易的集约边际和扩展边际产生的差异化的偏效应提供了第一个证据;(iii)与最近的理论预测一致,发现了两个边际的偏效应具有差异化的“时序性”,其中集约边际产生的影响往往比扩展边际效应更早发生。当采取相应手段纠正潜在的样本选择,企业异质性和反向因果关系偏差后,本文的结论依然是稳健的。

Title：Optimal design of trade agreements in the presence of renegotiation

Author：Giovanni Maggi，Robert W. Staiger

Periodical：American Economic Journal：Microeconomics

Date：Jul. 2015

Abstract：We study the optimal design of trade agreements in a setting where governments can renegotiate the agreement ex-post subject to a key transaction cost，namely that com-pensation between governments is inefficient. The model delivers predictions concerning the optimal form of the agreement，the conditions under which the agreement will be rene-gotiated in equilibrium，and the form that such renegotiation will take. A key question on which we focus is whether the agreement should be structured as a system of "property rules or liability rules，and in this respect we forge a link between the theory of trade agreements and the law-and-economics theory of optimal legal rules.

题目：重新协商谈判情况下的贸易协议优化设计

作者：乔瓦尼·马吉，罗伯特·史泰格

期刊：美国经济学杂志：微观经济学

日期：2015 年 7 月

摘要：我们研究了在政府可以按照核心交易成本重新谈判协议（政府间的补偿效率低下）这一情境下对贸易协定的最优化设计。该模型对涉及贸易协定的最佳形式，协议在均衡状况下被重新谈判时所处的条件，以及重新谈判将采取的形式这些问题提供了预测。我们关注的一个关键问题是，协议是否应该被结构化为财产规则或责任规则的制度，在这方面我们建立了贸易协定理论与最优法律规则的法律与经济学理论之间的联系。

Title：Trade integration，market size，and industrialization：evidence from China's national trunk highway system

Author：Benjamin Faber

Periodical：Review of Economic Studies

Date：Jan. 2014

Abstract：Large-scale transport infrastructure investments connect both large metropolitan centres of production as well as small peripheral regions. Are the resulting trade cost reductions a force for the diffusion of industrial and total economic activity to peripheral regions, or do they reinforce the concentration of production in space? This article exploits China's National Trunk Highway System as a large-scale natural experiment to contribute to our understanding of this question. The network was designed to connect provincial capitals and cities with an urban population above 500,000. As a side effect, a large number of small peripheral counties were connected to large metropolitan agglomerations. To address non-random route placements on the way between targeted city nodes, I propose an instrumental variable strategy based on the construction of least cost path spanning tree networks. The estimation results suggest that network connections have led to a reduction in GDP growth among non-targeted peripheral counties. This effect appears to be driven by a significant reduction in industrial output growth. Additional results present evidence in support of a trade-based channel in the light of falling trade costs between peripheral and metropolitan regions.

题目:贸易一体化、市场规模和产业化:来自中国国家干线公路系统的证据

作者:本杰明·法伯

期刊:经济研究评论

日期:2014 年 1 月

摘要:大型运输基础设施投资不但连接了大都市生产中心,还连接了小型周边地区。贸易成本的降低到底是推动了工业和总体经济活动扩散到周边地区的一种力量,还是加强生产的空间集聚?本文利用中国国家干线公路系统进行了大规模的自然实验,有助于我们对这一问题的理解。该网络旨在连接城市人口超过 50 万的省会城市。而作为副作用,大量小型周边县市被连接到大城市群。为了解释目标城市节点之间的非随机布局演进,我提出了一种基于最小成本路径生成的树型网络构建的工具性多样化策略。估计结果表明,网络连接导致非目标外围地区 GDP 增长率下降。这种影响似乎是由于工业产出增长的大幅度减少所致。鉴于外围和大都市地区的贸易成本下降,其他额外结果提供了支持贸易渠道的证据。

Title: Distributional preferences, reciprocity-like behavior, and efficiency in bilateral exchange

Author: Daniel J. Benjamin

Periodical: American Economic Journal : Microeconomics

Date：Jul. 2015

Abstract：Under what conditions do distributional preferences, such as altruism or a concern for fair outcomes, generate efficient trade? I analyze theoretically a simple bilateral exchange game：each player sequentially takes an action that reduces his own material payoff but increases the other player's. Each player's preferences may depend on both his/her own material payoff and the other player's. I identify two key properties of the second-mover's preferences：indifference curves kinked around "fair" material-payoff distributions, and materials payoffs entering preferences as "normal goods." Either property can drive reciprocity-like behavior and generate a Pareto efficient outcome.

题目：分配偏好、互惠行为和双边交易效率

作者：丹尼尔·本杰明

期刊：美国经济学杂志：微观经济学

日期：2015 年 7 月

摘要：分配偏好，如利他主义或对公平成果的关注，在什么条件下会产生有效的贸易？我在理论角度上分析一个简单的双边交易博弈：每个参与者按顺序采取行动以减少自己的物质收益，而增加另一参与者的。每个参与者的偏好可能取决于他/她自己的物质收益和另一参与者的喜好。我确定了第二动机偏好的两个关键属性：无差异曲线扭曲"公平"的物质收益分配，而物质报酬以"正常货物"的形式进入偏好。任何一种财产都可以驱使类似的互动行为，并最终产生帕累托有效的结果。

Title：Estimates of the trade and welfare effects of NAFTA

Author：Lorenzo Caliendo，Fernando Parro

Periodical：Review of Economic Studies

Date：May. 2014

Abstract：We build into a Ricardian model sectoral linkages, trade in intermediate goods, and sectoral heterogeneity in production to quantify the trade and welfare effects from tariff changes. We also propose a new method to estimate sectoral trade elasticities consistent with any trade model that delivers a multiplicative gravity equation. We apply our model and use our estimated elasticities to identify the impact of NAFTA's tariff reductions. We find that Mexico's welfare increases by 1.31%, U. S.'s welfare increases by 0.08%, and Canada's welfare declines by 0.06%. We find that intra-bloc trade increases by 118% for Mexico, 11% for Canada, and 41% for the U. S. We show that welfare effects from tariff reductions are reduced when the structure of production does not take into account intermediate goods or input-output linkages. Our results highlight the importance of sectoral heterogeneity, intermediate goods, and sectoral linkages for the quantification of the welfare gains from tariffs reductions.

题目:对"北美贸易协定"贸易效应和福利效应的估计

作者:洛伦佐·卡利嫩多,费尔南多·帕罗

期刊:经济研究评论

日期:2014 年 3 月

摘要:我们建立了一个以中间产品贸易和生产部门异质性为特征的李嘉图模式的部门联系,以量化关税变化对贸易和福利的影响。我们还提出了一种新的方法来估计部门贸易弹性,与任何提供乘法引力方程的贸易模型相一致。我们应用该模型,并使用我们估计的弹性来确定 NAFTA 关税削减的影响。我们发现墨西哥的福利增加了 1.31%,美国福利增加了 0.08%,加拿大的福利下降了 0.06%。我们发现,墨西哥国内贸易增长了 118%,加拿大为 11%,美国为 41%。我们的结果表明,当生产结构不考虑中间商品或投入产出关联时,减免关税削减的福利效应会减少。我们的结果强调了部门异质性,中间产品和部门联系对关税福利收益减免的量化的重要性。

Title: International lending, sovereign debt and joint liability

Author: Kaushik Basu, Joseph E. Stiglitz

Periodical: The Economic Journal

Date: 2015

Abstract: As the Eurozone crisis drags on, it is evident that a part of the problem lies in the architecture of debt and its liabilities within the Eurozone and, more generally, the European Union. This paper argues that a large part of the problem can be mitigated by permitting appropriately-structured cross-country liability for sovereign debt incurred by individual nations within the European Union. In brief, the paper makes a case for amending the Treaty of Lisbon. The case is established by constructing a game-theoretic model and demonstrating that there exist self-fulfilling equilibria, which would come into existence if cross-country debt liability were permitted and which are Pareto superior to the existing outcome.

题目:国际贷款、主权债务及连带责任

作者:卡希克・巴斯,约瑟夫・E. 斯蒂格利茨

期刊:经济学杂志

日期:2015 年

摘要:因为欧元区危机的拖累,显而易见的是,该问题的一部分在于债务结构及其在欧元区以及欧洲联盟范围内的负债。本文认为,通过对欧盟内各个国家所承担的主权债务进行适当的跨国赔偿责任结构化,可以缓解该问题的很大一部分。简言之,本论文建议修改里斯本条约。该建议建立在通过构建一个理论博弈模型,并证明存在自我实现的平衡的基础之上,如果允许跨国债务,改进后的结构将帕累托优于现有结果。

第三章

世界经济学科 2014—2015 年出版图书精选

第一节　中文图书精选

书名:国际货币体系未来变革与人民币国际化

作者:潘英丽

出版社:格致出版社

出版时间:2014 年 1 月 1 日

Title:The future of the international monetary system reform and internationalization of RMB

Author:Yingli Pan

Publisher:Gezhi Press

Date:Jan,2014

内容摘要:《国际货币体系未来变革与人民币国际化》(套装共 3 册)试图探索一种"临床政治经济学",将现代经济学、政治经济学、国际政治学和经济货币史研究结合起来,以现代微观经济学的最优化理论作为国际货币体系问题与改革目标的合理性分析基础;以宏观动态一般均衡理论作为探讨经济变量、政策变量之间内在逻辑关系的基础,强化研究的系统性,突出改革时序、政策选择、政策组合和政策协调等问题的重要性和复杂性。

书名:公共利益视野下的国际投资协定新发展

作者:张庆麟

出版社:中国社会科学出版社

出版时间:2014 年 11 月 1 日

Title:New development of international investment agreement from the perspective of public interest

Author:Qinglin Zhang

Publisher:China Social Sciences Press

Date:Nov,2014

内容摘要:《公共利益视野下的国际投资协定新发展》主要讲述了,近几年国际投资法得到了较大的发展,一方面是国际投资协定的大量签订,从传统的双边投资协定(BIT)到包含投资内容的自由贸易协定(FTA);另一方面则是国际投资协定中出现了较多的所谓非投资内容的条款,如环境、人权(包括劳工)、收支平衡等,以及原有条款在内涵上的新发展,如公平公正待遇条款、征收条款等;第三个方面是投资争端解决机制方面的较大发展,其既表现为国际投资协定中争端解决机制条款的变化,也表现为投资争端仲裁实践的发展。所以,国际投资法目前成为中外国际法领域的显学。

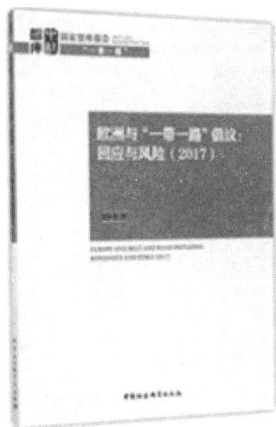

书名:欧洲与"一带一路"倡议:回应与风险(2017)

作者:刘作奎

出版社:中国社会科学出版社

出版时间:2015 年 12 月 1 日

Title:Europe and One Belt OneRoad initiative:response and risk

Author:Zuokui Liu

Publisher:China Social Sciences Press

Date:Dec,2015

内容摘要:《欧洲与"一带一路"倡议:回应与风险(2017)》基本上以实地调研和访谈为依托,并以每年一度针对欧洲国家精英开展的"一带一路"问卷调查为基底,以风险评估为主要研究内容和研究特色,以政策建议为报告的亮点,集中为"一带一路"倡议在欧洲的布局提供理论和实践参考。

书名:中国新一轮对外开放

作者:樊纲,马蔚华

出版社:中国经济出版社

出版时间:2015 年 1 月 1 日

Title:The new round of opening to the outside world in China

Author:Gang Fan,Weihua Ma

Publish:China Economic Publishing Press

Date:Jan,2015

内容摘要:本书以"中国新一轮对外开放:机遇与挑战"为主题,旨在探讨如何建立对全球高端生产要素富有吸引力的体制环境,提高我国整合国际资源的能力;如何通过进一步对外开放促进国内经济体制改革,释放改革红利;如何适应新的国际贸易与投资环境,建立有效的风险防范体系;如何发挥上海自贸区和深圳前海试验区的作用,推动服务业尤其是金融业领域的扩大开放。本书致力于为政策制定者提供决策参考。

书名:全球化变局与中国新一轮对外开放

作者:徐占枕

出版社:中国经济出版社

出版时间:2014 年 10 月 1 日

Title:The changing situation of globalization and China's new round of opening to the outside world

Author:Zhanzhen Xu

Publisher:China Economic Press

Date:Oct,2014

内容摘要:《全球化变局与中国新一轮对外开放》是中国国际经济交流中心智库丛书第一本。研究视角体现了战略和政策一体化的高度,现实性、针对性强。中国国际经济交流中心智库丛书遵循"创新、求实、睿智、兼容"的智库发展理念,即将推出多种质量好、水平高、价值大的优秀作品。研究领域覆盖战略问题、国际经济问题、国内经济问题,具体涉及经济发展战略、外交、法治建设、区域发展、能源资源、金融、创新驱动等多方面。本套丛书的面世,期望能够引起国内智库同行以及社会各界的关注,从而共同推进全社会对相关问题研究的不断深入,形成更多、更高质量和更具影响力的应对全球性问题的"中国方案"和解决现实中国问题的"中国智慧"。

书名:世界经济体系变迁与两岸经济关系发展

作者:汪立峰

出版社:南开大学出版社

出版时间:2014 年 10 月 1 日

Title:Changes of world economic system and development of economic relations across the Taiwan Straits

Author:Lifeng Wang

Publisher:Nankai University Press

Date:Oct,2014

内容摘要:《世界经济体系变迁与两岸经济关系发展》将进一步尝试从世界经济体系变迁的角度,分析两岸经济关系转折与发展的时空背景。此外,《世界经济体系变迁与两岸经济关系发展》还将结合当前世界经济体系的再调整以及两岸经济形势的新变化,为两岸经济关系的发展起指导作用。

书名:世界经济新格局下的中美经贸关系

作者:浦东美国经济研究所和武汉大学美国加拿大经济研究所

出版社:上海社会科学院出版社

出版时间:2014 年 8 月 1 日

Title:Sino US economic and trade relations under the new pattern of world economy

Author:Pudong Institute of American economics and the Institute of economic studies in the United States and Canada,Wuhan University

Publisher:Shanghai Academy of Social Sciences Press

Date:Aug,2014

内容摘要:《世界经济新格局下的中美经贸关系》主要围绕"世界经济新格局下美国经济发展"这一主题展开,邀请了包括陈宝森研究员、张宇燕研究员、华民教授在内的 16 位学者做了大会主题发言,分组讨论的议题涉及美国经济现状与再工业化趋势、美国宏观经济政策调整与改革、美国亚太战略与中美经贸关系等。在讨论中,与会专家学者畅所欲言,讨论热烈,针对美国经济走势、美国的再工业化与科技革命、美元国际货币地位、美国亚太战略以及中美经贸关系的发展等问题提出了许多颇有见地的观点和建设性对策建议。

书名:中国与拉丁美洲:未来 10 年的经贸合作

作者:苏振兴

出版社:中国社会科学出版社

出版时间:2014 年 8 月 1 日

Title:Chinese and Latin America:Economic and trade cooperation in the next 10 years

Author:Zhenxing Zhu

Publisher:China Social Sciences Press

Date:Aug,2014

内容摘要:《中国与拉丁美洲:未来 10 年的经贸合作》是关于中拉经贸关系发展的基础性研究,在总结 21 世纪以来拉美地区经济发展趋势和政策调整的基础上,通过对主要拉美国家资源禀赋、产业结构、经贸合作等多角度的案例分析,深入探讨了今后 10 年中拉经贸合作的前景和实现途径。《中国与拉丁美洲:未来 10 年的经贸合作》既有理论上的研究,也有历史的回顾和实证分析。全书资料丰富、数据翔实、论证扎实,是国内拉美研究学术界的一本优秀专著。

书名:中国对外贸易环境与贸易摩擦研究报告

作者:王孝松

出版社:中国人民大学出版社

出版时间:2015 年 6 月

Title:Research Report on China's foreign trade environment and trade friction

Author:Xiaosong Wang

Publisher:Renmin University of China press

Date:Jun,2015

内容摘要:中国外贸保持平稳发展具有一定基础和有利条件,但是制约外贸稳定发展的不确定和不稳定因素越来越多。中国外贸发展面临的主要风险来自于日趋复杂的外部环境。从国际来看,在目前各国宽松政策的刺激下,世界经济复苏步伐有所加快,发达国家经济有望延续回升向好态势。但全球经济仍处于政策刺激下的脆弱复苏阶段,发达国家经济仍低于潜在增长率,新兴经济体经济也难以恢复到前两年的高增速。美国即将退出量化宽松货币政策,将对全球经济和金融市场带来重大影响。全球范围内贸易保护主义仍在加剧,也将在一定程度上影响全球贸易复苏。对对外贸易环境及贸易摩擦的进行年度统计分析,有助于我们正确认识对外贸易面临的形势。本书运用统计数据所做对外贸易环境及贸易摩擦的进行年度统计分析,可以供商业企业、研究机构、投资机构、政府部门的决策参考。

书名:世贸规则与产业保护

作者:韩立余

出版社:北京大学出版社

出版时间:2014年10月1日

Title:WTO rules and industrial protectio

Author: Liyu Han

Publisher: Peking University Press

Date: Oct,2014

内容摘要:《世贸规则与产业保护》作者利用熟悉世贸规则和我国相关法律的优势,从产业保护和发展这一角度,对世贸规则进行彻底的、全面的、细致的梳理和分析,以探究世贸规则是如何具体影响到产业的,指出我国现有法规和政策存在的问题、可行的方法、发展的方向。

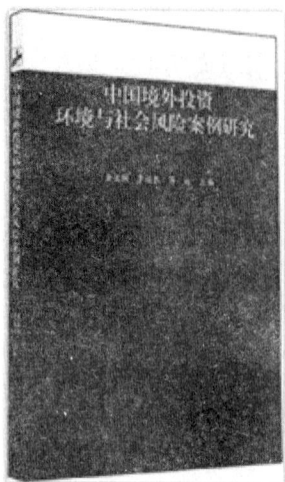

书名:中国境外投资环境与社会风险案例研究

作者:查道炯

出版社:北京大学出版社

出版时间:2014 年 9 月 1 日

Title:The case study of China's overseas investment environment and social risk

Author:Daojiong Cha

Publisher:Peking University Press

Date:Oct,2014

内容摘要:中国企业"走出去"进行海外投资已经到了十分重要的阶段,每年的增量显著,投资领域越来越广,涵盖能源矿产开发、农业、基础设施、跨国并购等,国有企业和民营企业"走出去"的势头都很强劲。与此同时,中资企业境外投资遇到的问题也越来越突出,面临着各种风险,其中突出的风险有环境风险、社会风险和冲突风险。

《中国境外投资环境与社会风险案例研究》选取中国境外投资中的十几个环境与社会风险案例,重点在东南亚、非洲、拉丁美洲和澳大利亚等地区,通过研究,深入探讨了这些风险的基本原理和规避方法,以期提高中国企业海外投资以及金融机构融资的风险管理水平。

参加本书编写的作者主要来自北京大学和国家发改委、商务部、环保部、进出口银行、国务院发展研究中心等政府智囊机构,也有国内一些国际组织的专家学者。本书可供国家宏观经济决策部门、"走出去"企业、教学及研究机构的有关人士阅读。

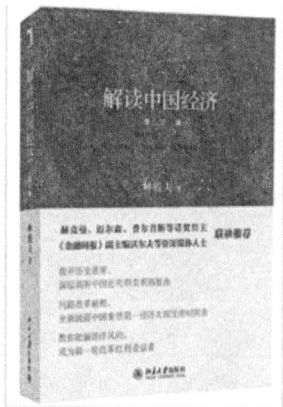

书名:解读中国经济(增订版)

作者:林毅夫

出版社:北京大学出版社

出版时间:2014 年 9 月 1 日

Title:Interpretation of China's economy

Author:Yifu Lin

Publisher:Peking University Press

Date:Sep,2014

内容摘要:《解读中国经济(增订版)》是解读中国经济最权威著作,总结了中国与其他国家、地区经济发展和改革活动的经验,提出了一个经济发展和转型的一般理论,并以此理论分析中国在改革和发展过程中取得的各项成就,面临的主要经济、社会问题,探讨其原因和解决问题的办法。书中用通俗的语言和生动的实例,系统地回顾了中国经济的发展历程与改革经验,深入浅出地讲解了中国经济发展的热点问题。新版新增了对最新经济形势的分析与预测,并就"资本账户"和"林张之争"等热点问题做出了重要评论。

书名:中国对外贸易对国民财富和福利增长的影响

作者:叶劲松

出版社:经济科学出版社

出版时间:2014 年 12 月 1 日

Title:The influence of China's foreign trade on national wealth and welfare growth

Author:Jinsong Ye

Publisher:Economic Science Press

Date:Dec,2014

　　内容摘要:《中国对外贸易对国民财富和福利增长的影响》主要分析对外贸易对一国国民财富增长的影响。介绍国民财富的内涵,给出了相关观测指标,结合中国所处发展阶段提出用收入差距来观测对外贸易的国民福利增长效应,分析了对外贸易影响一国财富和福利增长的主要途径,从进出口、工业制成品与初级产品相对比的角度实证分析了中国对外贸易对国民财富和福利增长的影响。

　　书名:中国市场准入环境与贸易投资新政——基于若干行业的实证研究

作者:郑建成

出版社:对外经济贸易大学出版社

出版时间:2015 年 7 月

Title:China's market access environment and tradeinvestment policy

Author:Jiancheng Zheng

Publisher:University of International Businessand Economics Press

Date：Jul，015

内容摘要：本书基于若干行业的实证研究，重新梳理了中国近年来高速发展的路线图。通过使用具有说服力的经济模型和分析方法，对上海自贸区等贸易新政实施以来探索我国对外开放的新路径和新模式，培育我国全球竞争新优势进行了缜密的研究分析。

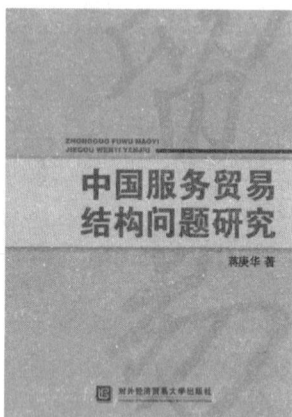

书名：中国服务贸易结构问题研究

作者：蒋庚华

出版社：对外经济贸易大学出版社

出版时间：2014 年 12 月 1 日

Title：The Study of Chinese Service Trade Structure

Author：Genghua Jiang

Publisher：University Of International Business And Economics Press

Date：Dec，2014

内容摘要：改革开放以来，随着经济开放程度的不断加深和产业结构升级步伐的不断加快，中国服务贸易得到了迅速发展。但我们应该看到，中国的服务贸易在快速发展过程中仍存在着许多问题，特别是服务贸易结构仍比较落后。中国服务贸易出口主要集中在旅游、运输和其他商业服务等传统的可以充分利用本国丰富的劳动力资源和自然资源的服务项目上；服务贸易逆差则主要集中在以运输、保险为代表的资本密集型和知识、技术密集型服务产品上。从服务贸易内部区域结构上看，主要集中在东部沿海发达地区，中、西部和东北地区的服务贸易与东部地区相比有较大差距；从外部区域结构上看，主要集中在美国、日本、欧盟和中国香港等发达国家和地区。中国服务贸易结构发展的不平衡直接关系到服务贸易的健康和可持续发展。《中国服务贸易结构问题研究》综合利用国际贸易学、经济地理学、产业经济学等相关学科的理论与方法，通过对改革开放以来中国服务贸易结构的变化趋势的分析，找出服务贸易结构变化的原因、未来发展趋势以及服务贸易结构与中国经济发展之间的关系，并相应地提出优化中国服务贸易结构的对策建议。

书名：多边贸易体制的理论与实践

作者：庄惠明

出版社：厦门大学出版社

出版时间：2015 年 12 月 1 日

Title：The theory and practice of multilateral trading system

Author：Huiming Zhuang

Publisher：Xiamen University Press

Date：Dec,2014

内容摘要：当前国内外学界对世界贸易体制的研究主要基于国际法学角度,国际贸易体系作为国际贸易研究的三大方向之一,其研究范式理应与传统国际经济学的研究框架保持一致。20 世纪 90 年代后期,多边贸易体制经济学研究范式的提出,使得对世界贸易体制的研究"回归"国际经济学研究框架中,初步实现了经济学与国际法学的交叉融合。本书主要从三个层次展开研究,一是基于经济学研究范式对多边贸易体制的理论基础、制度特征、多边贸易谈判的三大特征等进行分析;二是对多边贸易体制的实践与绩效进行考察,并从多哈发展议程视角剖析多边贸易体制的深层危机;三是在多边贸易体制框架下探讨中国参与 WTO 的绩效与应对策略。

书名：新功能主义理论与中日韩 FTA 建构模式

作者：李冬新

出版社：社会科学文献出版社

出版时间：2014 年 9 月 1 日

Title：The Neo-functionalism Theory and the Construction Mode of China-Japan-Korea FTA

Author：Dongxin Li

Publisher：Social Sciences Academic Press

Date：Sep,2014

内容摘要：本书主要内容是通过批判性研究有关区域一体化的理论范式,确立功能主义的理论范式是构建中日韩自由贸易区的适合路径,继而探讨中日韩自由贸易区的各种构想,包括中日韩三方各自提出了哪些战略性建议、具体方案以及三国各自的关注点和可能的利益冲突点,进而对中日韩三国在农业、服务业、制造业、水产业和投资领域等方面的合作进行损益比较,并通过借鉴欧盟和北美自由贸易区(NAFTA)的实践经验,构建"三高"的三国自由贸易区理论。

书名:我国对外贸易顺差研究 兼论我国经济的转型升级

作者:卢万青

出版社:中国经济出版社

出版时间:2014 年 8 月 1 日

Title:Study on the Foreign Trade Surplus in China Also on China's Economic Transformation and Upgrading

Author:Wanqing Lu

Publisher:China Economic Publishing House

Date:Aug,2014

内容摘要:《我国对外贸易顺差研究 兼论我国经济的转型升级》以对外贸易顺差问题为研究对象,主要研究我国外贸顺差的形成原因、变化趋势和解决对策。重点内容包括:第一,从东亚产品内分工、全球国际分工与全球经济失衡、相对国内供求关系和经济增长方式四方面解释我国贸易顺差的形成原因;第二,金融危机之后我国外贸顺差变化趋势是否会发生以及如何发生改变的问题;第三,如何调节我国的外贸失衡问题。

书名:欧债危机评估及中国对策

作者:中国国际经济交流中心课题组

出版社:社会科学文献出版社

出版时间:2014 年 9 月 1 日

Title:Evaluation on European Sovereign Debt Crisis and China's Policy

Author:China Center for International Economic Exchanges

Publisher:Social Sciences Academic Press

Date:Sep,2014

内容摘要:2013 年,中国国际经济交流中心把"欧债危机"列为一项重要研究课题。课题组吸收中国国际经济交流中心和中国人民银行有关人员参加,这是一个有实力的专业研究小组。经过一年的努力,"欧债危机"课题研究告一段落,中国国际经济交流中心课题组以《欧债危机评估及中国对策》为书名公开出版发行。该书从全球化角度,收集大量事实,分析了欧洲主权债务危机发生原因、危机过程和危害、化解欧债危机的主要措施,预测欧盟经济发展前景,用较多的文字研究并提出了中国与欧盟加强经贸、投资和金融合作的建议。这是一部有相当质量的专业著作。

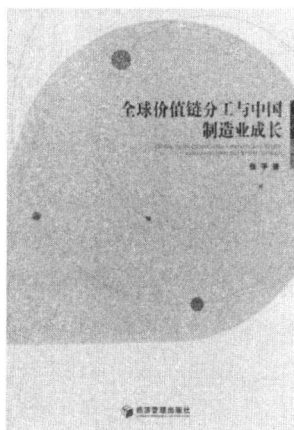

书名:全球价值链分工与中国制造业成长

作者:张平

出版社:经济管理出版社

出版时间:2014 年 5 月 1 日

Title: Global Value Chains Specizlization and China's Manufacturing Industries' Growth

Author:Ping Zhang

Publisher: Economic And Management Publishing Press

Date:May,2014

内容摘要:自第二次世界大战结束以来,国际分工发生了深刻的变革。全球价值链分工成为国际分工的主要形式,各国产业成长深受国际价值链分工的影响。中国改革开放以来,通过大力吸引外资、发展加工贸易,中国制造业已经深深嵌入全球价值链分工体系中,并获得了极大的发展,同时也面临着很大的风险。合理利用价值链分工,获取发展利益,成为中国当前国际化的战略目标。本书以全球价值链分工背景下发展中国家产业成长为主线,利用逻辑分析、历史经验分析和实证分析等方法,深入研究价值链分工对中国制造业成长的影响;结合国际成功经验和中国制造业实际发展状况,探讨我国在价值链分工背景下促进制造业健康成长的战略措施。

书名:基于交易决策的服务外包理论与实践创新研究

作者:姜维

出版社:浙江大学出版社

出版时间:2014 年 4 月 1 日

Title:Research on service outsourcing theory and practice innovation based on transaction decision

Author:Wei Jiang

Publisher:Zhejiang University Press

Date:Apr,2014

内容摘要:本书在全球产品内分工背景下,以新制度经济学和国际贸易理论为依据,探讨服务外包的微观主体——跨国公司的服务外包与一体化的决策理论创新,研究跨国公司在中国的服务外包模式和福利效应,并利用跨国外包决策思路,探讨中国的服务外包区域布局战略及区域创新发展实践,并提出政策集成与创新建议。

书名:对外直接投资与投资国产业升级——基于中国的实践分析

作者:李逢春

出版社:人民出版社

出版时间:2014 年 6 月 1 日

Title:External direct investment and investment country industry upgrading-based on China's practical analysis

Author:Fengchun Li

Publisher:People's Publishing House

Date:Jun,2014

内容摘要:本书总结了中国对外直接投资的特征以及变化趋势,并结合特征指标判断了中国对外直接投资推动产业升级具体的演进阶段,从企业视角、产业视角、全球价值链视角出发,运用国际投资理论、产业组织理论、国际贸易理论全面系统地探讨对外直接投资推动产业升级的作用机制。运用案例分析的方法解释对外投资推动产业升级的机制,并利用经典的经济模型,采用中国对外直接投资和产业升级的数据,验证对外直接投资推动产业升级的作用。其中发达国家和新兴经济体对外直接投资的经验、对中国对外直接投资推动产业升级的战略选择具有重要的借鉴意义。

书名:制度演化视角下的中国对外直接投资:主体结构分析与母国反哺效应检验

作者:姜亚鹏

出版社:中国社会科学出版社

出版时间:2014 年 5 月 1 日

Title: China's foreign direct investment under the perspective of institutional evolution—the main structure analysis and the maternal and state feedback effect test

Author: Yapeng Jiang

Publisher: China Social Sciences Press

Date: May,2014

内容摘要:本书主要关注对外直接投资与资本输出国间的互动。全书共十章,可大体分为三部分:制度安排在中国企业对外直接投资理论框架中的作用探讨、中国企业对外直接投资主体特征成因分析以及包括就业效应与技术溢出在内的中国对外直接投资母国反哺效应检验。

书名:中国跨国公司对外直接投资区位选择研究:制度距离的视角

作者:李凝

出版社:光明日报出版社

出版时间:2014 年 3 月 1 日

Title: Research on the location selection of foreign direct investment in China's transnational corporation

Author: Ning Li

Publisher: Guangming Daily Press

Date：Mar,2014

内容摘要：《中国跨国公司对外直接投资区位选择研究：制度距离的视角》在现有研究的基础上做出了如下扩展：首先，在理论基础方面，对母国制度影响制度距离与中国跨国公司 OFDI 区位选择关系的机制进行研究。其次，在理论分析和实证研究设计上对管制距离的方向进行区分，并以此来分析和检验管制距离与中国跨国公司 OFDI 区位选择之间的非线性关系。本书先后从外来者劣势视角、制度性优势视角以及制度逃离与制度套利视角分析制度距离对中国跨国公司 OFDI 区位选择的影响。在理论分析的基础上，实证研究发现，东道国与中国的正向管制距离与中国跨国公司对东道国直接投资倾向之间呈 U 形关系；负向管制距离没有显著影响；不区分方向的管制距离总体上会抑制中国跨国公司的 OFDI；文化距离的增加会抑制中国跨国公司 OFDI。

书名：中国地区差距与对外开放战略

作者：梁柱

出版社：社会科学文献出版社

出版时间：2014 年 5 月 1 日

Title：A Study on the Regional Disparity and Foreign Trade Strategy

Author：Zhu Liang

Publisher：Social Sciences Academic Press

Date：May,2014

内容摘要：本书认为单纯的地理位置不能够解释中国地区间差距问题。改革开放后，东部沿海地区在对外开放的背景下，凭借优越的地理位置和政策优惠，积极从事对外贸易，利用外商直接投资。对外贸易和外商直接投资作为对外开放的两个重要方面，在中国各省区的经济发展过程中发挥了重要作用，并且两者相互影响，在某种程度上形成了正反馈效应。在对外开放的过程中，由于产业集聚程度的差异，东部沿海地区逐渐拉开了和中西部地区的差距。

书名:对外开放关键领域的新突破

作者:赵晋平

出版社:中国发展出版社

出版时间:2015 年 8 月

Title:New breakthroughs in key fields of opening up

Author:Jinping Zhao

Publisher:China Development Press

Date:Aug,2015

内容摘要:对外开放关键领域的新突破包括在对外开放关键领域取得新突破、我国投资准入制度改革研究、境外投资管理制度改革研究、中国服务业扩大开放的若干问题研究、自由贸易试验区改革创新问题研究、高标准自由贸易区网络建设的目标、路径与政策举措、"一带一路"建设的政策支持体系研究、参考文献。

书名:以开放促改革——全球化新趋势与对外开放新阶段

作者:黄仁伟

出版社:上海社会科学院出版社

出版时间:2014 年 1 月 1 日

Title:To promote reform through opening-up—a new phase of globalization and opening to the outside worl

Author:Renwei Huang

Publisher:Shanghai Academy of Social Sciences Press

Date:Jan,2014

内容摘要:《以开放促改革——全球化新趋势与对外开放新阶段》阐述了经济全球化发展的新形势、新特征及其对中国开放战略转型升级提出的新挑战、新要求,在对中国参与全球经济一体化现状评估的基础上,提出中国以开放促改革的总体思路,以及上海在中国对外开放新战略中的功能定位和先行先试的作用。本书共分为上、中、下三篇,上篇对中国在全球经济一体化背景下实现的贸易、投资、金融发展以及参与国际事务、地区合作、对外援助和国际竞争力进行了比较系统的评估与分析;中篇总结分析了新一轮全球化的主题与趋势,提出中国以开放促改革的思路与内容;下篇综合分析了上海在中国扩大开放进程中的先行先试做法,提出要以上海自由贸易区建设为国家新一轮改革开放探索新经验、新做法。在中篇和下篇中,还对全球跨国公司的发展及其对全球化趋势演变的推动进行了专题分析,提出中国特别是上海市要加快培育本土跨国公司,以提升国家在全球价值链和国际分工体系中的地位,在新一轮国际竞争中赢得优势。

书名:全球经济失衡研究

作者:胡渊

出版社:社会科学文献出版社

出版时间:2014 年 4 月 1 日

Title:A Study of the Global Imbalances

Author:Yuan Hu

Publisher:Social Sciences Academic Press

Date:Apr,2014

内容摘要:本书针对当前世界经济失衡这一主题进行了阐述和分析,总结了造成这一状况的多方面原因不是一国或一个地区、单方面的问题所致。同时,世界经济失衡调整带来的冲击和风险也是世界各国需要共同面对的挑战。系统研究全球经济失衡调整路径、模式及其成本风险,必将推动对该问题理论认识的深入和发展,为制定科学的应对策略和措施提供研究资料,使全球经常账户失衡调整对中国的负面冲击最小化,这将有助于中国贯彻互利共赢对外开放观,促进中国经济的持续发展与繁荣。

书名：开放转型的政策创新——从经济大国到经济强国的战略升级

作者：张幼文

出版社：上海社会科学院出版社

出版时间：2014 年 1 月 1 日

Title：The policy innovation of open transformation-from economic power to economic power strategic upgrade

Author：Youwen Zhang

Publisher：Shanghai Academy of Social Sciences Press

Date：Jan,2014

　　内容摘要：改革开放以来，中国不仅基本完成了由计划经济向市场经济的渐进转型，而且形成了全方位、多层次、宽领域的对外开放格局和具有中国特色的开放型经济发展模式，取得了举世瞩目的成就。因此，在开放型经济的新阶段，中国就需要在目标、战略选择、政策等方面加以创新，以适应新的经济形势变化。

第二节　英文图书精选

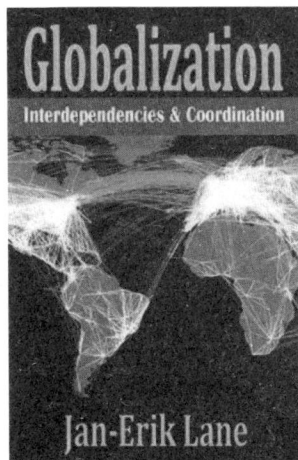

Title：Globalization：Interdependencies and Coordination

Author：Jan-Erik Lane

Publisher：Routledge

Date：July 30th,2014

书名：全球化：相互依存和协作

作者：简埃里克·莱恩

出版社：劳特利奇出版社

出版时间：2014 年 7 月 30 日

Contents: Efforts at coordination between nations are at the heart of the challenges of globalization. Despite steadily growing interdependencies, individual nations still have specific interests that present obstacles to globalization. While some challenges inspired by the need to coordinate are viewed as inevitable by many, they are less optimistic about prospects for success. Jan-Erik Lane argues that one should focus objectively upon the possibility of failures. Lane analyzes four kinds of challenges to interdependency, all of which are growing in geopolitical relevance. First, countries need to diminish their dependency on fossil fuel and shift to a reliable supply of energy, because fossil fuels are diminishing. Second, environmental degradation must be addressed, because it is accelerating under the strain of earth's population. Lane advocates an ecological footprint approach. Third, a single global market economy and its complexities must be addressed, as national economies are increasingly opened. Finally, as traditional state sovereignty weakens, foreign military intervention in both international and intra-state conflicts increases. Governments are attempting to address these interdependencies, or reply to the challenges they pose, mainly through international organizations and regionalism. These efforts are discussed at length. In addition, problems with international law are reviewed, as Lane warns against the utopian hopes of global constitutionalism. Globalization also examines the potential consequences of failing to address the need for coordination in efforts to address shared global challenges.

书籍简介:国家间协作的努力是全球化挑战的核心。尽管相互依存关系不断增强,但是个体国家仍然有特定的利益,这阻碍了全球化进程。虽然许多人认为协作需求带来的挑战是不可避免的,但是人们对成功的前景并不乐观。简埃里克·莱恩认为,应该客观地看待失败的可能性。莱恩分析了相互依存的四种挑战,所有这些挑战在地缘政治关联上不断增强。第一,各国需要减少对化石燃料的依赖,转向可靠的能源供应,因为化石燃料正在减少。第二,必须解决环境退化问题,因为在地球人口的压力下环境正在加速退化。莱恩倡导生态足迹法。第三,随着越来越多的国家经济开放,单一的全球市场经济及其复杂性必须得到解决。第四,由于传统的国家主权的弱化,外国对国际和国内冲突的军事干预日益增多。各国政府正试图主要通过国际组织和区域主义来解决这些相互依存关系,或对他们提出的挑战做出回应。这些努力被充分地讨论。此外,莱恩评述了与国际法相关的问题,同时作者对全球宪政主义的乌托邦式的希望提出警告。全球化也考察了为应对全球共同挑战而没能满足努力协作的需求的潜在后果。

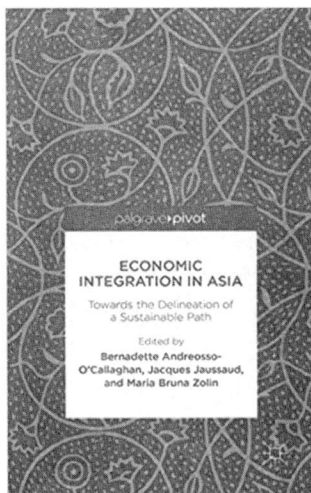

Title：Economic Integration in Asia：Towards the Delineation of a Sustainable Path

Author：Bernadette Andreosso-O'Callaghan，Jacques Jaussaud，Maria Bruna Zolin

Publisher：Palgrave Pivot

Date：January 1st，2014

书名：亚洲的经济一体化：走向可持续发展道路的蓝图

作者：伯纳黛特·安德烈斯－奥卡拉汉，雅克·加索，玛丽亚·布鲁娜·佐林

出版社：帕尔格雷夫出版社

出版时间：2014 年 1 月 1 日

Contents：This study assesses the current state of economic integration in Asia-in particular in East and South East Asia-and analyzes the prerequisites for a sustainable path of economic integration，using the background of the EU experience as a benchmark.

书籍简介：这项研究评估了亚洲特别是东亚和东南亚经济一体化的现状，以及以欧盟经验的背景为基准分析了经济一体化可持续发展的先决条件。

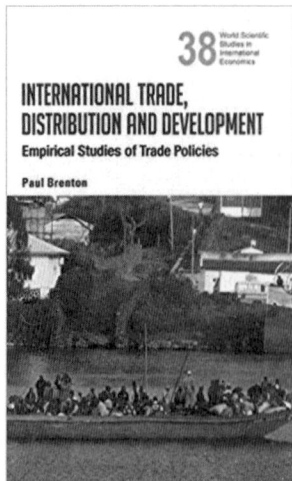

Title：International Trade, Distribution And Development：Empirical Studies Of Trade Policies

Author：Paul A. Brenton

Publisher：World Scientific Publishing Co Pte Ltd

Date：August 18th, 2014

书名：国际贸易、收入分配和经济发展：贸易政策的实证研究

作者：保罗·布伦特

出版社：世界科技出版公司

出版时间：2014 年 8 月 18 日

Contents：International Trade, Distribution and Development brings together a collection of papers that have sought to assess empirically the impacts of policy measures affecting trade. The carefully selected papers analyze the impact of trade barriers and their removal, with a focus on distributional consequences and economic development. Grounded in rigorous empirical analysis, this book covers a range of policy issues such as impacts of trade on wages, non-tariff barriers, trade preferences, export survival and carbon labelling. An invaluable reference for readers seeking to understand the impact of trade policies, the book also seeks to shed light on future research, especially for research on developing countries.

书籍简介：《国际贸易、收入分配和经济发展：贸易政策的实证研究》汇集了一组论文，试图对与贸易相关的政策措施的影响进行实证评估。经仔细挑选的论文分析了贸易壁垒及其消除的影响，重点是分配后果和经济发展。基于严格的实证分析，本书涵盖了一系列的政策问题，如贸易对工资的影响、非关税壁垒、贸易优惠、出口生存和碳标识。为寻求理解贸易政策的影响的读者提供有价值的参考，本书还试图阐述未来研究的方向，尤其是对发展中国家的研究。

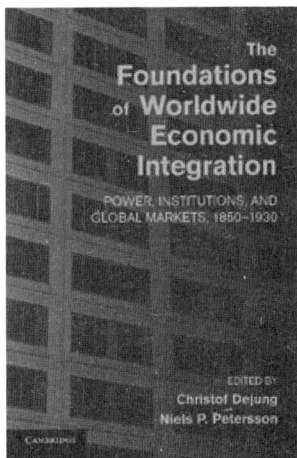

Title：The Foundations of Worldwide Economic Integration

Author：Christof Dejung，Niels P. Petersson

Publisher：Cambridge University Press

Date：August 21th，2014

书名：世界经济一体化的基础

作者：克里斯托夫·德容，尼尔斯·彼特森

出版社：剑桥大学出版社

出版时间：2014 年 8 月 21 日

Contents：The essays in this volume discuss worldwide economic integration between 1850 and 1930，challenging the popular description of the period after 1918 as one of mere deglobalisation. The authors argue that markets were not only places of material exchange，but also socially structured entities，shaped by the agency of individual actors and by complex structures of political and economic power. Economic transactions were supported by an array of different institutions，ranging from formalised regulations to informal relations of personal trust. They argue that these networks were strong enough to prosper even during and after World War I，in a political climate often hostile to foreign trade. The Foundations of Worldwide Economic Integration shows that institutionalism altered its shape in the face of circumstances that increasingly challenged international trade. By presenting case studies from various countries，this book offers a fresh perspective on crucial periods of economic globalisation.

书籍简介：本书讨论了 1850—1930 年间的世界范围内的经济一体化，反驳了 1918 年以后是一个纯粹的去全球化的时期的主流观点。作者认为，市场不仅是物质交换的场所，而且是社会结构实体，由个体行为者的代理以及政治和经济权力的复杂结构所塑造。经济交易是由一系列机构所支持，从正式制度到个体信用的非正式关系。他们认为，在一个常常敌视对外贸易的政治环境中，这些网络关系甚至在第一次世界大战期间和之后也很强大。《世界经济一体化的基础》表明，在面对越来越多的反对国际贸易的环境下，制度主义理论改变了制度结构。通过展示来自不同国家的案例研究，本书提供了一个关于经济全球化关键时期的新视角。

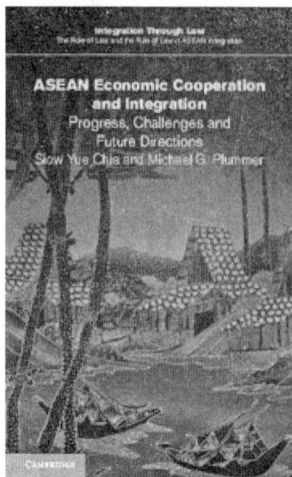

Title：ASEAN Economic Cooperation and Integration

Author：Siow Yue Chia，Michael G. Plummer

Publisher：Cambridge University Press

Date：April 16th，2015

书名：东盟经济合作与一体化

作者：行悦嘉，迈克尔·普卢默

出版社：剑桥大学出版社

出版时间：2015 年 4 月 16 日

Contents：ASEAN economic cooperation and integration have come a long way since the organisation's early days，when cooperation was more political and diplomatic than economic in nature. ASEAN now constitutes the most ambitious organisation of regional cooperation and integration in the developing world. This book investigates the economics of various ASEAN and ASEAN-centric economic integration initiatives，focusing in particular on the ASEAN Economic Community（AEC）. In addition to assessing the potential effects of the AEC on the economies of the ten ASEAN member states via changes in trade，foreign direct investment and economic structure，this book underscores the implementation challenges ASEAN faces as it completes the AEC project. It also considers the AEC in the context of the Regional Comprehensive Economic Partnership（RCEP）. This comprehensive study is written for academic researchers and students，as well as for policy makers in ASEAN as they chart the future policy path of the region.

书籍简介：自从东盟成立初期，东盟的经济合作和一体化已经走过了漫长的道路，当时的合作比经济更具有政治性和外交性。如今，东盟是发展中世界区域合作和一体化的最雄心勃勃的组织。本书考察了东盟和以东盟为中心的经济一体化举措的经济意义，特别是侧重于东盟经济共同体。除了通过贸易、外国直接投资和经济结构的变化来评估东盟经济共同体对 10 个东盟成员国经济的潜在影响外,本书还强调了东盟在完成东盟经济共同体计划时所面临的执行挑战。在区域全面经济伙伴关系的背景下本书也考虑了东盟经济共同体。这项综合性研究是为学术研究人员和学生以及东盟政策制定者编写的,他们将制定该区域未来的政策路径。

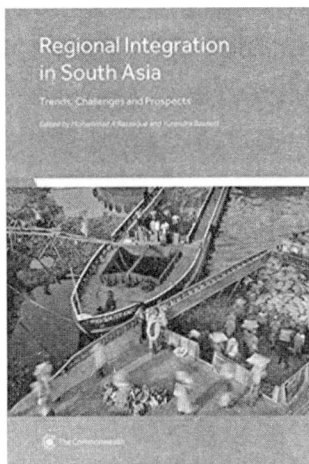

Title：Regional Integration in South Asia：Trends，Challenges and Prospects

Author：Mohammad A. Razzaque，Yurendra Basnett

Publisher：Commonwealth Secretariat

Date：November 1st，2014

书名:南亚的区域一体化:趋势、挑战和前景

作者:穆罕默德·拉扎克,约仁达·巴斯尼特

出版社:英联邦秘书处

出版时间:2014 年 11 月 1 日

Contents：Regional Integration in South Asia：Trends，Challenges and Prospects presents an objective assessment of trade and economic co-operation among South Asian nations and highlights policy issues to foster regional integration. The analyses presented in this volume go beyond the usual discussions on trade-in-goods to provide insightful perspectives on potential new areas of co-operation，emerging challenges，and country-specific views on regional and bilateral trade co-operation issues. Written by influential analysts and researchers，the volume's 24 chapters include perspectives from Bangladesh，India，Maldives，Nepal，Pakistan and Sri Lanka，and examinations of new areas of co-operation such as investment，regional supply chains，energy and cross-border transport networks.

　　书籍简介:《南亚的区域一体化:趋势、挑战和前景》客观评价了南亚国家之间的贸易和经济合作,并强调促进区域一体化的政策问题。本书的分析超越了通常关于货物贸易的讨论,就潜在的新合作领域、新出现的挑战和针对区域和双边贸易合作问题的国别观点提供了深刻的思考。本书由有影响力的分析家和研究人员撰写,全书24章包括来自孟加拉、印度、马尔代夫、尼泊尔、巴基斯坦和斯里兰卡的国别观点,以及考察了诸如投资、区域供应链、能源和跨境运输网络等合作的新领域。

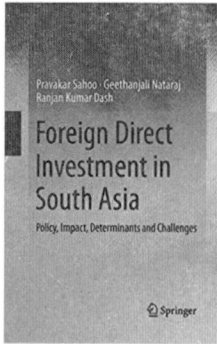

Title:Foreign Direct Investment in South Asia:Policy, Impact,Determinants and Challenges

Author:Pravakar Sahoo, Geethanjali Nataraj, Ranjan Kumar Dash

Publisher:Springer

Date:December,2014

书名:南亚的外国直接投资:政策、影响、决定因素和挑战

作者:普拉瓦卡·萨胡,格萨嘉里·纳塔瑞杰,兰詹·库玛·达什

出版社:施普林格

出版时间:2014年12月

Contents:During the 1990s,the governments of South Asian countries acted as 'facilitators' to attract FDI. As a result,the inflow of FDI increased. However,to become an attractive FDI destination as China,Singapore,or Brazil,South Asia has to improve the local conditions of doing business. This book,based on research that blends theory, empirical evidence,and policy,asks and attempts to answer a few core questions relevant to FDI policy in South Asian countries:Which major reforms have succeeded? What are the factors that influence FDI inflows? What has been the impact of FDI on macroeconomic performance? Which policy priorities/reforms needed to boost FDI are pending? These questions and answers should interest policy makers,academics,and all those interested in FDI in the South Asian region and in India,Pakistan,Bangladesh,Sri Lanka and Pakistan.

书籍简介:20世纪90年代,南亚各国政府充当了吸引外国直接投资的促进者。因此,外国直接投资的流入增加了。然而,为了成为一个像中国、新加坡或巴西一样有吸引力的投资目的地,南亚必须改善本国的营商环境。基于理论、经验证据和政策相结合的研究,本书提出并试图回答与南亚国家的外国直接投资政策有关的几个核心问题:哪些重大改革取得成功? 什么因素影响了外国直接投资流入? 外国直接投资对宏观经济绩效的影响是什么? 促进外国直接投资需要哪些政策优先/改革? 这些问题和答案应该引起决策者、学者以及所有关注东南亚地区、印度、巴基斯坦、孟加拉、斯里兰卡和巴基斯坦的外国直接投资的人的兴趣。

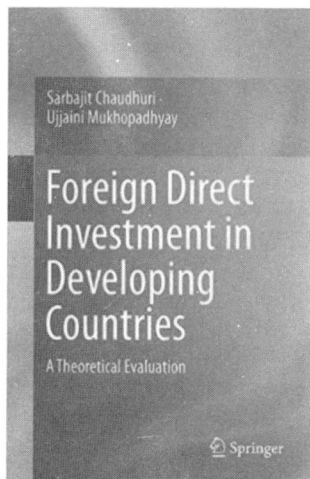

Title：Foreign Direct Investment in Developing Countries：A Theoretical Evaluation

Author：Sarbajit Chaudhuri, Ujjaini Mukhopadhyay

Publisher：Springer

Date：July 28th,2014

书名:发展中国家的对外直接投资:一个理论评价

作者:萨巴杰提·乔杜里,乌贾因·穆克帕德亚

出版社:施普林格

出版时间:2014年7月28日

Contents：In development literature Foreign Direct Investment(FDI)is traditionally considered to be instrumental for the economic growth of all countries,particularly the developing ones. It acts as a panacea for breaking out of the vicious circle of low savings/low income and facilitates the import of capital goods and advanced technical knowhow. This book delves into the complex interaction of FDI with diverse factors. While FDI affects the efficiency of domestic producers through technological diffusion and spill-over effects,it also impinges on the labor market,affecting unemployment levels,human capital formation,wages(and wage inequality)and poverty;furthermore,it has important implications for socio-economic issues such as child labor,agricultural disputes over Special Economic Zones(SEZ)and environmental pollution. The empirical evidence with regard to most of the effects of FDI is highly mixed and reflects the fact that there are a number of mechanisms involved that interact with each other to produce opposing results. The book highlights the theoretical underpinnings behind the inherent contradictions and shows that the final outcome depends on a number of country-specific factors such as the nature of non-traded goods, factor endowments, technological and institutional factors. Thus, though not exhaustive, the book integrates FDI within most of the existing economic systems in order to define its much-debated role in developing economies. A theoretical analysis of the different facets of FDI as proposed in the book is thus indispensable, especially for the formulation of appropriate policies for foreign capital.

书籍简介:在发展经济学文献中,外国直接投资(FDI)历来被认为是促进所有国家特别是发展中国家经济增长的工具。它是一个打破低储蓄、低收入的恶性循环的灵丹妙药,并促进了资本品和先进技术知识的进口。这本书探讨了外国直接投资与多种因素复杂的相互作用。外国直接投资通过技术扩散和溢出效应影响国内生产企业的效率的同时,也冲击到劳动力市场,影响失业水平、人力资本形成、工资(和工资不平等)和贫困。此外,它对诸如童工、特区农产品贸易争端和环境污染等社会经济问题具有重要意义。关于外国直接投资的大部分效应的经验证据是高度混杂的,并且反映了一个事实,即存在许多涉及相互影响而产生相反的结果的作用机制。本书突出了内在矛盾背后的理论基础,表明最终的结果取决于大量的国别因素,如非贸易品的性质、要素禀赋、技术和制度因素。因此,本书虽然不是详尽无遗的,但它将外国直接投资并入了大部分现有经济体系中,从而确定其在发展经济学中备受争议的角色。在本书中提出的外国直接投资的不同方面的理论分析因此是必不可少的,特别是在制定适宜的外国资本政策方面。

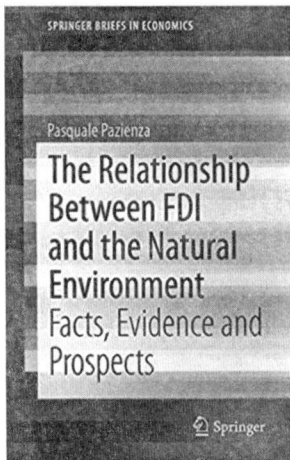

Title: The Relationship Between FDI and the Natural Environment: Facts, Evidence and Prospects

Author: Pasquale Pazienza

Publisher: Springer

Date: February 21th, 2014

书名:外商直接投资与自然环境的关系:事实、证据与前景

作者:帕斯夸莱·帕齐恩扎

出版社:施普林格

出版时间:2014 年 2 月 21 日

Contents:This work examines in depth the relationship between foreign direct investment and the environment. Over the last few decades, increasing levels of environmental degradation have been recorded and have been claimed to be particularly attributable to globalization and the widespread increase of economic activities, in particular foreign direct investments(FDIs). However, the environmental implications of FDIs are not easily identified and contradictory views and arguments have been presented. This work contributes to the debate by closely analyzing the specific literature produced over the last three decades, and by presenting and discussing recent trends and prospects with regard to the FDI phenomenon.

书籍简介:本书深入探讨了外国直接投资与环境之间的关系。在过去的几十年里,日益增加的环境退化得到确认,这被特别归因为全球化和经济活动的普遍增加,特别是外国直接投资(FDI)。但是,FDI 对环境的影响是不易识别的,并且提出了互相矛盾的观点和论证。通过仔细分析在过去三年中产生的具体文献,以及通过介绍和讨论最近关于外国直接投资现象的趋势和前景,本书对这些争论做出了贡献。

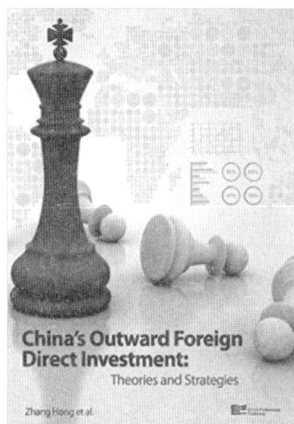

Title:China's Outward Foreign Direct Investment:Theories and Strategies

Author:Hong Zhang

Publisher:Enrich Professional Publishing,Inc. .

Date:December 5th,2014

书名:中国的对外直接投资:理论与策略

作者:张弘

出版社:天窗出版集团

出版时间:2014 年 12 月 5 日

Contents:This volume aims to combine global value chain(GVC)theories and foreign direct investment(FDI)theories and provide theoretical explanations for China's outward foreign direct investment activities from the perspective of the global value chain. The book addresses five areas: summary explanations for China's outward FDI activities offered by current theories of GVC and outward FDI; rationally understand China's position in GVC and characteristics of China's outward FDI in this new era; build and discuss theoretical models behind technology acquisition and upgrading in value chains through outward FDI; examine the impact of outward FDI on the domestic technologic progress; provide suggestions on China's outward FDI strategies from the perspective of GVC based on theoretical and empirical analyses.

书籍简介:本书旨在于将全球价值链(GVC)理论和对外直接投资(FDI)理论结合起来,并且从全球价值链的视角对中国的对外直接投资活动提供理论解释。本书涉及五方面:根据 GVC 和对外直接投资的当前理论对中国的对外直接投资活动给予了概要解释;客观地理解新时期中国在全球价值链中的地位以及中国的对外直接投资的特征;构建和讨论通过对外直接投资获取技术和提升价值链的理论模型;考察对外直接投资对国内技术进步的影响;基于理论和实证分析,从全球价值链的视角对中国的对外直接投资策略提供政策建议。

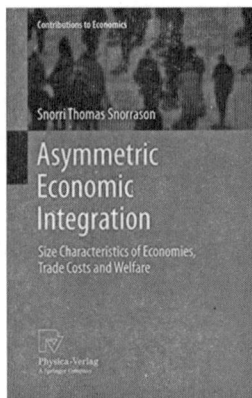

Title: Asymmetric Economic Integration: Size Characteristics of Economies, Trade Costs and Welfare

Author: Snorri Thomas Snorrason

Publisher: Physica-Verlag Heidelberg

Date: August 9th, 2014

书名:不对称的经济一体化:经济规模特征、贸易成本和福利

作者:史诺里·托马斯·斯诺拉森

出版社:施普林格经济出版社

出版时间:2014 年 8 月 9 日

Contents: This book investigates whether the effects of economic integration differ according to the size of countries. The analysis incorporates a classification of the size of countries, reflecting the key economic characteristics of economies in order to provide an appropriate benchmark for each size group in the empirical analysis of the effects of asymmetric economic integration. The formation or extension of Preferential Trade Areas (PTAs) leads to a reduction in trade costs. This poses a critical secondary question as to the extent to which trade costs differ according to the size of countries. The extent to which membership of PTAs has an asymmetric impact on trade flow according to the size of member countries is analyzed by employing econometric tools and general equilibrium analysis, estimating both the ex-post and ex-ante effects of economic integration on the size of countries, using a data set of 218 countries, 45 of which are European.

书籍简介：本书考察了经济一体化的影响是否因国家的规模而不同。分析采用了国家规模的分类，其反映了各经济体的主要经济特征，从而在对非对称经济一体化的影响进行实证分析中为每个规模组提供一个适宜的基准。特惠贸易区（PTAs）的形成或扩大引致贸易成本的下降。这就提出了至关重要的另一个问题，即各国的贸易成本因国家的规模有多大程度的不同。通过运用计量经济学工具和一般均衡分析考察了特惠贸易区的成员因成员国的规模对贸易流量具有多大程度的非对称影响，使用 218 个国家（包括了 45 个欧洲国家）的数据集估计了经济一体化对国家规模的事后和事前影响。

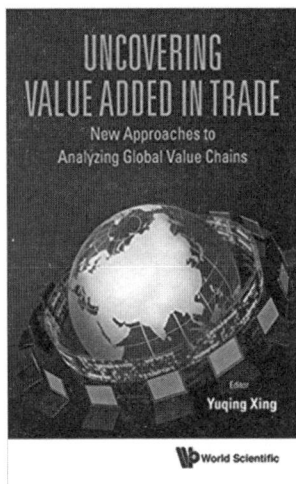

Title：Uncovering Value Added In Trade：New Approaches To Analyzing Global Value Chains

Author：Kae Sugawara，Yuqing Xing

Publisher： World Scientific Publishing Co Pte Ltd

Date：July 27th，2015

书名：揭示贸易增加值：分析全球价值链的新方法

作者：菅原香枝，邢予青

出版社：世界科技出版公司

出版时间：2015 年 7 月 27 日

Contents：Value chain trade has challenged economic implications of conventional trade statistics and transformed bilateral trade relationships into multilaterals. Conventional trade statistics exaggerate trade volumes and bilateral trade imbalances. It is imperative to measure trade in value-added and examine trade relations in the context of global value chains. This book is a collection of research papers on new approaches to measure trade in value added and the role of global value chains in modern international trade. It introduces the input output method for measuring trade and a direct approach for measuring the domestic value added of the People's Republic of China-the center of global assembly. In addition, it shows how to analyze trade relations in the context of global value chains.

书籍简介:价值链贸易对传统的贸易统计的经济含义提出了挑战并且将双边贸易关系转化为多边贸易关系。传统的贸易统计夸大了贸易额和双边贸易不平衡。所以必须在全球价值链的范围内测算贸易增加值并考察贸易关系。本书是一本关于在现代国际贸易中测算贸易增加值和全球价值链作用的新方法的研究论文集。它介绍了衡量贸易的投入产出方法和测算中国(全球装配中心)的国内贸易增加值的直接方法。此外,还展示了如何在全球价值链的背景下分析贸易关系。

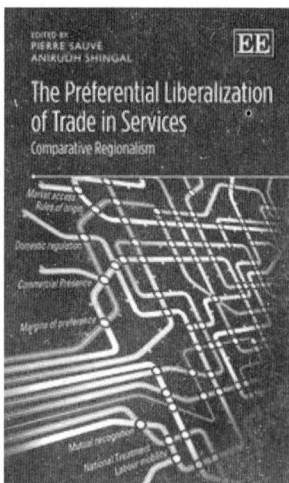

Title: The Preferential Liberalization of Trade in Services

Author: Pierre Sauve, Anirudh Shingal

Publisher: Edward Elgar Publishing Ltd

Date: April 25th, 2014

书名:服务贸易的特惠自由化

作者:皮埃尔·索韦,安尼路德·辛加尔

出版社:爱德华埃尔加出版有限公司

出版时间:2014 年 4 月 25 日

Contents: This book fills an important gap in the trade literature by offering a comprehensive cross-regional comparison of approaches to preferential market opening and rule-making in the area of trade in services. Chronicling the spectacular recent rise of preferential trade agreements(PTAs) in services and with contributions from some of the world's leading experts, the book examines the forces shaping the demand for preferences in services trade. It asks whether and how preferential advances differ from, go further than, and might ultimately inform the development of multilateral disciplines on services under the World Trade Organization's (WTO) General Agreement on Trade in Services(GATS). The book's core focus is on comparative scholarship, directing attention to the substantive features of services PTAs around the globe and exploring the iterative nature of rule-making and market opening in a still nascent field of trade diplomacy. It advances a number of ideas on how to multilateralize PTA advances in services and takes stock of the likely impact on the WTO system of ongoing attempts at crafting a plurilateral agreement on trade in services. Trade negotiators and policy officials working in the field of trade and investment in services as well as academics in the fields of law, economics and international political economy will find much of use in this authoritative study.

书籍简介:通过对服务贸易领域特惠市场的开放和规则制定提供一个全面的跨区域比较,本书填补了贸易文献中的一个重要空白。本书记述了近来在服务贸易领域中特惠贸易协定的大量兴起和一些世界领先的专家取得的成果,并考察了塑造服务贸易偏好需求的因素。它提出特惠的进展是否以及为何不同,更进一步地可能最终预知世界贸易组织的《服务贸易总协定》下服务贸易多边规则的发展情况。本书的核心重点是比较研究,引导关注全球的服务特惠协定的大量特征,以及探索一个新兴领域的贸易外交中的制定规则和市场开放的更替性质。它提出了关于如何多边化服务特惠协定发展的若干思路,估计对正在进行尝试起草服务贸易多边协定的世界贸易组织体制的可能影响。在服务贸易和投资领域工作的贸易谈判者和政策官员,以及法律、经济学和国际政治经济学领域的研究人员将在这一权威性研究中会发现大量的使用价值。

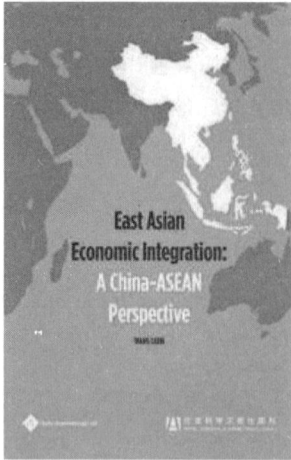

Title: East Asian Economic Integration: A China-ASEAN Perspective

Author: Wang Liqin

Publisher: Paths International Ltd

Date: October 1st, 2014

书名:东亚经济一体化:中国—东盟视角

作者:王丽琴

出版社:帕斯国际出版社

出版时间:2014 年 10 月 1 日

Contents: This book reviews and analyses East Asian economic integration by looking at China-ASEAN economic relations and the China-ASEAN Free Trade Area (CAFTA). The book explores the economic relations between China and ASEAN after the Cold War ended, investigates China's motives to establish the CAFTA (China-ASEAN Free Trade Area) and evaluates economic integration in East Asia, in which both China and ASEAN hold key roles. Much of the research is based upon interviews which the author conducted with key policy makers in China. After providing a theoretical framework and discussing methodology the author provides a background on economic cooperation between China and ASEAN from the 1980's onwards. China's role in trade and investment cooperation before and after 2001 is also analyzed as are China's shifting motives for cooperating with ASEAN. The author also looks at the features and the future for East Asian economic integration. Much of the research is based on Chinese language sources which are not usually referred to in western works in this field.

书籍简介:本书通过观察中国—东盟的经济关系和中国—东盟自由贸易区评述和分析了东亚经济一体化。本书探讨了冷战结束后中国与东盟之间的经济关系,考察了中国建立 CAFTA(中国—东盟自由贸易区)的目标并且评估了中国和东盟在其中扮演重要角色的东亚经济一体化。大部分的研究是基于作者与中国的重要的政策制定者进行的访谈。在给出了理论框架和探讨了方法论之后,作者提供了一个关于自 20 世纪 80 年代中国与东盟之间经济合作的背景。也分析了2001 年前后中国在贸易和投资合作中的作用,因为中国正在转变与东盟合作的目标。作者还对东亚经济一体化的特点和未来进行了展望。大部分的研究都是基于中国的语言来源,这在西方的研究领域中通常是不被提及的。

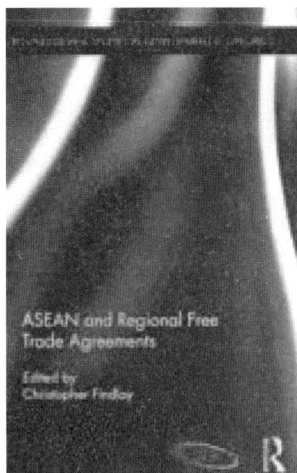

Title:ASEAN and Regional Free Trade Agreements

Author:Christopher Findlay

Publisher:Routledge

Date:May 21th,2015

书名:东盟与区域自由贸易协定

作者:克里斯托夫·芬德利

出版社:劳特利奇出版社

出版时间:2015 年 5 月 21 日

Contents:Efforts to use existing trade agreements to build a larger regional agreement face many challenges. This book considers this problem with reference to ASEAN's current agreements with key partners and the interest to build the Regional Comprehensive Economic Partnership(RCEP). The analysis of the options is framed by a focus on the use of supply chains in international business. Issues considered include those related to reductions in tariffs,trade facilitation,the treatment of investment and of services and the definition of rules of origin. The work is informed by case studies of supply chains in automobile and electronics,and in a professional service sector. The book provides a set of priority actions for better progress in taking a bottom-up approach to building RCEP.

书籍简介:使用现有贸易协定建立一个更大的区域协定的努力面临许多挑战。本书考察了关于东盟与关键合作伙伴目前的协议的问题以及建立区域全面经济伙伴关系的利益。选择的分析框架是以国际商务中供应链的使用为重点的。所考虑的问题包括关税削减、贸易便利化、投资和服务待遇以及原产地规则的界定。这项工作来源于汽车和电子产品以及专业服务部门供应链的案例研究。本书提供了一套促进采用自下而上的方法构建区域全面经济伙伴关系的优先行动方案。

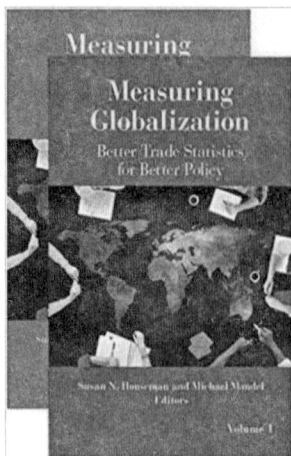

Title:Measuring Globalization:Better Trade Statistics for Better Policy. 2 vols.

Author:Houseman Susan N. ;Mandel Michael

Publisher:W. E. Upjohn Institute for Employment Research

Date:2015

书名:衡量全球化:更好的贸易统计政策(共两卷)

作者:苏曼.苏珊.N;曼德尔.迈克尔

出版社:W. E. 恩乔恩就业研究所

出版时间:2015 年

Contents:Seventeen papers in two volumes,originally presented at a 2013 research conference funded by the Alfred P. Sloan Foundation,document data gaps and biases in national statistics rising from the growth of globalization and propose solutions for statistical agencies. Papers in volume 1 discuss sourcing substitution and related price index biases;assessing price indexes for markets with trading frictions—a quantitative illustration;specific trade costs,quality,and import prices;measuring manufacturing—how the computer and semiconductor industries affect the numbers and perceptions;import sourcing bias in manufacturing productivity growth—evidence across advanced and emerging economies;biases to manufacturing statistics from offshoring—evidence from Japan;import allocation across industries,import prices across countries,and estimates of industry growth and productivity;the impact of globalization on prices—a test of hedonic price indexes for imports;and producing an input price index. Papers in volume 2 discuss factoryless goods production in the US statistical system;measuring "factoryless" manufacturing—evidence from US surveys;the scope of US "factoryless manufacturing";incomes and jobs in global production of manufactures—new measures of competitiveness based on the world input-output database;measuring trade in value-added and beyond;import uses and domestic value-added in Chinese exports—what can be learned from Chinese microdata;a formulary approach for attributing measured production to foreign affiliates of US parents;and data,trade,and growth. Houseman is a senior economist at the W. E. Upjohn Institute for Employment Research. Mandel is Chief Economic Strategist at the Progressive Policy Institute.

书籍简介：本书分为两卷，收录的 17 篇论文最初发布于 2013 年研究会，该研究会由阿尔弗雷德·斯隆基金会资助。这些论文记录了全球统计数据的数据差距和偏差，并为统计机构提出了解决方案。第一卷论文包括：采购替代和相关价格指数偏差；评估交易摩擦市场的价格指数——定量说明；具体贸易成本、质量和进口价格；测量制造——计算机和半导体行业如何影响数量和看法；进口采购偏向制造业生产率增长——跨越先进和新兴经济体的证据；偏离离岸外包制造统计资料——来自日本的证据；行业进口分配，国家进口价格，行业增长和生产力估算；全球化对价格的影响——进口享乐价格指数测验；产生投入物价指数。第二卷论文包括：美国统计系统中的无因次货物生产；测量"无因素"制造——美国调查的证据；美国"不可生产制造"的范围；全球制造业生产中的收入和就业机会——基于世界投入产出数据库的新的竞争力衡量标准；衡量增值和超越贸易；中国出口的进口使用量和国内增加值——从中国微观数据可以得到什么？将测量生产归因于美国母公司的外国子公司的处方方法；数据、贸易与增长。苏曼是 W. E. Upjohn 就业研究所的高级经济学家。曼德尔是进步政策研究所的首席经济战略家。

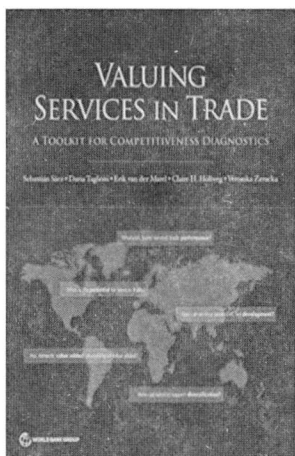

Title：Valuing Services in Trade：A Toolkit for Competitiveness Diagnostics

Author：Saez Sebastian；Taglioni Daria；van der Marel Erik；Hollweg Claire H

Publisher：World Bank

Date：2014

书名：服务贸易评估：竞争力诊断工具包

作者：塞斯·塞巴斯蒂安；塔格里奥妮·达丽娅；范德马雷尔；霍尔韦格·克莱尔·H

出版社：世界银行

出版时间：2014 年

Contents:Provides a framework,guidance,and tools to conduct an analysis and diagnostics of the trade competitiveness of a country's services sector,identifying the main constraints to improved competitiveness and the appropriate policy responses. Discusses assessing services trade and competitiveness outcomes;services as a source of competitiveness in the whole economy;assessing the potential for trade in services;and policy options for increasing competitiveness and trade in the services sector. Appendixes present the export of value added database;and the trade in services database. Saaez is a senior trade economist in the International Trade Unit at the World Bank. Hollweg is a consultant in the International Trade Unit at the World Bank. Taglioni is a senior economist in the International Trade Unit at the World Bank. Van der Marel is a senior economist at the European Centre for International Political Economy. Zavacka is a board operations officer at the International Monetary Fund.

书籍简介:本书提供一个框架、指导和工具,对一个国家服务部门的贸易竞争力进行分析和诊断,确定提高竞争力的主要制约因素和适当的政策对策。讨论评估服务贸易和竞争力的结果。本书说明服务贸易作为整个经济的竞争力来源、评估服务贸易的潜力以及提高服务业竞争力和贸易的政策选择。附录列出增值数据库的出口和服务数据库贸易。塞斯是世界银行国际贸易股的高级贸易经济学家。霍尔韦格是世界银行国际贸易股的顾问。塔格里奥尼是世界银行国际贸易股的高级经济师。范德马雷尔是欧洲国际政治经济中心的高级经济学家。扎瓦卡是国际货币基金组织的董事会运营官员。

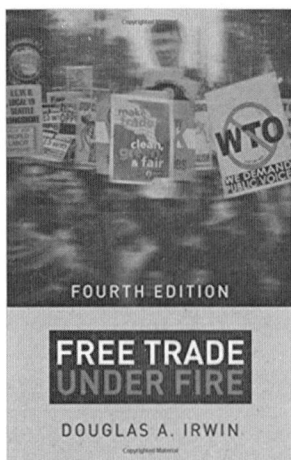

Title: Free Trade under Fire

Author: Irwin Douglas A

Publisher: Princeton University Press

Date:2015

书名:自由贸易的试炼

作者:欧文·道格拉斯·A

出版社:普林斯顿大学出版社

出版时间:2015 年

Contents:Updated fourth edition provides an introduction to basic economic principals and empirical evidence regarding international trade and trade policy, including protectionism, the Great Recession, and economic research on trade, wages, and jobs. Discusses the question of the United States in a new global economy; the case for free trade—old theories, new evidence; protectionism—the question of economic costs and political benefits; trade, jobs, and income distribution; relief from foreign competition—antidumping and the escape clause; developing countries and open markets; and the world trading system—the World Trade Organization, trade disputes, and regional agreements. Irwin is Professor of Economics at Dartmouth College.

书籍简介：本书已更新至第四版，介绍了有关国际贸易和贸易政策的基本经济原则和经验证据，包括保护主义、大衰退，以及对贸易、工资和就业的经济研究。讨论美国在全球经济中的新问题，自由贸易的理由——旧理论、新证据，保护主义——经济成本和政治利益的问题，贸易、就业和收入分配，减免竞争——反倾销和逃避条款，发展中国家和公开市场，世界贸易体系——世界贸易组织，贸易争端和地区协议。欧文是达特茅斯学院经济学教授。

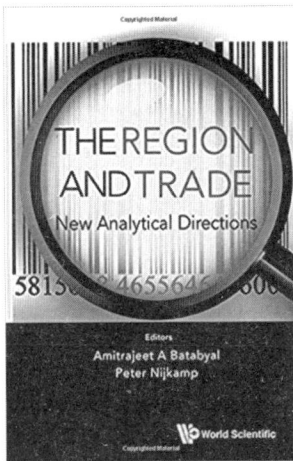

Title：The Region and Trade: New Analytical Directions

Author：Batabyal Amitrajeet A; Nijkamp Peter

Publisher：World Scientific

Date：2015

书名：区域与贸易：新分析方向

作者：巴塔布耶尔·阿米特拉吉特·A；尼杰卡普·皮特

出版社：世界科学

出版时间：2015 年

Contents: Eleven papers analyze theoretical and empirical research questions in interregional trade. Papers discuss statistical discrimination, endogenous quality, and North-South trade; regional trade in a three country model; voluntary formation of a free trade area in a third country market model; exploring the spatial connectivity of US states, 1993 – 2007; manufacturing fetishism—the neomercantilist preoccupation with protecting manufacturing; the evolution of freight movement and associated non-point-source emissions in the Midwest-Northeast transportation corridor of the United States, 1977 – 2007; multipliers in an island economy—the case of the Azores; interregional trade in research-based knowledge—the case of the European Incoherent Scatter Scientific Association radar system; trade openness and city interaction; infrastructure and the international export performance of Turkish regions; and trade in services and regional specialization—evidence and theory. Batabyal is in the Department of Economics at the Rochester Institute of Technology. Nijkamp is in the Department of Spatial Economics at Vrije Universiteit University Amsterdam.

书籍简介:本书包含 11 篇论文,分析了区域贸易中的理论和实证研究问题。论文讨论内容包括:统计歧视、内生质量和南北贸易,区域贸易三国模式,在第三国市场模式自愿形成自由贸易区,探索 1993—2007 年美国的空间连通性,制造拜物教——保护制造业的新偶像者关注焦点,1977—2007 年美国中西部——东北运输走廊货运和相关非点源排放的演变,岛屿经济中的乘数——亚速尔群岛的情况,基于研究的知识的区域间贸易——欧洲不相干散射科学协会雷达系统的情况,贸易开放与城市互动,土耳其地区的基础设施和国际出口业绩,服务贸易和区域专业化——证据与理论。巴塔布耶尔在罗切斯特理工学院的经济系。尼杰卡普在阿姆斯特丹弗里耶大学的空间经济系。

Title: Neither Free Trade Nor Protection: A Critical Political Economy of Trade Theory and Practice

Author: Dunn Bill

Publisher: Cheltenham, UK and Northampton, MA: Elgar

Date: 2015

书名:既不自由贸易也非保护主义:批判性政治贸易理论与实践经济

作者:邓恩·比尔

出版社:切尔滕纳姆,英国和北安普顿,马萨诸

塞州:埃尔加

出版时间:2015 年

Contents:Provides a critical exploration of mainstream and alternatives theories of international trade in a social, economic, and historical context. Discusses the making of world trade; free trade theory and its critics; market imperfections and state strategies; Marxism, trade, and the limits of radical nationalism; evaluating trade and growth; factor endowments, trade, and growth; international trade and inequality within countries; trade opening and the decline of industrial action; and global restructuring, trade, and the crisis of 2007 – 2009. Dunn is in the Department of Political Economy at the University of Sydney.

书籍简介:本书在社会、经济和历史背景下对国际贸易的主流和替代理论进行批判性的探索。内容包括:世界贸易的形成,自由贸易理论及其批判,市场缺陷和国家战略,马克思主义、贸易和激进民族主义的局限性,贸易和增长的评估,要素禀赋、贸易和增长,国际贸易与国家内部的不平等,贸易开放和工业生产的衰落,全球贸易重组和 2007—2009 年的危机。邓恩在悉尼大学政治经济系。

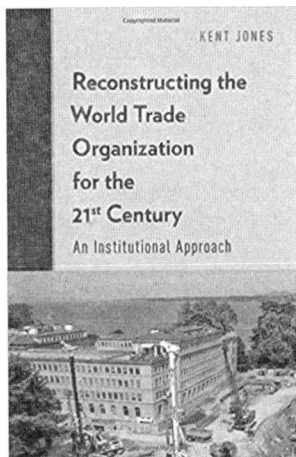

Title:Reconstructing the World Trade Organization for the 21st Century:An Institutional Approach
Author:Jones Kent
Publisher:Oxford University Press
Date:2015

书名:重塑 21 世纪世界贸易组织:制度化进程
作者:琼斯·肯特
出版社:牛津大学出版社
出版时间:2015 年

Contents:Presents an institutional framework with which to examine the difficulties of the World Trade Organization in completing multilateral trade negotiations and possible ways ease them. Discusses the Doha Round—what went wrong and what's at stake;

institutional foundations of the General Agreement on Tariffs and Trade/WTO system; the GATT to WTO transition and institutional crisis in the Doha Round; impediments to Doha Round consensus and the search for WTO solutions; WTO governance and committee chair representation; regional versus multilateral trade liberalization; trade, embedded liberalism, and development; and pathways back to Geneva. Jones is Professor of Economics at Babson College.

书籍简介:本书提出了一个体制框架,用于审查世界贸易组织完成多边贸易谈判的困难和解决的可能方法。本书讨论了多哈回合:问题与危机,"关税贸易总协定"/WTO 体系的体制基础,关贸总协定与 WTO 转型和多哈回合制度危机,阻碍多哈回合协商一致的原因——寻求 WTO 解决方案,WTO 治理和委员会主席代表,区域对多边贸易自由化的影响,贸易、嵌入式自由主义和发展,并返回日内瓦的途径。琼斯是巴布森学院经济学教授。

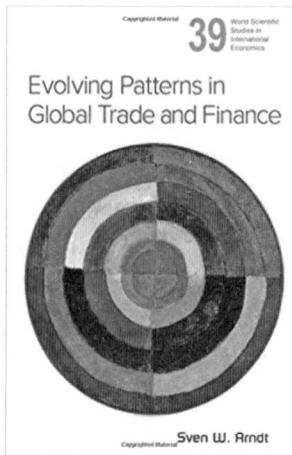

Title:Evolving Patterns in Global Trade and Finance

Author:Arndt Sven W

Publisher:World Scientific

Date:2015

书名:全球贸易与金融发展格局

作者:阿恩特·斯文·W

出版社:世界科学

出版时间:2015 年

Contents:Twenty-one papers, most previously published, focus on the meaning and implications of evolving and emerging patterns in international trade and finance. Papers discuss free trade and its alternatives; discriminatory versus nonpreferential tariff policies; customs union and the theory of tariffs; domestic distortions and trade policy; fragmentation; super-specialization and the gains from trade; global production networks and regional integration; production networks in an economically integrated region; trade diversion and production sharing; production networks, exchange rates, and macroeconomic stability; trade, production networks, and the exchange rate; intraindustry trade and the open economy; fragmentation, imperfect competition, and heterogeneous firms; policy choices in an open economy—some dynamic considerations; joint balance—capital mobility and the monetary system of a currency area; international short-term capital movements—a distributed lag model of speculation in foreign exchange; regional currency arrangements in North America; adjustment in an open economy with two exchange rate regimes; stabilization policy in an economy with two exchange rate regimes; policy challenges in a dual exchange rate regime; and the "Great Moderation" in a dual exchange rate regime. Arndt is Professor of Money, Credit, and Trade at Claremont McKenna College.

书籍简介:本书的 21 篇论文大部分已经发表过,侧重于国际贸易和国际金融的发展和新兴模式的意义和影响。论文讨论内容包括:自由贸易及其替代品,歧视性与非优惠关税政策,关税同盟和关税理论,国内扭曲和贸易政策,碎裂,超专业化和贸易收益,全球生产网络和区域一体化,经济一体化与地区生产网络,贸易转移和生产分享,生产网络、汇率和宏观经济稳定,贸易、生产网络和汇率,内部贸易和开放经济,分裂、不完全竞争和异质企业,开放经济中的政策选择———一些动态考虑,联合平衡———资本流动和货币区域的货币体系,国际短期资本流动——外汇投机分布式滞后模型,北美区域货币安排,以两种汇率制度调整开放型经济,一个具有两个汇率制度的经济体的稳定政策,双重汇率制度的政策挑战,双重汇率制度中的"大赦"。阿恩特是麦克纳学院的金融、信贷和贸易的教授。

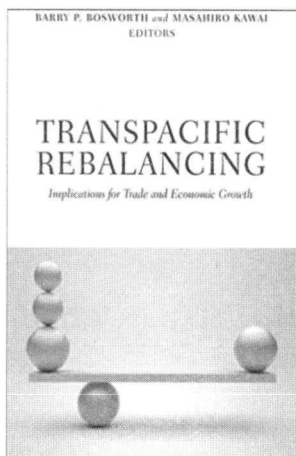

Title: Transpacific Rebalancing: Implications for Trade and Economic Growth

Author: Bosworth Barry; Kawai Masahiro

Publisher: Brookings Institution Press; Asian Development Bank

Date: 2015

书名:跨太平洋再平衡:对贸易和经济增长的影响

作者:博斯沃斯·巴里;河合正弘

出版社:布鲁金斯学会出版社;亚洲开发银行

出版时间:2015 年

Contents:Eight papers examine how to rebalance transpacific trade in the aftermath of the global financial crisis of 2007 – 2009. Papers discuss exchange rates and global rebalancing;the effect of exchange-rate changes on transpacific rebalancing;rebalancing the US economy in a postcrisis world;Japan's current account rebalancing;the role of factor market distortion in the People's Republic of China's external imbalances;the Asian tiger economies' choices;the Association of Southeast Asian Nations's need to rebalance—whether it is more regional than global;and crisis, imbalances, and India. Bosworth is Robert Roosa Chair for International Economics at the Brookings Institution. Kawai is Professor in the Graduate School of Public Policy at the University of Tokyo.

书籍简介:本书八篇论文研究 2007—2009 年全球金融危机之后跨太平洋贸易再平衡。论文讨论汇率和全球再平衡;汇率变动对跨太平洋再平衡的影响;在后危机时代美国经济再平衡;日本经常账户再平衡;中华人民共和国外部失衡因素市场扭曲的作用;亚洲虎经济的选择:东南亚国家联盟需要再平衡——区域化与全球化;危机、失衡和印度。博斯沃斯是罗伯特·罗莎布鲁金斯学会国际经济学主席。河合是东京大学公共政策研究科教授。

Title:Trade and Development Report 2014;Global Governance and Policy Space for Development

Author:United Nations Conference on Trade and Development

Publisher:United Nations Publications

Date:2014

书名:2014 年贸易和发展报告:全球治理与政策发展空间

作者:联合国贸易和发展会议

出版社:联合国出版社
出版时间:2014 年

Contents:Assesses recent trends and prospects in the global economy,focusing on the case for coordinated expansion, the importance of policy space, and strengthening multilateral mechanisms. Discusses recent trends in the world economy;moving toward a sustained economic recovery—a review of policy options;policy space and global governance—the issues at stake;policy space and the origins of the multilateral economic system;trade and industrial policies in an evolving global governance regime;international finance and policy space;and fiscal space for stability and development—contemporary challenges.

书籍简介:本书评估近期全球经济的趋势和前景,重点关注协调扩张的情况,政策空间的重要性,加强多边机制的必要性。讨论世界经济的趋势,走向持续的经济复苏——对政策选择的回顾,政策空间和全球治理所涉及的问题,政策空间和多边经济体系的起源,不断变化的全球治理制度中的贸易和工业政策,国际金融政策空间;稳定发展的财政空间——当代挑战。

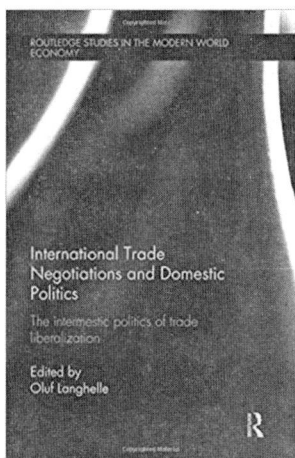

Title:International Trade Negotiations and Domestic Politics;The Intermestic Politics of Trade Liberalization

Author:Oluf Larghelle

Publisher:Routledge

Date:2014

书名:国际贸易谈判与国内政治:贸易自由化的国际政治

作者:奥朗夫朗格勒

出版社:劳特利奇出版社

出版时间:2014 年

Contents:Eight papers explore why resistance to increased market liberalization is strong, focusing on the "intermestic" character of trade politics—the way in which international and domestic aspects of politics and policies have been woven together and become related to one another. Papers discuss the intermestic politics of trade—institutions, ideas, interests, and actors; the global trade agenda; multilevel negotiations in American trade policy—free trade agreements from George W. Bush to Barack Obama; the European Union—balancing trade liberalization and protectionism; India's trade politics—continuity and change; China—an open, confident, and booming trading nation; Norway—agricultural exceptionalism and the quest for free trade; and the intermestic politics of trade. Langhelle is Professor of Political Science at the University of Stavanger.

书籍简介:本书的八篇论文探讨了为什么阻力反而强化市场自由化,重点关注贸易政治的"国际化"特征:国际和国内的政治和政策方面相互影响与关联。论文讨论包括了贸易机构、观念、兴趣和行为者的国际政治,全球贸易议程,美国贸易政策的多层次谈判——乔治·W.布什对巴拉克·奥巴马的自由贸易协定,欧盟——平衡贸易自由化和保护主义,印度的贸易政治——连续性与变化,中国——一个开放、自信、蓬勃发展的贸易国,挪威:农业例外主义和追求自由贸易,贸易的国际政治。朗切尔是斯塔万格大学政治学教授。

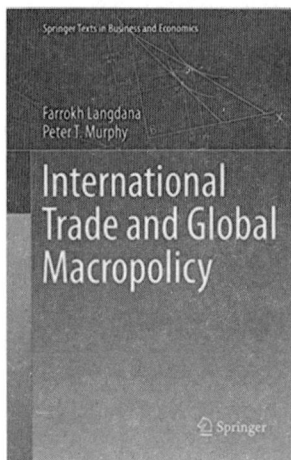

Title:International Trade and Global Macropolicy
Author:Langdana, Farrokh; Murphy, Peter T.
Publisher:Springer
Date:2014

书名:国际贸易与全球宏观政策
作者:朗丹阿·洛可;墨菲·彼得·T
出版社:施普林格
出版时间:2014 年

Contents:Explores the theoretical models that drive trade and global macroeconomics in the real world. Discusses the origins of international trade theory; the Ricardian trade model; factor intensity; stripping away David Ricardo's assumptions; trade barriers and protectionism; global macroeconomics; exchange rates; the Investment Saving/Liquidity Preference Money Supply-Balance of Payments model—the goods market, the money market, and the balance of payments; exports and imports, real exchange rates; incorporating inflation into the model; capital flows—perfectly and imperfectly mobile capital; and the global monetary system. Langdana is Professor in the Finance/Economics Department and Director of the Executive MBA Program at Rutgers Business School. Murphy is an operating partner with Dubilier and Company and President and CEO of DC Safety.

书籍简介:本书探讨了推动世界贸易和全球宏观经济学的理论模型。讨论内容包括:国际贸易理论的起源,理嘉贸易模式,因子强度,舍弃大卫·李嘉图的假设,贸易壁垒和保护主义,全球宏观经济学汇率,投资储蓄与流动性优先货币供应:国际收支模式——货物市场、货币市场和国际收支,出口和进口、实际汇率,考虑通货膨胀的模式,资本流动——完全不完全流动的资本,全球货币体系。朗丹阿是财务/经济系教授,罗格斯商学院执行 MBA 课程主任。墨菲是迪比尔公司的运营合伙人,DC 安全总裁兼首席执行官。

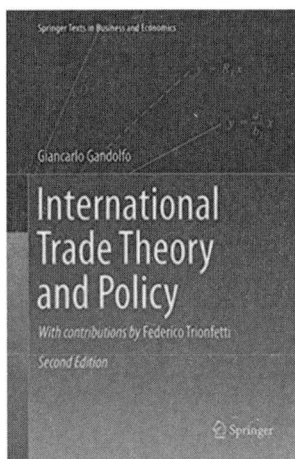

Title: International Trade Theory and Policy

Author: Gandolfo, Giancarlo

Publisher: Springer

Date: 2014

书名:国际贸易理论与政策(第二版)

作者:甘道夫·吉安卡洛

出版社:施普林格

出版时间:2014 年

Contents: Revised and expanded second edition presents an introduction to the theory and policy of international trade. Discusses the classical theory of comparative costs; the neoclassical theory of international trade; the Heckscher-Ohlin model; the four core theorems; some refinements; an overview of new explanations for international trade; the precursors; the models; tariff and nontariff barriers; free trade versus protection and preferential trade cooperation; the "new" protectionism; international trade and growth—

comparative statics; international trade and growth—dynamics; endogenous growth and trade, old and new; globalization and economic geography; and trade integration and wage inequality. Gandolfo is with the Class of Moral Sciences at the National Academy of Lincei.

书籍简介：本书的第二版经过修订和扩大，主要介绍了国际贸易的理论与政策。讨论了经典比较成本理论，新古典主义国际贸易理论，赫克歇尔－俄林模型，四核定理与改进，国际贸易新解释概述——前提与模型，关税和非关税壁垒，自由贸易、保护主义与优惠贸易合作，"新"保护主义，国际贸易与增长——比较静态，国际贸易与增长——动力、内生增长和贸易，全球化和经济地理学，贸易一体化和工资不平等。甘道夫在林琴国立学院教授道德科学课程。

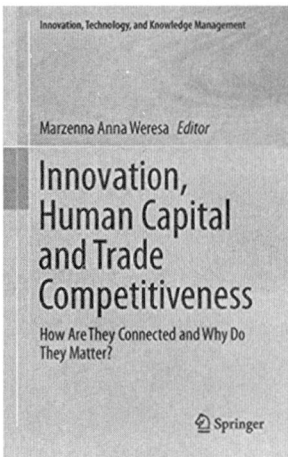

Title：Innovation, Human Capital and Trade Competitiveness

Author：Weresa, Marzenna Anna, ed.
Publisher：Springer
Date：2014

书名：创新、人力资本与贸易竞争力
作者：维尔利斯·马尔蒂娜·安娜
出版社：施普林格
出版时间：2014 年

Contents：Eight papers focus on the evaluation of the significance of two factors that are gaining importance in the international competitiveness of economies—human capital and innovation—using the national innovation system. Papers discuss the theoretical grounds of the development of long-term competitive advantages in international trade; human capital and innovation—basic concepts, measures, and interdependencies; a theoretical approach to the concept of the national innovation system and international competitiveness; human capital and innovations as determinants of competitiveness; the international competitiveness of countries with dynamic innovation systems; the international competitiveness of countries with performing innovation systems; the international competitiveness of countries with catching – up innovation systems；and the international competitiveness of countries with unbalanced innovation systems. Weresa is a professor and Director of the World Economy Research Institute at the Warsaw School of Economics.

书籍简介：本书包含的八篇论文侧重于利用国家创新体系评估人力资本与创新，这两个国际竞争力中日益重要的因素的意义。论文讨论了发展国际贸易长期竞争优势的理论依据，人力资本和创新——基本概念、措施和相互依存关系，国家创新体系和国际竞争力理论的理论方法，人力资本和创新行为——竞争力的决定因素，具有动态创新体系的国家国际竞争力，执行创新体系的国家国际竞争力，具有追赶创新体系的国家国际竞争力，以及不平衡创新体系国家国际竞争力。维尔利斯是华沙经济学院世界经济研究所教授和主任。

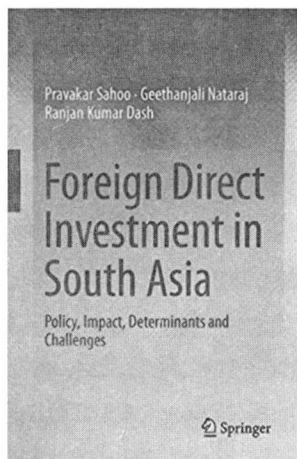

Title：Foreign Direct Investment in South Asia：Policy，Impact，Determinants and Challenges

Author：Sahoo，Pravakar；Nataraj，Geethanjali；Dash，Ranjan Kumar

Publisher：Springer

Date：2014

书名：对南亚的外国直接投资：政策、影响、决定因素和挑战

作者：舍户·普拉卢克；纳塔拉·蒂塔卓林；戴什·任杰·库玛

出版社：施普林格

出版时间：2014年

Contents：Addresses the policy，the impact，determinants，and challenges of foreign direct investment in South Asia. Discusses a macro overview of South Asia；FDI policy in South Asia；FDI inflows into South Asia；FDI in China—a comparative perspective with India；determinants of FDI in South Asia；FDI and economic growth in South Asia；the impact of FDI and domestic investment in South Asia—time series and panel evidence; the impact of FDI on domestic exports—time series and panel evidence from South Asia; and FDI reforms in South Asia—an unfinished agenda, future reforms, and challenges. Sahoo is Associate Professor with the Institute of Economic Growth at Delhi University. Nataraj is a Professor and Senior Fellow with the Observer Research Foundation in New Delhi. Dash is a fellow with the Indian Council for Research on International Economic Relations.

书籍简介:本书主要解决南亚外商直接投资的政策、影响、决定因素和挑战,讨论南亚的宏观概况,南亚的外商直接投资政策,外商直接投资流入南亚的情况,中国的外商直接投资——基于与印度的比较,南亚外商直接投资的决定因素,南亚的外商直接投资与经济增长,外商直接投资对南亚国内投资的影响——基于时间序列和小组证据,外商直接投资对国内出口的影响——来自南亚的时间序列和小组证据,南非的外商直接投资改革——未完成的议程、未来的改革和挑战。舍户是德里大学经济增长研究所的副教授。纳塔拉是新德里观察研究基金会的教授和高级研究员。戴什是印度国际经济研究理事会的研究员。

第四章

世界经济学科 2014—2015 年大事记

第一节　世界经济学科国内重大事件

1. 2014 年 1 月 11—12 日,由中国投资协会与中海投(北京)国际投资管理有限公司共同主办的"新丝绸之路——2014 中国海外投资新年论坛"在北京人民大会堂举行。

2. 2014 年 4 月 17 日,商务部发布《国别贸易投资环境报告 2014》,着重介绍美国、欧盟、日本、巴西、俄罗斯等我国 13 个主要贸易伙伴的贸易投资管理体制及措施的变化情况,分析其可能对我国对外贸易投资产生的壁垒,评估其贸易投资环境。

3. 2014 年 5 月 4 日,商务部(国际贸易经济合作研究院)发布 2014 年春季中国对外贸易形势报告。报告回顾了 2013 年及 2014 年一季度中国外贸运行情况,2013 年中国成为世界第一货物贸易大国。2014 年一季度,中国进出口数据表现不佳,主要是由于 2013 年同期套利贸易垫高了基数。剔出基数因素,一季度中国进出口总体符合预期。

4. 2014 年 5 月 28 日,第八届国际服务贸易论坛在北京举办。论坛由北京第二外国语学院与中国国际贸易学会、商务部研究院国际服务贸易研究所、《国际贸易》杂志社共同主办,全国各地服务贸易研究和实践领域的近 150 名专家代表参会。本届论坛在"文化贸易""服务外包"专题论坛的基础上,增设"城市开放与服务贸易"专题论坛。

5. 2014 年 6 月 15 日,中国新兴经济体研究会中青年论坛成立大会暨新兴经济体学术论坛在昆明举行。来自中国社会科学院、北京大学、清华大学、南开大学等高校和科研机构的30多位优秀中青年学者代表参加会议。会议围绕"APEC峰会"、国际与区域经济、金砖国家与区域经济合作、全球经济治理四个专题进行。

6. 2014年6月26—28日，美国国家经济研究局（NBER）、北京大学国家发展研究院（NSD）以及中国经济研究中心（CCER）联合举办的第十六届NBER-CCER"中国与世界经济"年会在北京举行。本届年会分为"金融市场""代际转移""国际贸易""国际金融I""国际金融II""市场与政策""退休"以及"高等教育"八大专场。

7. 2014年7月12日，2014年中国"区域科学与城市经济前沿"暨"自贸区经济"青年学者及研究生学术论坛在上海举行。上海财经大学自由贸易区研究院院长赵晓雷以《国际经贸新形势及中国上海自由贸易试验区建设》为题发言，本届论坛为全国区域科学、城市经济以及自贸区经济等领域的青年学者提供了一个很好的学术观点碰撞的平台。

8. 2014年7月19日，丝绸之路经济带（兰州新区）发展高层论坛在兰州召开。论坛主题为"共享丝绸之路经济带建设机遇：开放、合作、共赢"。

9. 2014年8月2日，第一届"东亚企业高峰会—青岛论坛"在青岛举行。山东省委书记姜异康、国土资源部部长姜大明、商务部部长高虎城、中国国际贸易促进委员会会长姜增伟等出席峰会。论坛包括金属机电塑化、观光餐饮文创、现代化服务业、地产建筑建材、农林渔牧食品、海洋经贸金融等议题。

10. 2014年8月20日，天津自由贸易区研究院在天津财经大学挂牌成立，中国社会科学院经济研究所所长裴长洪受聘为天津自由贸易区研究院院长。天津自由贸易区研究院的成立，旨在推动中国贸易投资自由化便利化改革，促进天津自贸区的申请和建设。

11. 2014年9月8—11日，中国国际投资贸易洽谈会在中国厦门举办。投洽会以国际投资促进为主线，以"引进来"和"走出去"为主题，以"投资和贸易展览、权威投资论坛研讨和项目对接会"为主要内容。本届投洽会将紧扣国际资本流动新趋势和全款产业发展新动向，围绕着展览展示、讨坛研讨、项目洽谈三大主题开展高端权威的活动。

12. 2014年9月10—12日，第八届世界经济论坛新领军者年会（夏季达沃斯论坛）在天津举行。来自100多个国家近2000名政、经、学界"领军人物"围绕"推动创新创造价值"主题展开探讨。续创新推动全球经济健康发展，成为与会嘉宾聚焦的一大热点。

13. 2014 年 9 月 11 日，丝绸之路经济带与新阶段西部大开发国际研讨会在西安召开。会议的主题为"丝绸之路经济带与新阶段西部大开发"。与会专家对丝绸之路经济带建设的理论内涵与实践研究、丝绸之路经济带建设与新阶段西部大开发的选择与启示等方面开展专题讨论。

14. 2014 年 9 月 20 日，全面提高开放型经济水平 2014 学术研讨会在北京举行，主题为"经济全球化新形势与中国贸易转型升级"。中国社科院经济所所长裴长洪、对外经济贸易大学副校长林桂军分别围绕"中国上海自贸区运行一年经验与前瞻""全球价值链对国际贸易政策的影响"做了主旨演讲。

15. 2014 年 9 月 16—19 日，2014 第 11 届中国—东盟博览会在广西南宁举办，设置商品贸易专题、投资合作专题、服务贸易专题、先进技术专题和"魅力之城"五个专题。新加坡出任第十一届博览会主题国。

16. 2014 年 9 月 27—29 日，由中国国际贸易学会、吉林图们江经济合作学会共同举办，中国国际贸易学会、吉林图们江经贸合作研究分会承办的"2014 中国国际贸易学会年会暨国际贸易发展论坛"在吉林省延吉市召开，同时还召开了"沿边开发开放、一带一路"研讨分论坛及"区域经贸合作"研讨会分论坛。

17. 2014 年 10 月 2 日，2014WTO 公众论坛"贸易与就业—中国的发展进程"论坛在上海举办，此次论坛聚焦中国的对外贸易与就业问题。瑞士国际贸易中心首席经济学家 Marion Jansen、法国经济社会研究院研究员 Peirre Conciald、复旦大学经济学院经济系副主任封进教授、复旦大学经济学院院长助理卢华博士分别从不同角度阐释了这一主题。

18. 2014 年 10 月 10 日，对外经济贸易大学举行了《中国外商投资发展报告(2014)》发布会暨"新一轮改革开放下的外商投资"研讨会。今年的主题为"新一轮改革开放下的外商投资"，研究了国际投资规则的变迁、外资管理制度变革、FDI 环境竞争力、FDI 与全球价值链等行业领域的 FDI 等问题，并就今年利用外资形势做了展望。

19. 2014 年 10 月 17 日，第五届中国商务发展上海论坛在上海举办，主题是：上海自贸区发展与中国开放型经济新体制建设。主旨是探讨商务领域的热点问题，促进国际贸易学科的发展，围绕开放经济与贸易领域的重点及热点问题展开研讨，为国际经贸领域的专家学者搭建学术交流的平台。

20. 2014 年 10 月 17 日，第十三届全国高校国际贸易学科协作组会议暨 2014 年中国国际贸易学科发展论坛在北京举行。大会主题是"中国对外开放新阶段与培育国际竞争新优势"。大会还有六场专家论坛，主题包括对外直接投资、多边贸易与区域经济一体化、服务业与服务贸易、贸易环境与创新、全球价值链与贸易利得等。

21. 2014 年 10 月 24 日,由中国世界经济学会主办的中国世界经济学会 2014 年年会在杭州举行,主题为:世界经济变革与中国开放型经济发展。年会按照学科划分与突出问题举办了多个分论坛讨论世界经济理论与现实问题,国际贸易,国际投资与跨国公司,中国开放型经济,自由贸易区发展。

22. 2014 年 11 月 5—11 日,2014 年 APEC 峰会在北京举行,包含领导人非正式会议、部长级会议等系列会议。其中领导人峰会于 10—11 日在北京雁栖湖举行,国家主席习近平主持峰会,主题是:共建面向未来的亚太伙伴关系。三大议题为"推动亚太区域经济一体化""促进经济创新发展、改革与增长""加强全方位基础设施与互联互通建设"。

23. 2014 年 11 月 6 日,商务部(国际贸易经济合作研究院)发布 2014 年秋季中国对外贸易形势报告。报告回顾了 2014 年前三季度中国外贸运行情况,面对错综复杂的国内外经济形势,中国政府及时出台支持外贸稳定增长的政策措施,推动了进出口增速逐步企稳回升、质量效益进一步提高。综合判断,2014 年中国对外贸易增速将低于 2013 年,但仍高于全球贸易平均增速,也高于大多数主要经济体对外贸易增速。

24. 2014 年 11 月 7—9 日,中国新兴经济体研究会 2014 年会暨 2014 新兴经济体合作与发展论坛在广州举行,会议主题为"新兴经济体的长期增长前景与 21 世纪海上丝绸之路建设",来自中国、孟加拉、巴西、希腊、缅甸、墨西哥、俄罗斯、南非、赞比亚和津巴布韦等国近 200 名学界、政届和商界代表出席了此次盛会。

25. 2014 年 11 月 10 日,第四届亚洲研究论坛在中国社会科学院举行,主题为"TPP 与 RCEP:竞争性与互补性",重点讨论了 TPP 和 RCEP 的最新进展、影响、未来展望,TPP 和 RCEP 的竞争性与互补性,以及亚太区域一体化的路径选择等多项议题。与会专家学者来自韩国、日本、新西兰、越南、中国社会科学院、商务部研究室等。

26. 2014 年 11 月 22 日,第三十二届"中国宏观经济论坛(2014—2015)"在北京举办。论坛上发布了《中国宏观经济分析与预测(2014—2015)》报告,报告预计 2014 年 GDP 增速为 7.4%,CPI 为 2.2%;预计在常态情形下,2015 年 GDP 增速为 7.2%,CPI 为 2.7%,投资增速为 12.3%,消费增速为 11.8%,出口增速为 5.6%。

27. 2014 年 11 月 28 日,由中央财经大学金融学院主办的第六届"亚太经济与金融论坛"在北京举行,主题是"中国经济的崛起及其对世界的影响"。论坛主要议题包括中国经济崛起的理论与实践、人民币汇率制度改革、外商直接投资的政策及其影响、金融创新与金融业改革的新动向等。

28. 2014年11月29—30日,由中国社科院经济研究所、复旦大学中国社会主义市场经济研究中心和厦门大学宏观经济研究中心联合主办的"首届中国宏观经济论坛(2014年)"在厦门召开。论坛以"全面深化改革与中国经济发展"为主题,围绕中国宏观经济的增长路径、财政政策、货币政策、市场结构等一系列热点问题展开研讨。

29. 2014年12月10日,第十四届中国经济论坛在北京举行,以"创新是中国发展的新引擎"为主题。论坛还进行了"中国—丹麦零碳对话""中国企业的全球化战略"及"新型城镇化的中国路径"三场高端峰会,中外嘉宾分别就环境问题、中国企业走出去、新型城镇化等与"新常态 可持续"密切相关的主题,进行了深入的交流。

30. 2014年12月13—14日,由中国经济学年会秘书处(北京大学国家发展研究院)与北京大学主办,北京大学汇丰商学院承办的第十四届中国经济学年会在深圳举行。600余位来自全国各地的经济专家、学者围绕"中国经济新常态与改革创新发展"的主题展开学术研讨和交流。

31. 2014年12月14日,"中国世界经济学科专家学术论坛——21世纪海上丝绸之路、贸易保护壁垒与中美贸易再平衡"学术研讨会在上海召开。会议邀请了国内著名高校和研究机构的专家学者30余名,围绕"一带一路"进行了学术研讨,提出应围绕"一带一路"倡议,具体实施中国新一轮的大变革、大突破和大布局。

32. 2014年12月15日,中国社科院在京发布《经济蓝皮书:2015年中国经济形势分析与预测》。蓝皮书指出,中国经济仍然进入结构趋于优化、物价涨幅趋于适度、新增就业趋于稳定、经济增速趋向潜在水平的"新常态"。2015年中国经济仍将保持平稳较快增长,预计增速为7%左右,出口和进口分别增长6.9%和4.6%。

33. 2014年12月15日,第三届金砖国家财经论坛在北京举行。中国财政部副部长朱光耀指出,金砖国家开发银行将落户中国上海,2015年年底之前投入运作,工作重心是破解发展中国家基础设施的发展难题。另外,《金砖国家更紧密伙伴关系框架》《金砖国家经济合作战略》两个文本的准备工作也已经就绪,有望在2015年正式通过并实施。

34. 2014年12月21日,由中国国际经济交流中心主办的2014—2015中国经济年会在北京举行。本次年会的主题为"新常态下中国经济的可持续发展"。中国国际经济交流中心理事长曾培炎致辞时表示,新常态突出表征为经济增长减速换挡,经济发展方式转向质量与效率型,产业链向高端迈进,高水平引进来、大规模走出去同步发生,中等收入群体成为稳定内需的主体,多样化消费渐成主流,中小企业和新业态成为增长新亮点。

35. 2015 年 1 月 15 日,第二届中国海外投资新年论坛在北京举行,主题为"丝路五通"。论坛还举办加强政策沟通——战略新兴产业合作,加强设施联通——丝路沿线基础设施投资,加强贸易畅通——境内外大宗商品交易互联互通,加强资金融通——跨国经营和投融资,加强民心相通——中外共建工业园等分论坛。

36. 2015 年 3 月 21 日,由国务院发展研究中心主办的"中国发展高层论坛2015 年会"在北京举行,主题为"新常态下的中国经济"。论坛围绕新常态下中国的发展与改革、实施积极财政政策、深化财税体制改革、新常态下的对外开放、深化互联互通,推进"一带一路"、调整产业结构,实施创新驱动发展等议题展开探讨。

37. 2015 年 3 月 26—29 日,博鳌亚洲论坛 2015 年年会在海南省博鳌召开,主题为"亚洲新未来:迈向命运共同体"。来自 49 个国家和地区的 2786 名政、商、学、媒界人士出席,议题涉及宏观经济、区域合作、产业转型、技术创新、政治安全、社会民生等六大领域。习近平主席发表了主旨演讲,围绕"迈向亚洲命运共同体、开创亚洲新未来"的主题发表看法。

38. 2015 年 3 月 29 日,厦门大学为厦门大学中国(福建)自贸区研究院、厦门大学富邦金融与产业研究中心、中国(福建)自贸区协同创新中心举行揭牌仪式暨首届福建自贸区高端论坛。专题涉及自贸区建设在国家对外经济中的战略意义、自贸区建设对各产业链的促进与推动、"一带一路"政策研究与分析、自贸区建设的两岸机遇与国际视野等。

39. 2015 年 5 月 5 日,商务部(国际贸易经济合作研究院)发布 2015 年春季中国对外贸易形势报告。报告回顾了 2014 年及 2015 年一季度中国外贸运行情况。2014 年,中国外贸总体保持平稳增长,国际市场份额进一步提高,贸易大国地位更加巩固,结构继续优化,质量和效益不断改善。2015 年一季度,在全球贸易总体下滑的背景下,中国出口保持增长势头,但受进口价格大幅下降、部分重要产品进口数量减少影响,进口降幅较大。

40. 2015 年 5 月 8 日,第二届上海国际投资论坛在上海举办。论坛聚焦跨境投资,剖析了在全球经济和政治充满不确定性因素的当下,投资者如何抓住投资良机、管理跨境风险。从全球自由贸易协定可能产生的影响,到各国自由贸易区所蕴藏的机遇,全面解读了跨境投资趋势,分享了实用投资策略。

41. 2015 年 5 月 13 日,由北京服务贸易协会、北京第二外国语学院、《国际贸易》杂志社、国家文化贸易学术研究平台共同主办的科博会·第九届国际服务贸易论坛在北京举办。

本届论坛围绕"经济新常态下的设计服务贸易"主题,探讨当前国际、国内在设计领域涉及的政策与理论重大问题。

42. 2015 年 5 月 30 日,由中国人民大学经济学院主办的首届中国人民大学"世界经济论坛"在北京举办,主题为"世界经济:探寻新的增长之路"。论坛邀请了国内著名高等院校和研究机构的专家齐聚一堂,探讨当前世界经济领域存在的问题,探寻新的增长之路,同时搭建国内外交流与合作的新平台。

43. 2015 年 6 月 2 日,中国社科院财经战略研究院承办的"CASS 财经战略论坛"在北京召开。主题是"一带一路"与人民币走出去战略。来自中国社科院、新华社、人民日报、光明日报、经济日报等 130 多人参加了论坛。

44. 2015 年 6 月 5 日,《中国海外投资国家风险评级报告(2015)》在北京发布。评级结果显示,发达国家评级结果普遍高于新兴经济体,投资风险较低。排列前 10 的国家中有 8 个国家为发达经济体,25 个新兴经济体中只有新加坡和韩国进入前 10 位,新兴经济体中金砖国家排名普遍处于中下游。

45. 2015 年 6 月 6 日,"第五届贸易与发展"国际学术会议在天津举行,主题为"新常态下的国际贸易与经济发展"。与会专家们就"中国企业出口行为的经验研究""对外贸易与中国经济发展""自贸区改革与'一带一路'""对外贸易与产业变动""贸易,竞争行为与环境变化""国际贸易专业教学"等议题展开研讨。

46. 2015 年 6 月 11 日,第五届亚洲研究论坛:"一带一路"与亚洲共赢国际研讨会在中国社会科学院举行。来自中国、俄罗斯、哈萨克斯坦、韩国、日本、印度、巴基斯坦等 14 个国家的研究机构和高校的 40 多位专家学者,围绕"一带一路"如何实现亚洲共赢进行了研讨,着重分析了面对的挑战并探讨了应对挑战的方法和途径。

47. 2015 年 6 月 18 日,由中国人民大学重阳金融研究院、义乌市政府、环球网举办的"2015 丝绸之路经济带城市国际论坛"在义乌举办,主题为"贸易畅通、共建繁荣",来自全球 40 多个国家的政府官员、商界代表及专家学者,就如何共建"一带一路"国际贸易支点城市,以及加强跨国金融合作、贸易投资等话题建言献策。

48. 2015 年 7 月 18 日,2015 国际货币论坛暨《人民币国际化报告》发布会在北京举行。圆桌研讨 I 以"人民币、SDR 与国际货币体系改革"为主题,圆桌研讨 II 聚焦"人民币国际化:机遇与挑战",圆桌研讨 III 主题为"人民币国际化与'一带一路'倡议"。

49. 2015 年 7 月 19 日,国研智库论坛·2015·创新金融助力中国"一带一路"倡议峰会在北京国家会议中心举行。峰会由国务院发展研究中心作为指导单位,中国发展出版社和新华社新媒体中心联合主办,钰诚集团及 e 租宝等单位承办。与会有关领导和专家就在"一带一路"的时代背景下,中国企业如何更好地走出去,如何发挥好互联网＋金融以及境外自贸区＋跨境贸易等创新举措,更好地服务实体经济,进行了权威、深入的解析和研讨。

50. 2015 年 8 月 11 日,2015 年中巴经济走廊论坛在新疆克拉玛依市举行。论坛由新疆维吾尔自治区人民政府、中国社科院主办,主题为"共商中巴合作,共建繁荣走廊,共享和谐发展"。来自中巴两国政府、企业、智库、社会组织、媒体机构等约 300 位代表就"城市合作""产业对接""信息走廊""人文社会"等议题展开讨论。

51. 2015 年 8 月 21 日,中国社会科学论坛(2015):"一带一路"与周边国际区域合作在北京举行。中国边疆研究所所长邢广程表示,作为国际、国内两个空间结合部和契合点的边疆地区,是"一带一路"建设的重要组成部分。其他学者也为"一带一路"建设及周边国际区域合作提出了许多新见解、新思路。

52. 2015 年 9 月 4 日,新发展观与金砖合作国际研讨会在上海举行。来自巴西、俄罗斯、南非、英国、加拿大、印度及中国的 100 多位学者、外交官参会,围绕"全球治理新格局""新发展观与金砖国家的崛起""新发展观与中国的实践""新发展观与金砖银行"四个专题展开研讨。

53. 2015 年 9 月 9—11 日,2015 年夏季达沃斯论坛在大连举行。以"描绘增长新蓝图"为主题的本届论坛吸引了包括各国政要、商界领袖等在内的 1700 余嘉宾参加,围绕"科学的变革""被颠覆的行业""经济不确定性""中国新常态""环境界限""人的意义"六方面进行了深入探讨,研究如何应对增长面临的各种挑战。

54. 2015 年 9 月 13 日,2015 中国宏观经济论坛在武汉举行,经济学家们围绕新常态下经济转型升级、宏观经济及金融改革、长江经济带发展等问题展开研讨,为经济新常态下地方政府与企业的发展建言献策。

55. 2015 年 9 月 16 日,由广西大学中国—东盟研究院、中国—东盟区域发展研究协同创新中心共同撰稿,中国社科出版社出版发行的《中国—东盟合作发展报告 2014—2015》首发仪式在广西大学中国—东盟研究院举行。《报告》旨在加强中国—东盟合作研究,更好地为中国企业"走出去"提供咨询,服务国家战略。

56. 2015年9月21日,中国社科院经济所和社会科学文献出版社共同举办了《经济蓝皮书夏季号:中国经济增长报告(2014—2015)》发布会。蓝皮书主报告预测,2015年GDP增长率预计为6.9%,2016年我国劳动力投入增长率将为负。报告还分析指出,经济减速将成清理"僵尸企业"的"清洁机制"。

57. 2015年9月23日,由中国国际经济交流中心与新西兰—中国关系促进委员会共同主办的第二届"中国—新西兰伙伴关系论坛"在北京召开。来自中新两国政府、工商界、科教文化界的高层人士近120人参加论坛。此次论坛以"携手合作 走向成功"为主题,就食品安全、旅游、人文交流、投资等议题展开了广泛深入的讨论。

58. 2015年11月5日,商务部(国际贸易经济合作研究院)发布2015年秋季中国对外贸易形势报告。报告回顾了2015年前三季度中国外贸运行情况,并展望了2015年全年和2016年中国外贸发展趋势。2015年前三季度,面对严峻复杂的国内外形势,中国政府加大外贸稳增长调结构政策力度,推动出口占国际市场份额进一步提高,外贸结构不断优化,质量和效益继续改善。

59. 2015年11月25日,对外经济贸易大学国际经济研究院近日发布的《中国外商投资发展报告(2015)》显示:在全球国际直接投资流出额较大幅度下降的环境下,我国吸收外商直接投资微幅增长,但吸收外商直接投资环境竞争力排名相对下降,被对外直接投资超越,成为直接投资净流出国。这是该校连续第五年推出外商投资年度研究报告,今年的主题是"国际规则变迁下的外商投资"。

60. 2015年12月4—至6日,中国新兴经济体研究会2015年会暨2015新兴经济体论坛在广州举办,主题为"新兴经济体创新发展与中国自由贸易试验区建设"。来自来中国、孟加拉国、巴西、智利、印度、俄罗斯和美国等国200余名学界、政届和商界代表出席了此次盛会。共同探讨新兴经济体的结构改革与制度创新。

61. 2015年12月26日,由中国国际经济交流中心主办的"2015—2016中国经济年会"在京召开。会议以"引领新常态,决胜'十三五'"为主题,围绕"创新、协调、绿色、开放、共享"五大理念,聚焦结构性改革、供给侧管理和增长新动能,展开深入热烈讨论。

第二节 世界经济学科国外重大事件

2014 January

1. World Economic Forum Annual Meeting

January 22 – 25,2014

Davos-Klosters,Switzerland

Hosted By:World Economic Forum

"The Reshaping of the World:Consequences for Society,Politics and Business" is therefore the thematic focus of the World Economic Forum Annual Meeting 2014. Our aim is to develop the insights,initiatives and actions necessary to respond to current and emerging challenges.

2. World Bank Public Seminar on Global Economic Prospects

January 27,2014

Tokyo

3. 2014 International Business Research,Economics,Finance and MIS Conference

February 14 – 16,2014

Honolulu,Hawaii

The BREFM offers a great opportunity to bring together professors,researchers and scholars around the globe a great platform to deliver the latest innovative research result and the most recent development and trends in business field.

4. 2014 Asia-Pacific Conference on Economics,Trade and Regional Development

February 20 – 22,2014

Hainan,China

The aim objective is to provide a platform for researchers,engineers,academicians as well as industrial professionals from all over the world to present their research results and development activities in Networking and Digital Society.

5. The Future of Asia's Finance:IMF-HKMA Joint Conference:Helping Asia Invest,Integrate and Innovate,While Remaining Resilient

February 28,2014

Hong Kong

6. International Symposium on Society, Economy and Urban Studies

February 28 – March 3, 2014

Xian, China

ISSEUS is an International conference for those who wish to present their projects and discuss the latest innovations and results in the field of Society, Economy and Urban Studies.

7. The Second International Conference on Education, Economic, Psychology and Society

March 14, 2014

Phuket, Thailand

ICEEPS 2014 aims to foster research relations between universities and the industry around the world. This conference provides opportunities for delegates to exchange innovative ideas face to face, hoping to establish global collaboration in the future.

8. International Finance and Macroeconomics

March 28, 2014

Hosted By: Gita Gopinath of Harvard University and Hélène Rey of London Business School

9. International Trade and Investment

March 28 – 29, 2014

Hosted By: David Richardson, Syracuse University, and Matthew Slaughter, Dartmouth College.

10. World Economic Forum on Latin America

April 1 – 3, 2014

Panama City, Panama

Hosted By: World Economic Forum

11. The 77th International Atlantic Economic Conference

April 2, 2014

Madrid, Spain

Hosted By: International Atlantic Economic Society

Economists from around the world will be brought together in Madrid to discuss the challenges of tomorrow.

12. Twenty-ninth Annual Conference on Macroeconomics

April 11 – 12,2014

Hosted By:Jonathan Parker of MIT and Michael Woodford of Columbia University.

13. Twenty-First Century Trade Policy:Pushing the Limits of International Cooperation

April 22,2014

Hosted By:International Cooperation and Global Public Goods

14. The 2nd International Conference on Social Science and Management

May 7 – 9,2014

Kyoto,Japan

ICSSAM 2014 is an international conference for state-of-the-art research in Social
Science and Management. It is one of the leading international conferences for presenting novel and fundamental advances in the fields of Social Science and Management.

15. World Economic Forum on Africa

May 7 – 9,2014

Abuja,Nigeria

Hosted By:World Economic Forum

16. World Economic Forum on East Asia

May 21 – 23,2014

Metro Manila,Philippines

Hosted By:World Economic Forum

Fresh demand in Europe and the United States,along with recently concluded trade
agreements,are expected to boost production and consumption in East Asia. Almost all
of the 10 ASEAN economies are expecting growth above 5% in 2014.

17. 2014 Canadian Economics Association(CEA)Annual Conference

May 30 – June 1,2014

Vancouver,Canada

Hosted By:Canadian Economics Association

18. Cowles Summer Conferences

June 2 – 6,2014

Topic:Conference on Economics

New Perspectives on Macroeconomics,Trade,and Developmnet

Structural Empirical Microeconomic Models

Conference on Economic Theory

19. The 17th conference of international economic association

June 6 – 10 ,2014

Dead Sea ,Jordan

Hosted By：International economic association

20. Global Conference on the G – 20 Data Gaps Initiative

June 25 – 26 ,2014

Basel ,Switzerland

21. NBER Conference in China

June 25 – 28 ,2014

Hosted By：Shang-Jin Wei of NBER and Columbia University ,Yang Yao of CCER ,
and Chong-En Bai of Tsinghua University.

22. International Seminar on Macroeconomics

June 27 – 28 ,2014

Hosted By：Richard Clarida of Columbia University ,Jeffrey Frankel of Harvard U-
niversity ,Francesco Giavazzi of Bocconi University ,and Hélène Rey of London Business
School.

23. The 4th International Conference on Social Sciences and Business

June 27 – 29 ,2014

Bali ,Indonesia

Hosted By：Asia-Pacific Education & Research Association

ICSSB is a forum of communication for academics ,researchers ,practitioners ,and
policy makers in the areas of Business ,Accounting ,Finance ,Economics ,Information
Management ,Education ,Psychology ,Communication ,Law ,and Politics.

24. 2014 International Symposium on Society ,Economics and Urban Studies

June 27 – 29 ,2014

Bali ,Indonesia

Hosted By：Asia-Pacific Education & Research Association

ISSEUS is an International conference for those who wish to present their projects
and discuss the latest innovations and results in the field of Society ,Economics and Urban Studies.

25. The Global Symposium on Social Sciences

July 11,2014

Bangkok, Thailand

IBSSS Conferences have an intellectual hub for academic discussions for the colleagues in the areas of business, economics, society, politics, law, finance, culture, education, management and psychology, participants have found an excellent opportunity for presenting new researches.

26. The 3rd International Symposium on Business and Social Sciences

July 22,2014

Sapporo, Japan

Hosted By: Asia-Pacific Education & Research Association

2014 International Symposium on Business and Social Sciences(ISBSS2014) aims to provide a forum for researchers, practitioners, and professionals from the industry, academia and government to discourse on research and development, professional practice in the related field of study.

27. 2014 International Symposium on Business, Banking, Marketing and Economy

August 15 – 17,2014

Singapore

2014 International Symposium on Business, Banking, Marketing and Economy(ISBBME 2014) aims to provide a forum for researchers and professionals from the industry, academia and government to discourse on research and development, professional practice in Business, Banking, Marketing and Economy.

28. Global Competitiveness Report 2014—2015

August 21,2014

The Global Competitiveness Report 2014 – 2015 assesses the competitiveness landscape of 144 economies, providing insight into the drivers of their productivity and prosperity.

29. International Business Research, Economics, Finance and MIS Conference

September 4 – 6,2014

Okinawa, Japan

Hosted By: Asia-Pacific Education & Research Association

The BREFM offers a great opportunity to bring together professors, researchers and scholars around the globe a great platform to deliver the latest innovative research result and the most recent development and trends in business field.

30. 2014 Global economic conference

September 6, 2014

Kuala Lumpur, Malaysia

Hosted By: Leibniz Information Centre for Economics, Universiti Teknologi MARA (UiTM)

Overcoming these problems requires us to restructure our economies to promote effective and sustainable growth, and transform our social practices to balance the pursuit of financial wealth with recognition of the value of equity, community and the quality of life.

31. Annual Meeting of the New Champions

September 10 – 12, 2014

Tianjin, China

Hosted By: World Economic Forum

The Annual Meeting of the New Champions convenes the next generation of fast-growing enterprises shaping the future of business and society together with leaders from major multinationals as well as government, media, academia and civil society.

32. 2014 Shanghai International Conference on Social Science

September 13 – 15, 2014

Shanghai, China

Hosted By: Asia-Pacific Education & Research Association

The 2014 SICSS is to offer scholars, professionals, academics and graduate students to present, share, and discuss their studies from various perspectives in the aspects of social sciences, including: Communication, Culture, Economy, Education, Finance, Law, Management, Politics, Psychology, Society and so forth.

33. Food Price Volatility, Food Security and Trade Policy Conference

September 18 – 19, 2014

World Bank Headquarters, Washington, D. C.

34. WTO Public Forum 2014

October 1 – 3, 2014

Geneva, Switzerland

Topic："Why trade matters to everyone". It showcases the myriad connections between trade and people's daily lives and demonstrates how trade improves the day-to-day lives of citizens around the globe. Under this thematic umbrella, three sub-themes are covered: trade and jobs, trade and consumers, trade and Africa.

35. 2014 Annual Meetings of the International Monetary Fund(IMF) and the World Bank Group

October 10 – 12,2014

Washington,D. C.

36. 14th Eurasia Business and Economics Society

October 23,2014

Barcelona,Spain

Participants will find opportunities for presenting new research, exchanging information, and discussing current issues. .

37. 2014 High Level Caribbean Forum: Unlocking Economic Growth,

October 23 – 24,2014

Montego Bay,Jamaica

38. Capacity Building Seminar on Monetary Policy in Transition: The Case for a Two-Pillar Monetary Regime

October 23 – 24,2014

Bali,Indonesia

39. Technology,Trade Costs,and the Pattern of Trade with Multi-Stage Production

October 30,2014

Hosted By: World Bank

40. International Finance and Macroeconomics

October 31,2014

Hosted By: Charles Engel, University of Wisconsin, Madison, and Emmanuel Farhi, Harvard University. World Economic Forum

41. World Bank Seminar "South Asia Economic Focus(SAEF): The Export Opportunity"

October 31,2014

Tokyo

42. India Economic Summit

November 4 – 6,2014

New Delhi,India

Hosted By:World Economic Forum

Marking the thirtieth year of the World Economic Forum's active engagement in India,taking place at a time when the energetic optimism for India which has been prevalent in the past decade has given way to questions about the country's true potential,the Forum will provide the foremost platform bringing together international and national leaders in New Delhi who are invested in building a sustainable roadmap for India's future.

43. Doing Business 2015 Report presentation in Geneva at the World Trade Organization

November 5,2014

Hosted By:World Trade Organization

44. Third IMF/WB/WTO Joint Trade Workshop

November 6 – 7,2014

Washington,DC

45. Asia-pacific economic cooperation(APEC)summit in 2014

November 10 – 11,2014

The theme of the summit are:to build the Asia-pacific partnership for the future

46. The asean summit 2014

November 13,2014

Myanmar

47. Macroeconomic Rebalancing for Sustainable Growth

November 20 – 21,2014

Seoul,Korea

48. 2014 Asia-Pacific Conference on Business & Social Science

November 21 – 23,2014

Taipei,Taiwan

Hosted By:Asia-Pacific Education & Research Association

This conference aims to provide a communication platform for academics,researchers,graduates and industry professionals to not only present their recent and latest researches but also discuss the future development.

49. International Trade and Investment

December 5 – 6,2014

Hosted By:Gordon Hanson,University of California,San Diego.

50. Trade,Poverty,and Shared Prosperity Conference

December 10 – 11,2014

World Bank Headquarters,Washington,D. C.

51. The International Symposium on Social Sciences

December 29,2014

Hong Kong,Hong Kong

Hosted By:Asia-Pacific Education and Research Association

The conference will highlight on research topics that cover every discipline in all fields of social science,economics and management.

52. World Economic Forum Annual Meeting 2015

January21,2015

Davos-Klosters,Switzerland

53. Launch of the World Bank Global Economic Prospects Report 2015

January 21,2015

Warsaw,Poland

54. World Economic Forum Annual Meeting

January 21 – 24,2015

Davos-Klosters,Switzerland

Hosted By:World Economic Forum

The Annual Meeting in Davos-Klosters remains the foremost creative force for engaging the world's top leaders in collaborative activities focused on shaping the global, regional and industry agendas.

55. "World Development Report(WDR)2015:Mind,Society,and Behavior"

February 4,2015

Tokyo

56. Annual 2015 session of the Parliamentary Conference on the WTO

February16,2015

Geneva,Switzerland

57. Annual Meeting 2015:The New Global Context

February 25 ,2015

At the Annual Meeting 2015 , global leaders from government , business and civil society took advantage of the Forum's unique platform to address profound political , economic , social and technological transformations that are affecting the world.

58. High-level conference : Managing Capital Flows : Lessons from Emerging Markets for Frontier Economies?

March 2 ,2015

Mauritius

59. International Trade and Investment

March 20 – 21 ,2015

Hosted By : Robert Feenstra of the University of California

60. International Finance and Macroeconomics

March 27 ,2015

Hosted By : Gita Gopinath and Laura Alfaro of Harvard University.

61. 30th Annual Conference on Macroeconomics

April 17 – 18 ,2015

Hosted By : Martin Eichenbaum of Northwestern University and Jonathan Parker of MIT.

62. World Economic Forum on East Asia

April 19 – 21 ,2015

Jakarta , Indonesia

Hosted By : World Economic Forum

East Asia continues to be the world's economically fastest-growing region and its most populous. Projected to maintain an average growth rate above 7% in 2015 , it boasts some of the world's most prosperous economies such as Australia , China , Japan , Singapore and South Korea.

63. 3rd International Symposium on Business and Social Science

April 22 – 24 ,2015

Chengdu , China

Hosted By : Higher Education Forum

The ISBASS Conference aims to provide a communication platform for scholars , professionals , academics and graduate students not only to present their recent and latest researches but also share their thoughts and discuss the future development in the field of business and social science, and to discuss the future developments and possible challenges faced.

64. The 2015 International Symposium on Business and Social Science

April 23 – 25, 2015

Shanghai, China

Hosted By: Asia-Pacific Education & Research Association

The ISBASS Conference aims to provide a communication platform for scholars, professionals, academics and graduate students not only to present their recent and latest researches but also share their thoughts.

65. Investor Sophistication and Capital Income Inequality

May 6, 2015

Hosted By: World Bank

66. World Economic Forum on Latin America

May 6 – 8, 2015

Riviera Maya, Mexi

Hosted By: World Economic Forum

67. Impact Evaluation in Trade & Competitiveness

May 11 – 14, 2015

Istanbul, Turkey

68. Harnessing Digital Trade for Competitiveness and Development

May 19, 2015

Washington, DC

69. Taste Heterogeneity, Trade Costs, and Global Market Outcomes in the Automobile Industry

May 21, 2015

Hosted By: World Economic Forum

70. World Economic Forum on the Middle East and North Africa

May 21 – 23, 2015

Dead Sea, Jordan

Hosted By: World Economic Forum

At a decisive time for the region and with the full support and presence of Their

Majesties King Abdullah II and Queen Rania Al Abdullah, the World Economic Forum is convening over 800 key leaders from government, business and civil society to support a comprehensive and forward-looking vision for prosperity and peace.

71. World Economic Forum on Africa

June 3 – 5, 2015

Cape Town, South Africa

Hosted By: World Economic Forum

Over the past decade and a half, Africa has demonstrated a remarkable economic turnaround, growing two to three percentage points faster than global GDP. Regional growth is projected to remain stable above 5% in 2015, buoyed by rising foreign direct investment flows, particularly into the natural resources sector; increased public invest-ment in infrastructure; and higher agricultural production.

72. Cowles Summer Conferences

June 8 – 12, 2015

Topic: Conference on Economics

New Perspectives on Macroeconomics, Trade, and Developmnet

Structural Empirical Microeconomic Models

Conference on Economic Theory

Hosted By: Lorenzo Caliendo and Francisco(Paco)Buera

73. Engaging the African Diaspora: Partnering for Long-term Trade, Investment and Skills for Workforce Development in Africa

June 10, 2015

Washington DC

Hosted By: World Bank

74. New Perspectives in Macroeconomics, Development and International? Trade

June 10 – 11, 2015

Organizers: Michael Peters and Richard Rogerson

75. Macro, Trade, and Finance Seminar

June 18, 2015

Andrew Atkeson will share the results of recent research.

76. East Asian Seminar on Economics

June 18 – 19, 2015

Hosted By: Takatoshi Ito, University of Tokyo, and Andrew K. Rose, University of California, Berkeley.

77. International Seminar on Macroeconomics

June 26 – 17, 2015

Hosted By: Jeffrey Frankel of Harvard University, Francesco Giavazzi of Bocconi University, Hélène Rey of London Business School, and Kenneth West, University of Wisconsin.

78. Fifth Global Review of Aid for Trade

June 30 – July 02, 2015

Geneva, Switzerland

79. 2015 International Conference on Social Sciences and Business

June 27 – 29, 2015

Bangkok, Thailand

Hosted By: Asia-Pacific Education & Research Association

The ICSSB Conference aims to provide a communication platform for scholars, professionals, academics and graduate students not only to present their recent and latest researches but also share their thoughts and discuss the future development in the field of Business, Accounting, Finance, Economics.

80. 5th Global Review on Aid for Trade – Formal Meeting

July 1, 2015

Geneva, Switzerland

81. 5th Annual Conference on Global Economics, Business, and Finance

July 6 – 8, 2015

Hong Kong, Hong Kong

Hosted By: Asia-Pacific Education & Research Association

The main objective of this conference is to provide a platform for engineers, academicians, scientists, industrial professionals and researchers from over the world to present the result of their research activities in the field of Economics, Business, Finance, and Management.

82. Economic Fluctuations and Growth

July 11, 2015

Hosted By：Giovanni Violante of New York University and Ivan Werning of MIT.

83. IMF Launches New Public Investment Management Assessment，Addis Ababa，Ethiopia

July 15，2015

84. The 4th International Symposium on Business and Social Sciences

July 20，2015

Hokkaido，Japan

85. 2015 International Business Research，Economics，Finance and MIS Conference

July 20 – 22，2015

Hokkaido，Japan

Hosted By：Asia-Pacific Education & Research Association

The BREFM offers a great opportunity to bring together professors，researchers and scholars around the globe a great platform to deliver the latest innovative research result and the most recent development and trends in business field.

86. 2015 International Academic Conference on Social Sciences and Management

July 29 – 31，2015

Okinawa，Japan

2015 International Academic Conference on Social Sciences and Management (IACSSM 2015)aims to provide a forum for researchers，practitioners，and professionals from the industry，academia and government to discourse on research and development，professional practice in social sceinces and management.

87. Annual Meeting of the New Champions

September 9 – 11，2015

Dalian，China

Hosted By：World Economic Forum

Established in 2007 as the foremost global gathering on science，technology and innovation，the Annual Meeting of the New Champions convenes the next generation of fast-growing enterprises shaping the future of business and society，and leaders from major multinationals as well as government，media，academia and civil society.

88. Sierra Leone Diaspora Investment and Trade Stakeholder Forum

September 30，2015

Washington DC

89. Sustainable Asia Conference 2015

September 19,2015

Gansu,China

Hosted By:Asian business BBS,Lan Zhou University of Finance and Economics.

90. The Global Competitiveness Report 2015

September 22,2015

The Global Competitiveness Report 2015 – 2016 assesses the competitiveness land-scape of 140 economies,providing insight into the drivers of their productivity and prosperity. The Report series remains the most comprehensive assessment of national competitiveness worldwide.

91. International Trade,Income Distribution and Welfare

October 22,2015

Hosted By:World Economic Forum

92. Summit on the Global Agenda

October 25 – 27,2015

Abu Dhabi,United Arab Emirates

Hosted By:World Economic Forum

The Summit on the Global Agenda,established as a unique partnership between the World Economic Forum and the United Arab Emirates since 2008,is the annual gathering of the Network of Global Agenda Councils.

93. World Trade Report 2015

October 26,2015

The WTO released World Trade Report 2015.

94. What Companies Want from the World Trading System

October 26,2015

The post – war world has seen a remarkable advance in prosperity and trade,while private enterprise has flourished as never before. However,with technology and the globalization of production the demands on the trading system for deeper and more comprehensive disciplines have increased greatly,and the system is evolving far too slowly. For reasons of efficiency and equity,the consequences of this troubling situation for smaller enterprises is of special concern.

95. The scale and speed of urbanization in China

October 29,2015

Southampton,Britain

The scale and speed of urbanization in China is unprecedented in the history of human development. It is not only a major driver of the country's extraordinary economic growth but also for reshaping both the physical environment and the cultural fabric of China.

96. How Important are Terms of Trade Shocks?

October 29,2015

Hosted By:World Economic Forum

97. International Finance and Macroeconomics

October 30,2015

Hosted By:Ariel Burstein of University of California,Los Angeles,and Charles Engel of University of Wisconsin.

98. WTO Chairs Programme Annual Conference 2015

November 2,2015

Geneva,Switzerland

99. Alternative Investments 2020:The Future of Alternative Investments

November 2,2015

The goal of this report is to provide readers in the global investment and financial services industries with a perspective on how the industry may evolve over the coming decade and which business and investment models successful alternative investors and capital providers will employ to navigate the changing ecosystem.

100. Trade and Labor Market Dynamics

November 19,2015

Hosted By:World Economic Forum

101. 18th china-asean(10 + 1)leaders' meeting

November 21,2015

Kuala Lumpur,Malaysia

102. 20th anniversary of the WTO

November 29,2015

103. Lessons from the Crisis for Macroeconomics

December 4,2015

Hosted By:NBER

104. World Bank Group TICAD Seminar Series "Investment in Nutrition:Initiatives in Africa"

December 4,2015

Tokyo

105. International Trade and Investment

December 4 – 5,2015

Hosted By:Robert Feenstra of the University of California, Davis, Ana Fernandes and Martha Pierola, World Bank; Peter Klenow, Stanford University and NBER; Sergii Meleshchuk, University of California, Berkeley, and Andrés Rodríguez-Clare, University of California, Berkeley and NBER.

106. 2016 International Business Research, Economics, Finance and MIS Conference

December 31,2015

Hokkaido, Japan

Hosted By:Higher Education Forum

107. 2015 Asia-Pacific Symposium on Social Science and Management

December 31,2015

Singapore

Hosted By:Higher Education Forum

2015 Asia-Pacific Symposium on Social Science and Management(APCSSM) is to offer scholars, professionals, academics and graduate students to present, share, and discuss their studies from various perspectives in the aspects of social sciences, including: Business, Communication, Culture, Economics, Education, Finance, Law, Management, Politics, Psychology, Society and so forth.

第五章

世界经济学科 2014—2015 年文献索引

第一节　中文期刊索引

[1]安树伟."一带一路"对我国区域经济发展的影响及格局重塑[J].经济问题,2015(4):1-4.

[2]白玫.中国对外直接投资对产业结构调整影响研究[J].国际贸易,2014(2):38-43.

[3]白洁.企业异质性与服务贸易保护水平的决定——基于中国数据的实证检验[J].经济经纬,2015,第32卷(2):62-67.

[4]白云真."一带一路"倡议与中国对外援助转型[J].世界经济与政治,2015(11):53-73.

[5]包群,叶宁华,邵敏.出口学习、异质性匹配与企业生产率的动态变化[J].世界经济,2014(4):26-48.

[6]蔡宏波,刘杜若,张明志.外商直接投资与服务业工资差距——基于中国城镇个人与行业匹配数据的实证分析[J].南开经济研究,2015(4):109-120.

[7]蔡濛萌,薛福根.贸易开放、产业结构调整与环境质量——来自省级面板数据的经验研究[J].湖北民族学院学报(哲学社会科学版),2015,第33卷(5):34-39.

[8]蔡松锋,张亚雄.跨大西洋贸易与投资伙伴协议(TTIP)对金砖国家经济影响分析——基于含全球价值链模块的动态GTAP模型[J].世界经济研究,2015(8):79-89.

[9]岑丽君.中国在全球生产网络中的分工与贸易地位——基于 TiVA 数据与 GVC 指数的研究[J].国际贸易问题,2015(1):3-14.

[10]曾福生,郭珍,高鸣.中国农业基础设施投资效率及其收敛性分析——基于资源约束视角下的实证研究[J].管理世界,2014(8):173-174.

[11]曾国彪,姜凌.贸易开放、地区收入差距与贫困:基于 CHNS 数据的经验研究[J].国际贸易问题,2014(3):72-85.

[12]陈虹,杨成玉."一带一路"国家战略的国际经济效应研究——基于 CGE 模型的分析[J].国际贸易问题,2015(10):4-13.

[13]陈俭,布娲鹣·阿布拉,陈彤.中国与中亚五国农产品贸易模式研究[J].国际贸易问题,2014(4):78-89.

[14]陈林,罗莉娅.中国外资准入壁垒的政策效应研究——兼议上海自由贸易区改革的政策红利[J].经济研究,2014,卷缺失(4):104-115.

[15]陈雯,李强.全球价值链分工下我国出口规模的透视分析——基于增加值贸易核算方法[J].财贸经济,2014(7):107-115.

[16]陈曦."市场换技术"视野中的我国对外开放技术安全问题分析[J].湖北行政学院学报,2015(2):65-69.

[17]陈怀超,范建红.制度距离、中国跨国公司进入战略与国际化绩效:基于组织合法性视角[J].南开经济研究,2014(2):99-117.

[18]陈继勇,吴颂.TPP 促进东亚经济再平衡的不确定性及中国的对策[J].武汉大学学报,2014,第 67 卷(6):5-11.

[19]陈景华.中国 OFDI 来源的区域差异分解与影响因素——基于 2003—2011 年省际面板数据的实证研究[J].数量经济技术经济研究,2014(7):21-37.

[20]陈景华.企业异质性视角下中国服务贸易出口的影响因素——基于服务业行业面板数据的实证检验[J].世界经济研究,2014(11):55-62.

[21]陈俊聪,黄繁华.对外直接投资与贸易结构优化[J].国际贸易问题,2014(3):113-122.

[22]陈丽丽.国际投资模式与中国"走出去"企业绩效异质性:基于 KS 检验及分位数估计[J].国际贸易问题,2015(7):118-127.

[23]陈宁.我国国际贸易发展模式与路径分析[J].求索,2015(2):76-80.

[24]陈淑梅,倪菊华.中国加入"区域全面经济伙伴关系"的经济效应——基于 GTAP 模型的模拟分析[J].亚太经济,2014(2):125-133.

[25]陈涛涛,陈晓.吸引外资对对外投资能力的影响机制——机制分析框架

的初步构建[J].国际经济合作,2015(5):4-11.

[26]陈文府.中国制造业参与全球价值链的竞争力——基于世界投入产出表的国际比较研究[J].产业经济研究,2015(5):1-12.

[27]陈勇兵,陈小鸿,曹亮,等.中国进口需求弹性的估算[J].世界经济,2014(2):28-49.

[28]陈勇兵,王晓伟,谭桑.出口持续时间会促进新市场开拓吗——来自中国微观产品层面的证据[J].财贸经济,2014(6):79-90.

[29]陈兆源,田野,韩冬临.双边投资协定中争端解决机制的形式选择——基于 1982—2013 年中国签订双边投资协定的定量研究[J].世界经济与政治,2015(3):122-149.

[30]陈志阳.多双边贸易协定中的国际核心劳工标准分析[J].国际贸易问题,2014(2):56-64.

[31]程宝栋,秦光远,宋维明."一带一路"战略背景下中国林产品贸易发展与转型[J].国际贸易,2015(3):22-25.

[32]程大中.中国参与全球价值链分工的程度及演变趋势——基于跨国投入—产出分析[J].经济研究,2015(9):4-17.

[33]程大中.中国增加值贸易隐含的要素流向扭曲程度分析[J].经济研究,2014(9):105-120.

[34]程俊杰.中国转型时期产业政策与产能过剩——基于制造业面板数据的实证研究[J].财经研究,2015,第 41 卷(8):131-144.

[35]程新章.发展中国家支持全球价值链升级的政策体系——基于演化经济学的视角[J].社会科学,2015(4):42-54.

[36]程云洁."丝绸之路经济带"建设给我国对外贸易带来的新机遇与挑战[J].经济纵横,2014(6):92-96.

[37]储殷,高远.中国"一带一路"战略定位的三个问题[J].国际经济评论,2015(2):90-100.

[38]崔凡,邓兴华.异质性企业贸易理论的发展综述[J].世界经济,2014(6):138-160.

[39]代法涛.跨越"中等收入陷阱"理论、经验和对策——基于 44 个国家的跨国实证分析[J].财经研究,2014,第 40 卷(2):54-66.

[40]戴觅,茅锐.产业异质性、产业结构与中国省际经济收敛[J].管理世界,2015(6):34-48.

[41]戴觅,茅锐. 外需冲击、企业出口与内销:金融危机时期的经验证据[J].世界经济,2015(1):81-104.

[42]戴觅,余淼杰,Maitra Madhura. 中国出口企业生产率之谜:加工贸易的作用[J].经济学(季刊),2014,第13卷(2):675-698.

[43]戴翔,金碚. 产品内分工、制度质量与出口技术复杂度[J].经济研究,2014(7):4-18.

[44]戴翔. 中国制造业国际竞争力——基于贸易附加值的测算[J].中国工业经济,2015(1):78-88.

[45]邓海清. 兵马未动,粮草先行:"一带一路"与金融基础设施建设[J].国际经济评论,2015(4):45-52.

[46]邓世专. 中国在全球价值链中的作用——基于零部件产品视角[J].经济问题,2015(11):83-89.

[47]邓晓虹,黄满盈. 基于扩展引力模型的中国双边金融服务贸易出口潜力研究[J].财经研究,2014,第40卷(6):48-59.

[48]邓晓兰,鄢哲明,武永义. 碳排放与经济发展服从倒U型曲线关系吗——对环境库兹涅茨曲线假说的重新解读[J].财贸经济,2014(2):19-29.

[49]邓新明,许洋. 双边投资协定对中国对外直接投资的影响——基于制度环境门槛效应的分析[J].世界经济研究,2015(3):47-56.

[50]刁莉,邰婷婷. 我国应在RCEP的区域服务贸易一体化发展中发挥更积极作用[J].经济纵横,2015(8):96-100.

[51]丁守海,陈秀兰,许珊. 服务业能长期促进中国就业增长吗? [J].财贸经济,2014(8):127-137.

[52]丁守海,熊宇,许珊. 产业内贸易对中国技能工资差距的影响[J].经济理论与经济管理,2014(10):60-76.

[53]东艳,张琳. 美国区域贸易投资协定框架下的竞争中立原则分析[J].当代亚太,2014(6):117-131.

[54]东艳. 全球贸易规则的发展趋势与中国的机遇[J].国际经济评论,2014(1):45-65.

[55]董锁成,黄永斌,李泽红,等. 丝绸之路经济带经济发展格局与区域经济一体化模式[J].资源科学,2014,第36卷(12):2452-2459.

[56]董有德,孟醒. OFDI、逆向技术溢出与国内企业创新能力——基于我国分价值链数据的检验[J].国际贸易问题,2014(9):120-129.

[57]杜江,宋跃刚.制度距离、要素禀赋与我国 OFDI 区位选择偏好——基于动态面板数据模型的实证研究[J].世界经济研究,2014(12):47-53.

[58]杜威剑,李梦洁.目的国市场收入分配与出口产品质量——基于中国企业层面的实证检验[J].当代财经,2015(10):89-96.

[59]杜威剑,李梦洁.出口失败经历对企业是"长痛"还是"短痛"?[J].财经论丛,2015(8):3-10.

[60]杜秀红."一带一路"背景下的中印货物贸易结构分析:2002—2014 年[J].审计与经济研究,2015(6):106-112.

[61]杜运苏.出口技术复杂度影响我国经济增长的实证研究——基于不同贸易方式和企业性质[J].国际贸易问题,2014(9):3-12.

[62]樊海潮,郭光远.出口价格、出口质量与生产率间的关系:中国的证据[J].世界经济,2015(2):58-85.

[63]樊茂清,黄薇.基于全球价值链分解的中国贸易产业结构演进研究[J].世界经济,2014(2):50-70.

[64]樊秀峰,程文先.中国制造业出口附加值估算与影响机制分析[J].中国工业经济,2015(6):81-93.

[65]范建亭,汪立.出口导向、技术类型与跨国公司内部技术转移——基于在华日资企业的实证分析[J].财经研究,2015,第 41 卷(10):83-95.

[66]范子英,田彬彬.出口退税政策与中国加工贸易的发展[J].世界经济,2014(4):49-68.

[67]冯雷.进口贸易是通向贸易强国的关键——转变外贸发展方式的战略研究[J].国际贸易,2014(12):51-56.

[68]冯根福,毛毅.外资进入对中国工业行业价格变动的影响机理及其效应[J].中国工业经济,2015(12):36-50.

[69]冯维江.丝绸之路经济带战略的国际政治经济学分析[J].当代亚太,2014(6):73-98.

[70]冯维江.试析美欧日自贸区战略及对中国的启示[J].亚太经济,2015(1):9-15.

[71]冯旭南.中国投资者具有信息获取能力吗?——来自"业绩预告"效应的证据[J].经济学(季刊),2014,第 13 卷(3):1065-1090.

[72]符磊,强永昌.OFDI 逆向技术溢出产生的内生机制:理论与启示[J].投资研究,2014,第 33 卷(7):94-109.

[73]付文林,赵永辉. 价值链分工、劳动力市场分割与国民收入分配结构[J]. 财经研究,2014,第 40 卷(1):50-61.

[74]傅缨捷,丁一兵. 中间品进口与经济结构转型[J]. 世界经济研究,2014(4):51-59.

[75]刚翠翠,任保平. 丝绸之路经济带背景的中亚五国发展模式[J]. 改革,2015(1):109-118.

[76]高越,任永磊,冯志艳. 贸易便利化与 FDI 对中国出口增长三元边际的影响[J]. 经济经纬,2014,第 31 卷(6):46-51.

[77]高帆. 中美两种经济"新常态"基本特征及交互作用[J]. 学术月刊,2015,第 47 卷(11):35-48.

[78]高凌云,屈小博,贾鹏. 中国工业企业规模与生产率的异质性[J]. 世界经济,2014(6):113-137.

[79]高志刚,张燕. 中巴经济走廊建设中双边贸易潜力及效率研究——基于随机前沿引力模型分析[J]. 财经科学,2015(11):101-110.

[80]葛振宇,湛泳. 中国对美国直接投资的影响因素研究[J]. 亚太经济,2015(2):85-91.

[81]宫占奎. APEC 与 FTAAP 平行推进问题研究[J]. 南开学报(哲学社会科学版),2015(2):15-26.

[82]郭晶,刘菲菲. 中国服务业国际竞争力的重新估算——基于贸易增加值视角的研究[J]. 世界经济研究,2015(2):52-61.

[83]郭晴,帅传敏,帅竞. 碳关税对世界经济和农产品贸易的影响研究[J]. 数量经济技术经济研究,2014(10):97-110.

[84]韩冰. 准入前国民待遇与负面清单模式:中美 BIT 对中国外资管理体制的影响[J]. 国际经济评论,2014(6):101-111.

[85]韩会朝,徐康宁. 中国产品出口"质量门槛"假说及其检验[J]. 中国工业经济,2014(4):58-70.

[86]韩先锋,惠宁,宋文飞. 贸易自由化影响了研发创新效率吗?[J]. 财经研究,2015,第 41 卷(2):15-26.

[87]韩永辉,罗晓斐,邹建华. 中国与西亚地区贸易合作的竞争性和互补性研究——以"一带一路"战略为背景[J]. 世界经济研究,2015(3):89-99.

[88]韩永辉,邹建华."一带一路"背景下的中国与西亚国家贸易合作现状和前景展望[J]. 国际贸易,2014(8):21-28.

［89］郝硕博,倪霓. 创新异质性、公共教育支出结构与经济增长［J］. 财贸经济,2014(7):37-49.

［90］何力. 多哈回合早期收获与《贸易便利化协定》［J］. 上海对外经贸大学学报,2014,第 21 卷(2):24-32.

［91］何林,任媛. 我国与中亚五国双边贸易成本的测度与分析［J］. 西安财经学院学报,2015,第 28 卷(6):78-84.

［92］何兴强,欧燕,史卫,等. FDI 技术溢出与中国吸收能力门槛研究［J］. 世界经济,2014(10):52-76.

［93］贺艳. 建设"丝绸之路经济带"自由贸易协定问题研究［J］. 国际经贸探索,2015,第 31 卷(6):87-101.

［94］洪世勤,刘厚俊. 中国制造业出口技术结构的测度及影响因素研究［J］. 数量经济技术经济研究,2015(3):77-93.

［95］胡兵,邓富华. 腐败距离与中国对外直接投资——制度观和行为学的整合视角［J］. 财贸经济,2014(4):82-92.

［96］胡翠,许召元,符大海. 中国出口"双重集聚"及其形成机制——基于出口溢出效应的视角［J］. 财贸经济,2015(1):117-131.

［97］胡安俊,孙久文. 中国制造业转移的机制、次序与空间模式［J］. 经济学(季刊),2014,第 13 卷(4):1533-1556.

［98］胡超. 中国—东盟自贸区进口通关时间的贸易效应及比较研究——基于不同时间密集型农产品的实证［J］. 国际贸易问题,2014(8):58-67.

［99］胡昭玲,张咏华. 中国制造业国际分工地位研究——基于增加值贸易的视角［J］. 南开学报(哲学社会科学版),2015(3):149-160.

［100］胡宗彪. 企业异质性、贸易成本与服务业生产率［J］. 数量经济技术经济研究,2014(7):68-84.

［101］黄灿. 垂直专业化贸易对我国就业结构的影响——基于省际面板数据的分析［J］. 南开经济研究,2014(4):64-77.

［102］黄建忠,占芬. 区域服务贸易协定的收敛研究——对"绊脚石"与"垫脚石"问题的一个观察［J］. 厦门大学学报(哲学社会科学版),2014(1):127-137.

［103］黄建忠,占芬. 区域服务贸易协定中的"GATS-"条款研究［J］. 国际商务研究,2015,第 36 卷(201):18-32.

［104］黄梅波,朱丹丹. 国际发展援助的出口多样化促进效应分析——基于

66 个受援国面板数据的实证研究[J].财贸经济,2015(2):97-108.

[105]黄梅波,朱丹丹."促贸援助"的贸易成本削减效应研究——基于 63 个受援国面板数据的实证研究[J].厦门大学学报(哲学社会科学版),2014(1):138-148.

[106]黄庆波,戴庆玲,李焱.中韩两国工业制成品产业内贸易水平的测度及影响因素研究[J].国际贸易问题,2014(1):92-98.

[107]黄伟新,龚新蜀.丝绸之路经济带国际物流绩效对中国机电产品出口影响的实证分析[J].国际贸易问题,2014(10):56-66.

[108]黄卫平.新丝绸之路经济带与中欧经贸格局新发展——兼论跨亚欧高铁的战略价值[J].中国流通经济,2015(1):84-90.

[109]黄卫平,黄都.中国如何因应亚太经贸格局新变化[J].学术前沿,2015(12):19-29.

[110]黄先海,胡馨月,刘毅群.产品创新、工艺创新与我国企业出口倾向研究[J].经济学家,2015(4):37-47.

[111]黄阳华.德国"工业 4.0"计划及其对我国产业创新的启示[J].经济社会体制比较,2015(2):1-10.

[112]黄益平.中国经济外交新战略下的"一带一路"[J].国际经济评论,2015(1):48-54.

[113]姬超.投资效率与全要素生产率的变化趋势考察——基于中国经济特区的差异比较分析[J].财贸经济,2014(3):91-99.

[114]计志英,毛杰,赖小锋.FDI 规模对我国环境污染的影响效应研究——基于 30 个省级面板数据模型的实证检验[J].世界经济研究,2015(3):56-65.

[115]冀相豹.中国对外直接投资影响因素分析——基于制度的视角[J].国际贸易问题,2014(9):98-108.

[116]贾利军,仝晓婷.碳关税的演化博弈分析[J].学术交流,2014(11):101-105.

[117]贾妮莎,韩永辉,邹建华.中国双向 FDI 的产业结构升级效应:理论机制与实证检验[J].国际贸易问题,2014(11):109-120.

[118]江希,刘似臣.中国制造业出口增加值及影响因素的实证研究——以中美贸易为例[J].国际贸易问题,2014(11):89-98.

[119]蒋姮."一带一路"地缘政治风险的评估与管理[J].国际贸易,2015(8):21-24.

[120]蒋为.环境规制是否影响了中国制造业企业研发创新——基于微观数据的实证研究[J].财经研究,2015,第 41 卷(2):76 - 87.

[121]蒋冠法,蒋殿春.中国工业企业对外直接投资与企业生产率进步[J].世界经济,2014(9):53 - 76.

[122]蒋冠宏,蒋殿春.中国企业对外直接投资的"出口效应"[J].经济研究,2014(5):160 - 173.

[123]蒋灵多,陈勇兵.出口企业的产品异质性与出口持续时间[J].世界经济,2015(7):3 - 26.

[124]金缀桥,杨逢珉.中韩双边贸易现状及潜力的实证研究[J].世界经济研究,2015(1):81 - 91.

[125]荆林波,袁平红.中国(上海)自由贸易试验区发展评价[J].国际经济评论,2015(5):78 - 90.

[126]鞠建东,余心玎.全球价值链上的中国角色——基于中国行业上游度和海关数据的研究[J].南开经济研究,2014(3):39 - 52.

[127]阚大学,吕连菊.中国服务贸易的本地市场效应研究——基于中国与31 个国家(地区)的双边贸易面板数据[J].财经研究,2014,第 40 卷(10):71 - 83.

[128]阚大学,吕连菊.对外贸易、地区腐败与环境污染——基于省级动态面板数据的实证研究[J].世界经济研究,2015(1):120 - 127.

[129]课题组."一带一路"战略实施与国际金融支持战略构想[J].国际贸易,2015(4):35 - 44.

[130]孔庆峰,董虹蔚."一带一路"国家的贸易便利化水平测算与贸易潜力研究[J].国际贸易问题,2015(12):158 - 168.

[131]孔庆峰,董虹蔚.中国加入 GPA 谈判的困境与对策——一个博弈论的经济分析[J].东岳论丛,2015,第 36 卷(9):165 - 170.

[132]赖琳慧,冯淇,郑方辉.基于宏微观视角的出口消费品质量评价实证研究——以 2012 年度广东为例[J].宏观质量研究,2014(3):67 - 74.

[133]雷昭明.东亚生产网络内分工格局的稳定性——基于贸易关系持续时间的分析[J].江西社会科学,2015(7):66 - 71.

[134]黎峰.全球价值链分工下的出口产品结构及核算——基于增加值的视角[J].南开经济研究,2015(4):67 - 79.

[135]黎峰.全球价值链下的国际分工地位:内涵及影响因素[J].国际经贸

探索,2015,第 31 卷(9):31 – 42.

[136]李静,陈思. 出口企业比非出口企业具有更高的环境友好度吗——基于微观企业数据的检验[J]. 财贸经济,2014(10):94 – 104.

[137]李娟,万璐. 贸易自由化加剧就业市场波动了吗? ——基于劳动需求弹性角度的实证检验[J]. 世界经济研究,2104(6):35 – 43.

[138]李军,刘海云. 生产率异质性还是多重异质性——中国出口企业竞争力来源的实证研究[J]. 南方经济,2015(3):1 – 23.

[139]李磊,包群. 融资约束制约了中国工业企业的对外直接投资吗? [J]. 财经研究,2015,第 41 卷(6):120 – 131.

[140]李平,孟寒,黎艳. 双边投资协定对中国对外直接投资的实证分析——基于制度距离的视角[J]. 世界经济研究,2014(12):53 – 60.

[141]李春顶. 中国企业"出口—生产率悖论"研究综述[J]. 世界经济,2015(5):148 – 175.

[142]李春顶,东艳. 2013 年国际贸易国外学术研究前沿[J]. 经济学,2015:78 – 90.

[143]李繁荣,韩克勇. 马克思国际贸易思想的生态蕴含及其现实意义[J]. 福建论坛·人文社会科学版,2014(12):5 – 12.

[144]李方静. 出口、出口目的地与工资水平——来自中国制造业企业微观层面证据[J]. 国际经贸探索,2014,第 30 卷(8):4 – 17.

[145]李宏兵,赵春明. 出口开放、市场邻近与异质性企业工资差距——基于中国工业企业数据的实证研究[J]. 国际贸易问题,2015(1):36 – 46.

[146]李宏兵,赵春明,文磊,等. 市场潜能促进了制造业女性就业吗? ——基于中国工业企业数据的实证分析[J]. 财经研究,2014,第 40 卷(3):52 – 62.

[147]李洪亚. R-D、企业规模与成长关系研究——基于中国制造业企业数据:2005—2007[J]. 世界经济文汇,2014(3):98 – 120.

[148]李怀建,沈坤荣. 出口产品质量的影响因素分析——基于跨国面板数据的检验[J]. 产业经济研究,2015(6):62 – 72.

[149]李计广,盖新哲. 基于全球生产网络视角的中美经济脱钩趋势分析[J]. 人民大学学报,2014(4):50 – 58.

[150]李计广,高宽. 中国自新兴市场国家进口潜力分析:基于引力模型[J]. 亚太经济,2014(5):60 – 64.

[151]李金昌,项莹. 中国制造业出口增值份额及其国别(地区)来源——基

于 SNA – 08 框架下《世界投入产出表》的测度与分析[J].中国工业经济,2014(8):84 – 96.

[152]李坤望,蒋为,宋立刚.中国出口产品品质变动之谜:基于市场进入的微观解释[J].中国社会科学,2014(3):80 – 104.

[153]李坤望,邵文波,王永进.信息化密度、信息基础设施与企业出口绩效——基于企业异质性的理论与实证分析[J].管理世界,2015(4):52 – 65.

[154]李丽.低碳经济对国际贸易规则的影响及中国的对策[J].财贸经济,2014(9):114 – 123.

[155]李墨丝.国际贸易体制的新变革与中国对外文化贸易的应对策略[J].福建论坛·人文社会科学版,2015(8):62 – 68.

[156]李清如,蒋业恒,董鹂馥.贸易自由化对行业内工资不平等的影响——来自中国制造业的证据[J].财贸经济,2014(2):85 – 95.

[157]李秋萍,李长健,肖小勇.产业链视角下农产品价格溢出效应研究——基于三元 VAR-BEKK – GARCH(1,1)模型[J].财贸经济,2014(10):125 – 136.

[158]李殊琦,赵仲匡,海闻.贸易企业"用脚投票"?——基于区域金融发展水平不均衡的视角[J].管理世界,2014(7):32 – 40.

[159]李未无,冯淑敏.金融危机期间中国对美国出口下跌分解研究[J].国际经贸探索,2014,第 30 卷(11):81 – 92.

[160]李文韬.中国参与 APEC 互联互通合作应对战略研究[J].南开学报(哲学社会科学版),2014(6):105 – 116.

[161]李向阳.论海上丝绸之路的多元化合作机制[J].世界经济与政治,2014(11):4 – 18.

[162]李向阳.构建"一带一路"需要优先处理的关系[J].国际经济评论,2015(1):54 – 64.

[163]李小平,王树柏,周记顺.碳生产率变动与出口复杂度演进:1992—2009 年[J].数量经济技术经济研究,2014(9):22 – 39.

[164]李小平,周记顺,卢现祥,等.出口的"质"影响了出口的"量"吗?[J].经济研究,2015(8):114 – 129.

[165]李小平,周记顺,王树柏.中国制造业出口复杂度的提升和制造业增长[J].世界经济,2015(2):31 – 57.

[166]李晓."一带一路"战略实施中的"印度困局"——中国企业投资印度的困境与对策[J].国际经济评论,2015(5):19 – 43.

[167]李晓峰,姚传高. 中印服务贸易竞争优势比较及影响因素的实证研究[J].学术研究,2014(9):79-88.

[168]李勇辉,袁旭宏. 企业非技术创新的价值实现机理与驱动机制——基于价值链的视角[J].财经研究,2014,第40卷(9):26-37.

[169]李云娥. 对外开放必然带来经济增长吗? ——基于二元经济转换的视角[J].南开经济研究,2014(1):59-73.

[170]李真. 进口真实碳福利视角下的中国贸易碳减排研究——基于非竞争型投入产出模型[J].中国工业经济,2014(12):18-30.

[171]梁颖. 打造中国—东盟自由贸易区升级版的路径与策略[J].亚太经济,2014(1):104-107.

[172]梁中华,余淼杰. 贸易自由化与中国劳动需求弹性:基于制造业企业数据的实证分析[J].南方经济,2014(10):1-12.

[173]廖显春,夏恩龙. 为什么中国会对FDI具有吸引力? ——基于环境规制与腐败程度视角[J].世界经济研究,2015(1):112-120.

[174]林江,范芹. 广东自贸区:建设背景与运行基础[J].广东社会科学,2015(3):21-27.

[175]林民旺. 印度对"一带一路"的认知及中国的政策选择[J].世界经济与政治,2015(5):42-59.

[176]林莎,雷井生. 贸易成本对跨国并购影响的实证性分析[J].湖南商学院学报(双月刊),2015,第22卷(3):19-26.

[177]林伯强,刘泓汛. 对外贸易是否有利于提高能源环境效率——以中国工业行业为例[J].经济研究,2015(9):127-141.

[178]林发彬. 全球价值链下中国提高出口依存度与其经济风险的防范研究[J].现代经济探讨,2015(10):35-39.

[179]林桂军,何武. 中国装备制造业在全球价值链的地位及升级趋势[J].国际贸易问题,2015(4):3-15.

[180]林珏. 区域自由贸易协定"负面清单"的国际比较研究[J].四川大学学报(哲学社会科学版),2015(5):120-129.

[181]林立国,楼国强. 外资企业环境绩效的探讨——以上海市为例[J].经济学(季刊),2014,第13卷(2):515-536.

[182]刘阿明. 亚太自由贸易区构建路径的比较分析——兼论中国的战略选择[J].世界经济与政治论坛,2015(2):41-57.

[183]刘慧,綦建红．我国工业企业在新产品出口中的次序选择——以对美国市场出口为例[J].财经研究,2014,第 40 卷(12):128 - 140.

[184]刘锦,王学军．寻租腐败与中国企业出口:促进还是抑制[J].国际经贸探索,2015,第 31 卷(3):42 - 53.

[185]刘锦,王学军．中国产品出口"质量门槛"假说及其检验[J].中国工业经济,2014(4):58 - 70.

[186]刘磊,张猛．贸易成本、垂直专业化与制造业产业集聚:基于中美数据的实证分析[J].世界经济研究,2014(4):58 - 65.

[187]刘琳．中国参与全球价值链的测度与分析——基于附加值贸易的考察[J].世界经济研究,2015(6):71 - 84.

[188]刘茜．经济结构与贸易失衡之间关系的理论辨析——西方经典贸易理论与马克思主义理论的比较[J].政治经济学评论,2014,第 5 卷(1):126 - 138.

[189]刘倩,粘书婷,王遥．国际气候资金机制的最新进展及中国对策[J].中国人口资源与环境,2015,第 25 卷(10):30 - 38.

[190]刘晴,李静,徐蕾．出口模式、企业异质性与行业内贸易环境效益——基于中国事实的理论与经验分析[J].世界经济文汇,2014(2):17 - 29.

[191]刘斌,王杰,魏倩．对外直接投资与价值链参与:分工地位与升级模式[J].数量经济技术经济研究,2015(12):39 - 56.

[192]刘瑶,丁妍．中国 ICT 产品的出口增长是否实现了以质取胜——基于三元分解及引力模型的实证研究[J].中国工业经济,2015(1):52 - 64.

[193]刘杜若,张明志,蔡宏波．贸易开放对我国制造业工人工资的影响研究——来自个体微观调查的证据[J].国际贸易问题,2014(5):3 - 12.

[194]刘海云,聂飞．中国制造业对外直接投资的空心化效应研究[J].中国工业经济,2015(4):83 - 96.

[195]刘琳．全球价值链、制度质量与出口品技术含量——基于跨国层面的实证分析[J].国际贸易问题,2015(10):37 - 47.

[196]刘朋春．TPP 背景下中韩自由贸易区的经济效应——基于 GTAP 模型的模拟分析[J].亚太经济,2014(5):20 - 25.

[197]刘啟仁,黄建忠．异质出口倾向、学习效应与"低加成率陷阱"[J].经济研究,2015(12):143 - 157.

[198]刘庆林,汪明珠．中国农产品市场准入政策的保护水平与结构——基于贸易限制指数的研究[J].经济研究,2014(7):18 - 30.

[199]刘仕国,吴海英,马涛,等.利用全球价值链促进产业升级[J].国际经济评论,2015(1):64－86.

[200]刘舜佳,生延超.服务贸易非物化型知识溢出的空间测度——基于修正的 Coe－Helpman 模型[J].南方经济,2014(11):43－66.

[201]刘维林.中国式出口的价值创造之谜:基于全球价值链的解析[J].世界经济,2015(3):3－28.

[202]刘维林,李兰冰,刘玉海.全球价值链嵌入对中国出口技术复杂度的影响[J].中国工业经济,2014(6):83－100.

[203]刘晓宁,魏子东.关税减让与异质性企业出口强度——基于中国制造业企业的实证研究[J].江西社会科学,2015(5):86－93.

[204]刘修岩,刘茜.对外贸易开放是否影响了区域的城市集中——来自中国省级层面数据的证据[J].财贸研究,2015(3):69－78.

[205]刘志成,刘斌.贸易自由化、全要素生产率与就业——基于 2003－2007 年中国工业企业数据的研究[J].南开经济研究,2014(1):101－117.

[206]刘重力,赵颖.东亚区域在全球价值链分工中的依赖关系——基于 Ti-VA 数据的实证分析[J].南开经济研究,2014(5):115－129.

[207]刘中伟.东亚生产网络、全球价值链整合与东亚区域合作的新走向[J].当代亚太,2014,(4):126－156.

[208]龙晓柏,洪俊杰.战略性贸易政策与出口绩效的关系研究——基于我国省际效应视角[J].南开经济研究,2014(3):84－99.

[209]卢锋,李昕,李双双,等.为什么是中国?——"一带一路"的经济逻辑[J].国际经济评论,2015(3):9－35.

[210]卢晶亮,冯帅章.贸易开放、劳动力流动与城镇劳动者性别工资差距——来自 1992—2009 年中国省际面板数据的经验证据[J].财经研究,2015,第41 卷(12):15－25.

[211]鲁晓东.技术升级与中国出口竞争力变迁:从微观向宏观的弥合[J].世界经济,2014(8):70－97.

[212]陆铭,冯皓.集聚与减排:城市规模差距影响工业污染强度的经验研究[J].世界经济,2014(7):86－114.

[213]陆南泉.丝绸之路经济带与欧亚经济联盟关系问题[J].西伯利亚研究,2015,第42 卷(5):5－8.

[214]逯建,杨小娟,程盈莹.中国边境贸易的交易成本有多高——基于海关

数据库的计算分析[J].世界经济文汇,2015(3):43-59.

[215]罗军,陈建国.研发投入门槛、外商直接投资与中国创新能力——基于门槛效应的检验[J].国际贸易问题,2014(8):135-146.

[216]罗长远,张军.附加值贸易:基于中国的实证分析[J].经济研究,2014(6):4-18.

[217]罗长远,智艳,王钊民.中国出口的成本加成率效应:来自泰国的证据[J].世界经济,2015(8):107-131.

[218]吕萍,郭晨曦.治理结构如何影响海外市场进入模式决策——基于中国上市公司对欧盟主要发达国家对外直接投资的数据[J].财经研究,2015,第41卷(3):88-99.

[219]吕越,罗伟,刘斌.异质性企业与全球价值链嵌入:基于效率和融资的视角[J].世界经济,2015(8):29-55.

[220]吕健.中国对外贸易增长分化:基于经济结构和人口红利的解释[J].国际贸易问题,2014(1):3-13.

[221]吕延方,王冬,陈树文.进出口贸易对生产率、收入、环境的门限效应——基于1992—2010年我国省际人均 GDP 的非线性面板模型[J].经济学(季刊),2015,第14卷(2):703-730.

[222]马鹏,肖宇.服务贸易出口技术复杂度与产业转型升级——基于 G20 国家面板数据的比较分析[J].财贸经济,2014(5):105-114.

[223]马涛.全球价值链下的产业升级——基于汽车产业的国际比较[J].国际经济评论,2015(1):98-112.

[224]马风涛.中国制造业全球价值链长度和上游度的测算及其影响因素分析——基于世界投入产出表的研究[J].世界经济研究,2015(8):3-11.

[225]马晶梅,王新影.基于 MRIO 模型的中美贸易内涵碳转移研究[J].统计与信息论坛,2015,第30卷(9):40-47.

[226]马林梅,张群群.中国企业规模异质性与间接出口模式——基于2013年世界银行数据的实证研究[J].国际贸易问题,2014(7):133-143.

[227]马相东,王跃生.全球贸易新常态与中国外贸发展新策略[J].中共中央党校学报,2015,第19卷(6):77-84.

[228]马学礼.重塑规则还是整合地缘:亚太经济深度一体化的模式之争[J].东南亚研究,2015(5):54-62.

[229]毛其淋,盛斌.贸易自由化与中国制造业企业出口行为"入世"是否促

进了出口参与？[J].经济学(季刊),2014,第13卷(2):647-674.

[230]毛其淋,许家云.中间品贸易自由化的生产率效应——以中国加入WTO为背景的经验研究[J].财经研究,2015,第41卷(4):42-53.

[231]毛其淋,许家云.中国企业对外直接投资是否促进了企业创新[J].世界经济,2014(8):98-125.

[232]毛其淋,许家云.中国对外直接投资促进抑或抑制了企业出口？[J].数量经济技术经济研究,2014(9):3-21.

[233]毛艳华,李敬子.中国服务业出口的本地市场效应研究[J].经济研究,2015(8):98-113.

[234]孟辽阔."一带一路"视野下的巴基斯坦战略地位及其实现路径探析[J].世界经济与政治论坛,2015(4):29-45.

[235]孟夏,陈立英.深化亚太区域经济一体化的路径选择——FTAAP问题分析[J].南开学报(哲学社会科学版),2014(6):95-104.

[236]孟祺.中国国际分工地位的演变——基于贸易附加值的视角[J].云南财经大学学报,2014(6):44-55.

[237]穆丽霞,胡敏敏.中国在国际碳交易定价中的应对策略[J].首都经济贸易大学学报(双月刊),2015,17(1):56-60.

[238]聂飞,刘海云.FDI、环境污染与经济增长的相关性研究——基于动态联立方程模型的实证检验[J].国际贸易问题,2015(2):72-83.

[239]聂聆,李三妹.制造业全球价值链利益分配与中国的竞争力研究[J].国际贸易问题,2014(12):102-113.

[240]聂平香,戴丽华.美国负面清单管理模式探析及对我国的借鉴[J].国际贸易,2014(4):33-36.

[241]潘锐,娄亚萍.中美自由贸易协定的动因与可行性[J].美国研究,2014(6):69-80.

[242]潘文卿.中国区域经济发展:基于空间溢出效应的分析[J].世界经济,2015(7):120-142.

[243]潘文卿,娄莹,李宏彬.价值链贸易与经济周期的联动:国际规律及中国经验[J].经济研究,2015(11):20-33.

[244]潘镇,金中坤.双边政治关系、东道国制度风险与中国对外直接投资[J].财贸经济,2015(6):85-97.

[245]庞明川,朱华,刘婧.基于准入前国民待遇加负面清单管理的中国外资

准入制度改革研究[J].宏观经济研究,2014(12):12-19.

[246]裴长洪,付彩芳.上海国际金融中心建设与自贸区金融改革[J].国际经贸探索,2014,第 30 卷(11):4-19.

[247]裴长洪,杨志远,刘洪愧.负面清单管理模式对服务业全球价值链影响的分析[J].财贸经济,2014(12):5-17.

[248]彭文斌,吴伟平,邝嫦娥.环境规制对污染产业空间演变的影响研究——基于空间面板杜宾模型[J].世界经济文汇,2014(6):99-110.

[249]蒲红霞,马霞.增加值贸易下金砖国家服务贸易竞争力比较分析[J].亚太经济,2015(1):82-87.

[250]朴光姬."一带一路"与东亚"西扩"——从亚洲区域经济增长机制构建的视角分析[J].当代亚太,2015(6):37-62.

[251]齐俊妍,王岚.贸易转型、技术升级和中国出口品国内完全技术含量演进[J].世界经济,2015(3):29-56.

[252]钱学锋,魏朝美.出口与女性的劳动参与率——基于中国工业企业数据的研究[J].北京师范大学学报(社会科学版),2014(6):95-110.

[253]乔晶,胡兵.中国对外直接投资:过度抑或不足[J].数量经济技术经济研究,2014(7):38-51.

[254]邱斌,刘修岩,吴飞飞,等."新常态背景下中国对外贸易转型升级的理论创新与政策研究"会议综述[J].经济研究,2015(7):188-192.

[255]邱斌,闫志俊.异质性出口固定成本、生产率与企业出口决策[J].经济研究,2015(9):142-155.

[256]裘莹,于立新."互联网+"新业态促进中国服务贸易与货物贸易协调发展研究——基于浙江省的经验[J].宏观经济研究,2015(12):14-22.

[257]全毅,汪洁,刘婉婷.21 世纪海上丝绸之路的战略构想与建设方略[J].国际贸易,2014(8):4-15.

[258]全毅.全球区域经济一体化发展趋势及中国的对策[J].经济学家,2015(1):94-104.

[259]任曙明,吕镯.融资约束、政府补贴与全要素生产率——来自中国装备制造企业的实证研究[J].管理世界,2014(11):10-24.

[260]阮宗泽.美国"亚太再平衡"战略前景论析[J].世界经济与政治,2014(4):4-21.

[261]桑百川.新一轮全球投资规则变迁的应对策略——以中美投资协定谈

判为视角[J].学术前沿,2014(1):82-89.

[262]上海社会科学院经济研究所课题.全球金融危机下在华外资企业撤资的影响分析与风险判断[J].上海经济研究,2014(12):3-14.

[263]邵桂兰,任越,李晨.中国与欧盟水产品产业内贸易研究[J].东岳论丛,2015,第36卷(8):157-161.

[264]邵金菊,姜丽花.中印服务贸易国际竞争力比较研究[J].商业时代,2015(25):40-43.

[265]邵军,吴晓怡,刘修岩.我国文化产品出口贸易联系持续期及影响因素分析[J].世界经济文汇,2014(4):36-47.

[266]佘群芝,贾净雪.中国出口增加值的国别结构及依赖关系研究[J].财贸经济,2015(8):91-103.

[267]申现杰,肖金成.国际区域经济合作新形势与我国"一带一路"合作战略[J].宏观经济研究,2014(11):30-38.

[268]沈琪,周世民.进口关税减免与企业全要素生产率:来自中国的微观证据[J].管理世界,2014(9):174-175.

[269]沈国兵.美元弱势调整对中韩双边产品贸易的影响[J].国际商务研究,2015,第36卷(206):5-18.

[270]沈铭辉.经济收益与政治博弈:跨太平洋伙伴关系协定的广谱视角[J].甲社会科学院研窀生院学报,2014(6):126-136.

[271]沈梓鑫,贾根良.增加值贸易、累积关税与关税结构扭曲[J].地点经济研究,2015(11):45-55.

[272]沈梓鑫,贾根良.增加值贸易与中国面临的国际分工陷阱[J].政治经济学评论,2014,第5卷(4):165-179.

[273]盛斌.迎接国际贸易与投资新规则的机遇与挑战[J].国际贸易,2014(2):4-9.

[274]盛斌,陈帅.全球价值链如何改变了贸易政策:对产业升级的影响和启示[J].国际经济评论,2015(1):85-98.

[275]盛斌,果婷.亚太区域经济一体化博弈与中国的战略选择[J].世界经济与政治,2014(10):4-22.

[276]盛斌,果婷.亚太地区自由贸易协定条款的比较及其对中国的启示[J].亚太经济,2014(2):94-101.

[277]盛斌,毛其淋.贸易自由化、企业成长和规模分布[J].世界经济,2015

(2):3-30.

[278]盛思鑫,曹文炼. 中国对外直接投资情况的再评估[J].宏观经济研究,2015(4):29-38.

[279]盛雯雯. 金融发展与国际贸易比较优势[J].世界经济,2014(7):142-166.

[280]施炳展,曾祥菲. 中国企业进口产品质量测算与事实[J].世界经济,2015(3):57-77.

[281]施炳展,邵文波. 中国企业出口产品质量测算及其决定因素——培育出口竞争新优势的微观视角[J].管理世界,2014(9):90-106.

[282]史青,李平,宗庆庆. 企业出口对劳动力就业风险影响的研究[J].中国工业经济,2014(7):71-83.

[283]史本叶,张永亮. 中国对外贸易成本分解与出口增长的二元边际[J].财经研究,2014,第40期(1):73-82.

[284]舒展,刘墨渊. 中国对外开放中的国家经济自主性问题探析[J].贵州社会科学,2015(9):114-120.

[285]宋国友. 中美经贸关系发展的新常态[J].复旦学报(社会科学版),2015(3):150-156.

[286]宋国友. 中美经贸关系的新变化与新趋势[J].复旦学报(社会科学版),2014(4):95-102.

[287]宋加强,王强. 现代服务贸易国际竞争力影响因素研究——基于跨国面板数据[J].国际贸易问题,2014(2):96-104.

[288]宋文飞,李国平,韩先锋. 价值链视角下环境规制对 R-D 创新效率的异质门槛效应——[基于工业 33 个行业 2004—2011 年的面板数据分析[J].财经研究,2014,第40卷(1):93-104.

[289]宋玉华,张海燕. 亚太价值链解构与中国的利得——基于 APEC 主要国家的投入产出分析[J].亚太经济,2014(2):52-59.

[290]苏杭."一带一路"战略下我国制造业海外转移问题研究[J].国际贸易,2015(3):18-21.

[291]苏剑. 语言距离影响国际贸易的理论机理与政策推演[J].学术月刊,2015,第47卷(12):59-64.

[292]随洪光,刘廷华.FDI 是否提升了发展中东道国的经济增长质量——来自亚太、非洲和拉美地区的经验证据[J].数量经济技术经济研究,2014(11):

3 - 20.

[293]孙瑾,刘文革. 国家竞争优势产业甄别与升级——基于新结构主义经济学方法[J]. 国际贸易,2014(4):11 - 17.

[294]孙瑾,刘文革,周钰迪. 中国对外开放、产业结构与绿色经济增长——基于省际面板数据的实证检验[J]. 管理世界,2014(6):172 - 173.

[295]孙楚仁,陈瑾,刘雅莹. 中国城市对外贸易结构:典型事实与初步解释[J]. 国际商务研究,2015,第 36 卷(4):16 - 35.

[296]孙少勤,邱斌. 金融发展与我国出口结构优化研究——基于区域差异视角的分析[J]. 南开经济研究,2014(4):17 - 31.

[297]孙少勤,邱斌,唐保庆. 法制建设强度与中国制造业出口动力新源泉研究[J]. 中国工业经济,2014(7):84 - 95.

[298]孙晓霓,刘晴. TPP 对我国对外贸易和投资的影响及对策:基于异质性企业理论的视角[J]. 经济经纬,2015,第 32 卷(2):50 - 55.

[299]孙文娜,毛其淋. 进口关税减免、企业异质性与新产品创新——基于中国企业层面的分析[J]. 中南财经政法大学学报,2015(6):100 - 108.

[300]覃毅. 企业异质性、所有制结构与 FDI 技术外溢——来自微观层面的证据[J]. 财贸经济,2014(3):100 - 111.

[301]谭人友,葛顺奇,刘晨. 全球价值链分工与世界经济失衡——兼论经济失衡的持续性与世界经济再平衡路径选择[J]. 世界经济研究,2015(2):32 - 43.

[302]谭秀杰,周茂荣. 21 世纪"海上丝绸之路"贸易潜力及其影响因素——基于随机前沿引力模型的实证研究[J]. 国际贸易问题,2015(2):3 - 12.

[303]汤毅,尹翔硕. 贸易自由化、异质性企业与全要素生产率——基于我国制造业企业层面的实证研究[J]. 财贸经济,2014(10):79 - 88.

[304]汤维祺,吴力波. 以自贸区建设为支点助力金砖合作的长期战略——"金砖国家发展与中国自贸区建设论坛"综述[J]. 经济研究,2015(1):183 - 186.

[305]唐东波. 垂直专业分工与劳动生产率:一个全球化视角的研究[J]. 世界经济,2014(11):25 - 52.

[306]唐杰英. 要素价格扭曲对出口的影响——来自中国制造业的实证分析[J]. 世界经济研究,2015(6):92 - 102.

[307]唐铁球. 全球价值链下中国制造业国际分工地位研究[J]. 财经问题研究,2015(6):3 - 8.

[308]陶春海,汤晓军. 中国制造业产品出口竞争力的评价研究[J]. 东岳论

丛,2015,第 36 卷(9):186 - 190.

[309]田巍,余淼杰.中间品贸易自由化和企业研发:基于中国数据的经验分析[J].世界经济,2014(6):90 - 112.

[310]田毕飞,李伟.内陆自贸区的建立与评价研究——以武汉为例[J].国际商务研究,2015,第 36 卷(4):47 - 55.

[311]田海峰,黄祎,孙广生.影响企业跨国并购绩效的制度因素分析——基于 2000—2012 年中国上市企业数据的研究[J].世界经济研究,2015(6):111 - 118.

[312]佟家栋,李连庆.贸易政策透明度与贸易便利化影响——基于可计算一般均衡模型的分析[J].南开经济研究,2014(3):3 - 16.

[313]佟家栋,刘竹青,黄平川.不同发展阶段出口学习效应比较——来自中国制造业企业的例证[J].经济评论,2014(3):75 - 86.

[314]童馨乐,徐菲菲,张为付,等.生产者服务出口贸易如何影响生产率增长?——基于 OECD 国家数据的实证检验[J].南开经济研究,2015(4):44 - 66.

[315]屠新泉,莫慧萍.服务贸易自由化的新选项:TISA 谈判的现状及其与中国的关系[J].国际贸易,2014(4):41 - 47.

[316]汪戎,李波.贸易便利化与出口多样化:微观机理与跨国证据[J].国际贸易问题,2015(3):33 - 43.

[317]汪建新.贸易自由化、质量差距与地区出口产品质量升级[J].国际贸易问题,2014(10):3 - 14.

[318]汪素芹.中国经济发展方式转变与外贸发展方式转变相互影响的实证分析[J].国际贸易问题,2014(1):51 - 60.

[319]王传剑.南海问题与中美关系[J].当代亚太,2014(2):4 - 26.

[320]王杰,刘斌.环境规制与企业生产率:出口目的地真的很重要吗?[J].财经论丛,2015(3):98 - 104.

[321]王杰,刘斌.环境规制与企业全要素生产率——基于中国工业企业数据的经验分析[J].中国工业经济,2014(3):44 - 56.

[322]王俊,杨恬恬.全球价值链、附加值贸易与中美贸易利益测度[J].上海经济研究,2015(7):115 - 128.

[323]王岚,李宏艳.中国制造业融入全球价值链路径研究——嵌入位置和增值能力的视角[J].戴翔,2015(2):76 - 88.

[324]王岚,盛斌.全球价值链分工背景下的中美增加值贸易与双边贸易利

益[J].财经研究,2014,第40卷(9):97-108.

[325]王敏,黄滢.中国的环境污染与经济增长[J].经济学(季刊),2015,第14卷(2):557-578.

[326]王勤,李南.东盟互联互通战略及其实施成效[J].亚太经济,2014(2):115-120.

[327]王青,秦琳贵.我国文化产品出口影响因素分析[J].西部论坛,2015,第25卷(5):99-108.

[328]王孝松,张国旺,周爱农.上海自贸区的运行基础、比较分析与发展前景[J].经济与管理研究,2014(7):52-64.

[329]王瑛,许可.食品安全标准对我国农产品出口的影响——基于引力模型的实证分析[J].国际贸易问题,2014(10):45-55.

[330]王直,魏尚进,祝坤福.总贸易核算法:官方贸易统计与全球价值链的度量[J].中国社会科学,2015(9):108-129.

[331]王碧珺.中国参与全球投资治理的机遇与挑战[J].国际经济评论,2014(1):94-111.

[332]王碧珺,谭语嫣,余淼杰,等.融资约束是否抑制了中国民营企业对外直接投资[J].世界经济,2015(12):54-78.

[333]王兵,刘光天.节能减排与中国绿色经济增长——基于全要素生产率的视角[J].中国工业经济,2015(5):57-69.

[334]王洪涛.文化差异是影响中国创意产品出口的阻碍因素吗——基于中国创意产品出口35个国家和地区的面板数据检验[J].国际经贸探索,2014,第30卷(10):51-62.

[335]王厚双,李艳秀,朱奕绮.我国服务业在全球价值链分工中的地位研究[J].世界经济研究,2015(8):11-19.

[336]王恕立,刘军,胡宗彪.FDI流入、动机差异与服务产品垂直型产业内贸易[J].世界经济,2014(2):71-94.

[337]王恕立,滕泽伟,刘军.中国服务业生产率变动的差异分析——基于区域及行业视角[J].经济研究,2015(8):73-84.

[338]王恕立,向姣姣.对外直接投资逆向技术溢出与全要素生产率:基于不同投资动机的经验分析[J].国际贸易问题,2014(9):109-119.

[339]王恕立,向姣姣.制度质量、投资动机与中国对外直接投资的区位选择[J].财经研究,2015,第41期(5):134-144.

[340]王维薇,李荣林.全球生产网络背景下中间产品进口对出口的促进作用——基于对中国电子行业的考察[J].南开经济研究,2014(6):74-90.

[341]王文举,向其凤.中国产业结构调整及其节能减排潜力评估[J].中国工业经济,2014(1):44-56.

[342]王小梅,秦学志,尚勤.金融危机以来贸易保护主义对中国出口的影响[J].数量经济技术经济研究,2014(5):20-37.

[343]王晓红,沈家文.我国利用外商直接投资的现状与趋势展望[J].国际贸易,2015,卷缺失(3):41-48.

[344]王孝松,翟光宇,林发勤.中国出口产品技术含量的影响因素探究[J].数量经济技术经济研究,2014,卷缺失(11):21-37.

[345]王孝松,翟光宇,谢申祥.中国贸易超调:表现、成因与对策[J].管理世界,2014(1):27-39.

[346]王雅琦,戴觅,徐建炜.汇率、产品质量与出口价格[J].世界经济,2015(5):17-35.

[347]王永钦,杜巨澜,王凯.中国对外直接投资区位选择的决定因素:制度、税负和资源禀赋[J].经济研究,2014(12):126-142.

[348]王玉燕,林汉川,吕臣.全球价值链嵌入的技术进步效应——来自中国工业面板数据的经验研究[J].中国工业经济,2014(9):65-77.

[349]王跃生.世界经济"双循环"、"新南南合作"与"一带一路"建设[J].新视野,2015(6):12-18.

[350]王正明,余为琴.中国稀土贸易定价地位及其成因的实证分析[J].国际经贸探索,2014,第30卷(5):49-61.

[351]王子先,张斌,邓娜.基于全球价值链的外贸转型战略[J].国际贸易,2014(12):14-19.

[352]王自锋,孙浦阳,张伯伟,等.基础设施规模与利用效率对技术进步的影响:基于中国区域的实证分析[J].南开经济研究,2014(2):118-135.

[353]卫瑞,张少军.中间品出口对中国就业结构的影响——基于技能、来源地和部门视角的分析[J].财经研究,2014,第40卷(11):133-144.

[354]卫瑞,张文城,张少军.全球价值链视角下中国增加值出口及其影响因素[J].数量经济技术经济研究,2015(7):3-20.

[355]卫瑞庄,宗明.生产国际化与中国就业波动:基于贸易自由化和外包视角[J].世界经济,2015(1):53-80.

[356]魏浩,李翀.中国制造业劳动力成本上升的基本态势与应对策略[J].国际贸易,2014(3):10-15.

[357]魏浩,李晓庆.中国进口贸易的技术结构及其影响因素研究[J].世界经济,2015(8):56-79.

[358]魏浩,叶子丹,赵春明.中国进口地区结构及其变化趋势的测算研究[J].世界经济与政治论坛,2014(5):1-21.

[359]魏浩.中国进口商品的国别结构及相互依赖程度研究[J].财贸经济,2014(4):69-81.

[360]文东伟,冼国明.中国制造业的空间集聚与出口:基于企业层面的研究[J].管理世界,2014(10):57-74.

[361]文东伟,冼国明.中国制造业产业集聚的程度及其演变趋势:1998—2009年[J].世界经济,2014(3):3-31.

[362]吴瑶,孙彤.出口企业升级的市场演化路径研究[J].国际商务研究,2015,第36卷(206):44-53.

[363]吴崇伯.福建构建21世纪海上丝绸之路战略的优势、挑战与对策[J].亚太经济,2014(6):109-113.

[364]吴力波,钱浩祺,汤维祺.基于动态边际减排成本模拟的碳排放权交易与碳税选择机制[J].经济研究,2014(9):48-62.

[365]席艳乐,胡强.企业异质性、中间品进口与出口绩效——基于中国企业微观数据的实证研究[J].产业经济研究,2014(5):72-82.

[366]夏明,张红霞.跨国生产、贸易增加值与增加值率的变化——基于投入产出框架对增加值率的理论解析[J].管理世界,2015(2):32-44.

[367]肖慧敏,刘辉煌.中国企业对外直接投资的学习效应研究[J].财经研究,2014,第40卷(4):42-55.

[368]肖雁飞,万子捷,刘红光.我国区域产业转移中"碳排放转移"及"碳泄露"实证研究——基于2002—2007年区域间投入产出模型的分析[J].财经研究,2014,第40卷(2):75-84.

[369]萧琛,赵恩娇.中韩FDI与产业内贸易转型[J].开放导报,2014(2):20-24.

[370]谢建国,姜珮珊.中国进出口贸易隐含能源消耗的测算与分解——基于投入产出模型的分析[J].经济学(季刊),2014,第13卷(4):1365-1392.

[371]谢建国,李梦月.中国零部件贸易比较优势与技术含量:结构与演变研

究[J].财经理论与实践(双月刊),2014,第 35 卷(6):89 - 95.

[372]谢建国,吴国锋.FDI 技术溢出的门槛效应——基于 1992—2012 年中国省际面板数据的研究[J].世界经济研究,2014(11):74 - 80.

[373]谢建国,赵锦春,林小娟.不对称劳动参与、收入不平等与全球贸易失衡[J].世界经济,2015(9):56 - 79.

[374]谢姗.比较优势理论过时了吗?——基于国内区际贸易的实证分析[J].经济与管理研究,2015,第 36 卷(10):71 - 79.

[375]谢申祥,王祯,胡凯.部分私营化国有企业中的外资份额、贸易政策与污染物排放[J].世界经济,2015(6):49 - 69.

[376]邢广程.理解中国现代丝绸之路战略——中国与世界深度互动的新型链接范式[J].世界经济与政治,2014(12):4 - 27.

[377]邢斐,宋毅.FDI 纵向一体化、技术转移与东道国产业发展[J].财经研究,2015,第 41 卷(5):123 - 133.

[378]徐婧,孟娟.贸易开放、经济增长与人力资本——基于面板门槛模型的研究[J].世界经济研究,2015(6):84 - 92.

[379]徐榕,赵勇.融资约束如何影响企业的出口决策?[J].经济评论,2015(3):108 - 120.

[380]徐美娜,彭羽.出口产品质量的国外研究综述[J].国际经贸探索,2014,第 30 卷(7):25 - 36.

[381]徐明君,黎峰.基于生产效率视角的全球价值链分工:理论解释及实证检验[J].世界经济与政治论坛,2015(6):74 - 94.

[382]徐宁,皮建才,刘志彪.全球价值链还是国内价值链——中国代工企业的链条选择机制研究[J].经济理论与经济管理,2014(1):62 - 74.

[383]许和连,孙天阳,成丽红."一带一路"高端制造业贸易格局及影响因素研究——基于复杂网络的指数随机图分析[J].财贸经济,2015(12):74 - 88.

[384]许家云,佟家栋,毛其淋.人民币汇率变动、产品排序与多产品的的出口行为——以中国制造业企业为例[J].管理世界,2015(2):17 - 31.

[385]许培源,魏丹.TPP 的投资区位效应及非 TPP 亚太国家的应对措施——基于多国自由资本模型的分析[J].财经研究,2015,第 41 卷(3):77 - 87.

[386]薛力.中国"一带一路"战略面对的外交风险[J].国际经济评论,2015(2):68 - 80.

[387]薛荣久,杨凤鸣.对中国特色社会主义国际经贸理论构建的思考[J].

国际贸易,2014(4):4-10.

[388]闫云凤.中日韩在全球价值链中的地位和作用——基于贸易增加值的测度与比较[J].世界经济研究,2015(1):74-81.

[389]严冰.中国贸易自由化与工业企业产品创新——基于熊彼特增长范式的分析[J].湖北行政学院学报,2015(1):79-85.

[390]严兵,张禹,韩剑.企业异质性与对外直接投资——基于江苏省企业的检验[J].南开经济研究,2014(4):50-63.

[391]杨骞,刘华军.污染排放约束下中国农业水资源效率的区域差异与影响因素[J].数量经济技术经济研究,201(1):114-129.

[392]杨春艳,綦建红.内资企业国际市场进入的动态选择——基于出口经验的视角[J].宏观经济研究,2015(9):151-159.

[393]杨逢珉,翟慧娟,毛一卿.我国农产品出口欧盟市场的二元边际分解[J].经济问题,2015(10):78-84.

[394]杨高举,黄先海.中国会陷入比较优势陷阱吗?[J].管理世界,2014(5):5-22.

[395]杨广贡,杨正位.全球经贸体系重塑的动因、趋势和对策[J].国际经济评论,2015(1):121-131.

[396]杨继军,范从来."中国制造"对全球经济"大稳健"的影响——基于价值链的实证检验[J].中国社会科学,2015(10):92-115.

[397]杨青龙,张为付.国际贸易的成本分析:视角与方法[J].财贸经济,2015(3):103-112.

[398]杨汝岱.中国制造业企业全要素生产率研究[J].经济研究,2015(2):61-74.

[399]杨少文,熊启泉.1994—2011年的中国经济开放度——基于GDP份额法的测算[J].国际贸易问题,2014(3):13-24.

[400]杨晓兰,张安全.经济增长与环境恶化——基于地级城市的经验分析[J].财贸经济,2014(1):125-134.

[401]杨校美.中欧服务贸易与中国制造业效率提升——基于行业面板数据的分析[J].国际商务研究,2015,第36卷(6):77-86.

[402]杨振兵.FDI是否会迅速逃离:基于工业行业根植性的视角[J].当代经济科学,2014,第36卷(4):1-10.

[403]杨志远,谭文君.技术进步、贸易波动与服务业增长[J].财贸经济,

2014(2):125 – 136.

[404]姚德权,黄学军. 我国与丝绸之路经济带国家的金融合作:现状、挑战与前景展望[J]. 国际贸易,2014(10):37 – 41.

[405]姚树洁,冯根福,王攀,等. 中国是否挤占了 OECD 成员国的对外投资?[J]. 经济研究,2014(11):43 – 57.

[406]姚毓春,袁礼,王林辉. 中国工业部门要素收入分配格局——基于技术进步偏向性视角的分析[J]. 中国工业经济,2014(8):44 – 56.

[407]姚战琪. 全球价值链背景下中国服务业的发展战略及重点领域——基于生产性服务业与产业升级视角的研究[J]. 国际贸易,2014(7):13 – 18.

[408]叶娇,王佳林. FDI 对本土技术创新的影响研究——基于江苏省面板数据的实证[J]. 国际贸易问题,2014(1):131 – 138.

[409]叶扬,张文. 新兴经济体对 WTO 规则的冲击与展望[J]. 西部论坛,2014,第 24 卷(5):59 – 69.

[410]叶宁华,包群,邵敏. 空间集聚、市场拥挤与我国出口企业的过度扩张[J]. 管理世界,2014(1):58 – 72.

[411]叶作义,张鸿下,田充,等. 全球价值链下国际分工结构的变化——基于世界投入产出表的研究[J]. 世界经济研究,2015(1):56 – 65.

[412]衣长军,李赛,张吉鹏. 制度环境、吸收能力与新兴经济体 OFDI 逆向技术溢出效应——基于中国省际面板数据的门槛检验[J]. 财经研究,2015,第 41 卷(11):4 – 19.

[413]易先忠,欧阳晓,傅晓岚. 国内市场规模与出口产品结构多元化:制度环境的门槛效应[J]. 经济研究,2014,(6):18 – 29.

[414]于斌斌. 产业结构调整与生产率提升的经济增长效应——基于中国城市动态空间面板模型的分析[J]. 中国工业经济,2015(12):83 – 98.

[415]于春海. 我国制造业增长的外部条件是否发生了变化?[J]. 国际贸易,2014(2):20 – 24.

[416]于春海,雷达. 新地区主义与美国的对外贸易政策协调[J]. 国际经济评论,2014(4):65 – 79.

[417]于津平,邓娟. 垂直专业化、出口技术含量与全球价值链分工地位[J]. 世界经济与政治论坛,2014(2):44 – 62.

[418]余振,葛伟. 经济一体化与产业区位效应:基于中国—东盟自贸区产业层面的面板数据分析[J]. 财贸经济,2014(12):87 – 98.

[419]余振,张萍,吴莹. 美国退出 QE 对中美两国金融市场的影响及中国的对策——基于 FAVAR 模型的分析[J]. 世界经济研究,2015(4):24 - 33.

[420]余娟娟. 全球价值链分工下中国出口技术结构的演进机理与路径[J]. 产业经济研究,2014(6):31 - 40.

[421]余官胜,杨文. 中国企业对外直接投资的国内决定因素——基于投资规模的实证研究[J]. 经济经纬,2015,第 32 卷(4):61 - 66.

[422]余淼杰,李晋. 进口类型、行业差异化程度与企业生产率提升[J]. 经济研究,2015(8):85 - 98.

[423]余淼杰,梁中华. 贸易自由化与中国劳动收入份额——基于制造业贸易企业数据的实证分析[J]. 管理世界,2014,(7):22 - 31.

[424]余泳泽. 中国区域创新活动的"协同效应"与"挤占效应"——基于创新价值链视角的研究[J]. 中国工业经济,2015(10):37 - 52.

[425]余长林. 知识产权保护如何影响了中国的出口边际[J]. 国际贸易问题,2015(9):43 - 54.

[426]喻坤,李治国,张晓蓉,等. 企业投资效率之谜:融资约束假说与货币政策冲击[J]. 经济研究,2014(5):106 - 120.

[427]袁东,李霖洁,余淼杰. 外向型对外直接投资与母公司生产率——对母公司特征和子公司进入策略的考察[J]. 南开经济研究,2015(3):38 - 58.

[428]袁胜育,汪伟民. 丝绸之路经济带与中国的中亚政策[J]. 世界经济与政治,2015(5):21 - 43.

[429]袁志刚,饶璨. 全球化与中国生产服务业发展——基于全球投入产出模型的研究[J]. 管理世界,2014,(3):10 - 30.

[430]岳咬兴,范涛. 制度环境与中国对亚洲直接投资区位分布[J]. 财贸经济,2014(6):69 - 78.

[431]张彬,孔祥贞,杨勇. 信贷融资对异质性企业出口参与的影响——基于商业信贷和银行信贷角度的理论和实证分析[J]. 经济理论与经济管理,2015(8):36 - 46.

[432]张彬,桑百川. 中美技术密集型产品双边贸易研究——显性比较优势、产业内贸易与贸易平衡研究[J]. 亚太经济,2015(1):43 - 49.

[433]张彬,桑百川. 中国制造业参与国际分工对升级的影响与审计路径选择——基于出口垂直专业化视角的研究[J]. 产业经济研究,2015(5):12 - 20.

[434]张宏,叶丽,杜学知. 国际分工演变对提升中国生产性服务贸易竞争力

的影响[J].亚太经济,2015(5):52-57.

[435]张杰,郑文平,陈志远.进口与企业生产率——中国的经验证据[J].经济学(季刊),2015,第 14 卷(3):1029-1052.

[436]张杰,郑文平,陈志远,等.进口是否引致了出口:中国出口奇迹的微观解读[J].世界经济,2014(6):3-26.

[437]张军,陈磊.中国出口贸易文化异质性效应研究——来自主要贸易伙伴国的经验证据[J].财贸经济,2015(7):123-136.

[438]张军.我国西南地区在"一带一路"开放战略中的优势及定位[J].经济纵横,2014(11):93-96.

[439]张琳,东艳.国际贸易投资规则的新变化:竞争中立原则的应用与实践[J].国际贸易,2014(6):48-51.

[440]张明,肖立晟.国际资本流动的驱动因素:新兴市场与发达经济体的比较[J].世界经济,2014(8):151-172.

[441]张亚军,干春晖,郑若谷.生产性服务业与制造业的内生与关联效应——基于投入产出结构分解技术的实证研究[J].产业经济研究,2014(6):81-90.

[442]张翊,陈雯,骆时雨.中间品进口对中国制造业全要素生产率的影响[J].世界经济,2015(9):107-129.

[443]张宇,蒋殿春.FDI_政府监管与中国水污染——基于产业结构与技术进步分解指标的实证检验[J].经济学(季刊),2014,第 13 卷(2):491-514.

[444]张云,唐海燕.经济新常态下实现碳排放峰值承诺的贸易开放效应——中国贸易开放环境效应与碳泄露存在性实证检验[J].财贸经济,2015(7):96-108.

[445]张伯伟,田朔,许家云.汇率变动、融资能力与中国企业出口[J].山西财经大学学报,2015,第 37 卷(3):11-21.

[446]张川川.出口对就业、工资和收入不平等的影响——基于微观数据的证据[J].经济学(季刊),2015,第 14 卷(4):1611-1630.

[447]张定胜,刘洪愧,杨志远.中国出口在全球价值链中的位置演变——基于增加值核算的分析[J].财贸经济,2015(11):114-130.

[448]张海燕.基于投入产出占用模型的中国开放收益测度[J].财贸经济,2014(5):93-104.

[449]张昊.国内市场如何承接制造业出口调整——产需匹配及国内贸易的

意义[J].中国工业经济,2014(8):70-83.

[450]张浩然.生产性服务业集聚与城市经济绩效——基于行业和地区异质性视角的分析[J].财经研究,2015,第41卷(5):67-77.

[451]张华."绿色悖论:之谜"地方政府竞争视角的解读[J].财经研究,2014,第40卷(12):114-127.

[452]张会清.中国铁矿石进口风险的量化评估——兼评进口多元化策略的成效[J].国际经贸探索,2014,第30卷(1):44-56.

[453]张季风.中日经贸关系70年回顾与思考[J].现代日本经济,2015(6):1-12.

[454]张杰.进口对中国制造业企业专利活动的抑制效应研究[J].中国工业经济,2015(7):68-83.

[455]张靖佳,姜小雨,孙浦阳.贸易风险与价格离散:基于企业—产品级别的验证[J].世界经济研究,2015(12):89-100.

[456]张靖佳,孙浦阳,刘澜飚.量化宽松政策、财富效应与企业出口[J].经济研究,2015(12):158-162.

[457]张琳.国际经贸新规则:中国自贸区的实践与探索[J].世界经济与政治论坛,2015(5):140-157.

[458]张明之,梁洪基.全球价值链重构中的产业控制力——基于世界财富分配权控制方式变迁的视角[J].世界经济与政治论坛,2015(1):1-23.

[459]张乃丽,石芳芳.中德机电产品的出口竞争力:基于美国市场的比较分析[J].山东大学学报(哲学社会科学版),2014(3):68-77.

[460]张晓静,李梁."一带一路"与中国出口贸易:基于贸易便利化视角[J].亚太经济,2015(3):21-27.

[461]张一博,祝树金.基于改进的嵌套Logit模型的中国工业出口质量测度研究[J].世界经济与政治论坛,2014(2):1-18.

[462]张咏华.制造业全球价值链及其动态演变——基于国际产业关联的研究[J].世界经济研究,2015(6):61-71.

[463]张友国.碳排放视角下的区域间贸易模式:污染避难所与要素禀赋[J].中国工业经济,2015(8):5-19.

[464]张友国.碳税对我国进出口贸易的影响研究[J].中国地质大学报(社会科学版),2015,第15卷(6):1-11.

[465]张幼文.生产要素的国际流动与全球化经济的运行机制[J].国际经济

评论,2013(5):30-41.

[466]张幼文.自贸区试验与开放型经济体制建设[J].学者论坛,2015:26-29.

[467]张玉娥,朱晶.基于三元差额视角的中国农产品贸易逆差结构[J].财经科学,2015(10):74-81.

[468]张毓卿,周才云.中国对外贸易成本的测度及其影响因素——基于面板数据模型的实证分析[J].经济学家,2015(9):11-20.

[469]张灼华,陈芃.中国香港:成为"一带一路"版图中的持续亮点[J].国际经济评论,2015(2):80-90.

[470]赵德昭.FDI、第三方效应与农村剩余劳动转移的空间集聚——基于中国省际面板数据的空间计量检验[J].南开经济研究,2014(6):105-124.

[471]赵亮,陈淑梅.经济增长的、"自贸区驱动"——基于中韩中日韩自贸区与 RCEP 的比较研究[J].经济评论,2015(1):92-102.

[472]赵文军,于津平.市场化进程与我国经济增长方式——基于省际面板数据的实证研究[J].南开经济研究,2014(3):3-22.

[473]赵英会.IAFTA 对我国经济的影响研究[J].山东科技大学学报(社会科学版),2015,第 17 卷(2):60-66.

[474]赵永亮,杨子晖,苏启林.出口集聚企业"双重成长环境"下的学习能力与生产率之谜——新—新贸易理论与新—新经济地理的共同视角[J].管理世界,2014(1):40-57.

[475]赵玉意.体制冲突视域中 GATS 与 BITs 准入规则冲突研究[J].国际经贸探索,2015,第 31 卷(8):65-76.

[476]赵增耀,章小波,沈能.区域协同创新效率的多维溢出效应[J].中国工业经济,2015(1):32-44.

[477]郑小碧.内生比较优势_国际贸易方式与收入分配:一个新兴古典框架[J].商业经济与管理,2015(2):87-97.

[478]郑辛迎,方明月,聂辉华.市场范围、制度质量和企业一体化:来自中国制造业的证据[J].南开经济研究,2014,(1):118-133.

[479]郑学党,庄芮.中国对其他金砖国家出口增长因素研究——基于修正的 CMS 模型分析[J].国际经贸探索,2015,第 31 卷(2):4-18.

[480]钟昌标,黄远浙,刘伟.外资进入速度、企业异质性和企业生产率[J].世界经济,2015(7):53-72.

[481]钟飞腾."一带一路"产能合作的国际政治经济学分析[J].山东社会科学,2015(8):40-49.

[482]仲鑫,丁秀飞.服务贸易技术结构优化的驱动因素研究[J].中国高校社会科学,2015(5):121-132.

[483]周丹.基于扩展的超越对数引力模型贸易成本弹性测度与分析——以中国与主要亚太国家间贸易为例[J].南开经济研究,2015(3):59-73.

[484]周丹,陆万军.中国与金砖国家间农产品贸易成本弹性测度与分析[J].数量经济技术经济研究,2015(1):20-35.

[485]周浩,余金利,郑越.网络销售对中国工业企业出口参与的影响[J].财经研究,2014,第40卷(10):46-58.

[486]周力,李静.外商直接投资与PM2.5空气污国——基于中国数据的"污染避难所"假说再检验[J].国际经贸探索,2015,第31卷(12):98-111.

[487]周申,李可爱,任希丽.贸易结构变动对我国能源消耗的影响[J].数量经济技术经济研究,2014(3):104-118.

[488]周大鹏.进口服务中间投入对我国制造业全球价值链分工地位的影响研究[J].世界经济研究,2015(8):27-37.

[489]周康."邻居"的影响有多大——出口企业集聚与海外市场扩张[J].国际贸易问题,2015(4):137-147.

[490]周茂荣.跨大西洋贸易与投资伙伴关系协定(TTIP)谈判及其对全球贸易格局的影响[J].国际经济评论,2014(1):77-94.

[491]周睿.中国加入TPP的经济效应分析——基于GTAP模型的模拟[J].世界经济与政治论坛,2014(6):45-57.

[492]周升起,兰珍先,付华.中国制造业在全球价值链国际分工地位再考察——基于Koopman等的"GVC地位指数"[J].国际贸易问题,2014(2):3-12.

[493]周云波,陈岑,田柳.外商直接投资对东道国企业间工资差距的影响[J].经济研究,2015(12):128-142.

[494]朱荃,张天华.中国企业对外直接投资存在"生产率悖论"吗——基于上市工业企业的实证研究[J].财贸经济,2015(12):103-117.

[495]朱剑冰,吕静.贸易便利化评价指标体系研究及其应用[J].湖南大学学报(社会科学版),2015,第29卷(6):70-75.

[496]朱启荣.中国外贸中虚拟水与外贸结构调整研究[J].中国工业经济,2014(2):58-70.

［497］朱启荣,袁其刚. 中国工业出口贸易中的灰色虚拟水及其政策含义［J］. 世界经济研究,2014(8):42 - 49.

［498］朱廷珺,林薛栋. 全球化下的经济赶超路径探索——基于 D - S 框架［J］. 南开经济研究,2014(4):32 - 49.

［499］朱维巍. 究竟谁才是中美贸易失衡的主因——来自中美分行业产品异质性视角的经验证据［J］. 世界经济研究,2014(9):41 - 49.

［500］竺彩华,韩剑夫.“一带一路”沿线 FTA 现状与中国 FTA 战略［J］. 亚太经济,2015(4):44 - 50.

［501］祝明侠. 国际经贸规则变化新趋势及我国的因应对策［J］. 烟台大学学报(哲学社会科学版),2015,第 28 卷(6):114 - 131.

［502］祝树金,尹似雪. 污染产品贸易会诱使环境规制“向底线赛跑”?——基于跨国面板数据的实证分析［J］. 产业经济研究,2014(4):41 - 51.

［503］邹宗森,原磊,薄晓东. 中国与东亚地区产业内贸易现状及影响因素分析［J］. 亚太经济,2014(1):53 - 59.

第二节　英文期刊索引

［1］Abbassi A,Tamini L D,Dakhlaoui A. Import quota allocation between regions under Cournot competition［J］. Economic Modelling,2015,51:484 - 490.

［2］Abotsi A K. Foreign ownership of firms and corruption in Africa［J］. 2015.

［3］Adamopoulos T,Restuccia D. The size distribution of farms and international productivity differences ［J］. The American Economic Review, 2014, 104 (6): 1667 - 1697.

［4］Adom P K,Amakye K,Doh E,et al. SMEs Record Keeping in Ghana:Has VAT Made It Better? ［J］. International Journal of Economics and Financial Issues, 2014,4(1):152.

［5］Afonso G,Lagos R. Trade dynamics in the market for federal funds［J］. Econometrica,2015,83(1):263 - 313.

［6］Akhmat G,Zaman K,Shukui T,et al. Exploring the root causes of terrorism in South Asia:everybody should be concerned［J］. Quality & Quantity,2014,48(6):

3065 - 3079.

[7]Alaei S,Setak M. Multi objective coordination of a supply chain with routing and service level consideration [J]. International Journal of Production Economics, 2015,167:271 - 281.

[8]Allegret J P,Mignon V,Sallenave A. Oil price shocks and global imbalances: Lessons from a model with trade and financial interdependencies[J]. Economic Modelling,2015,49:232 - 247.

[9]Allegret J P,Sallenave A. The impact of real exchange rates adjustments on global imbalances: A multilateral approach [J]. Economic Modelling, 2014, 37: 149 - 163.

[10]Allen T,Arkolakis C. Trade and the Topography of the Spatial Economy[J]. The Quarterly Journal of Economics,2014,129(3):1085 - 1140.

[11] Allen T. Information frictions in trade [J]. Econometrica, 2014, 82 (6): 2041 - 2083.

[12]Amighini A,Sanfilippo M. Impact of South - South FDI and trade on the export upgrading of African economies[J]. World Development,2014,64:1 - 17.

[13]Amiti M,Itskhoki O,Konings J. Importers,exporters,and exchange rate disconnect[J]. The American Economic Review,2014,104(7):1942 - 1978.

[14]Antras P,Foley C F. Poultry in motion:a study of international trade finance practices[J]. Journal of Political Economy,2015,123(4):853 - 901.

[15]Anwar S,Sun S. Heterogeneity and curvilinearity of FDI-related productivity spillovers in China's manufacturing sector[J]. Economic Modelling,2014,41:23 - 32.

[16]Armenter R,Koren M. A balls-and-bins model of trade[J]. The American Economic Review,2014,104(7):2127 - 2151.

[17]Arvas M A,Uyar B. Exports and firm productivity in Turkish manufacturing: an Olley-Pakes estimation[J]. International Journal of Economics and Financial Issues, 2014,4(2):243.

[18]Asche F,Bellemare M F,Roheim C,et al. Fair enough? Food security and the international trade of seafood[J]. World Development,2015,67:151 - 160.

[19]Azzimonti M,De Francisco E,Quadrini V. Financial globalization,inequality, and the rising public debt[J]. The American Economic Review,2014,104(8):2267 - 2302.

[20]Baccini L, Urpelainen J. International institutions and domestic politics: can preferential trading agreements help leaders promote economic reform? [J]. The Journal of Politics, 2014, 76(1): 195 – 214.

[21]Badau F. Ranking trade resistance variables using data envelopment analysis [J]. European Journal of Operational Research, 2015, 247(3): 978 – 986.

[22]Bagchi P, Lejeune M A, Alam A. How supply competency affects FDI decisions: some insights [J]. International Journal of Production Economics, 2014, 147: 239 – 251.

[23]Barthel F, Neumayer E, Nunnenkamp P, et al. Competition for export markets and the allocation of foreign aid: The role of spatial dependence among donor countries [J]. World Development, 2014, 64: 350 – 365.

[24]Bekhet H A, Al – Smadi R W. Determinants of Jordanian foreign direct investment inflows: Bounds testing approach[J]. Economic Modelling, 2015, 46: 27 – 35.

[25]Bekkers E, Stehrer R. Reallocation effects in the specific factors and Heckscher-Ohlin models under firm heterogeneity [J]. Economic Modelling, 2015, 49: 104 – 119.

[26]Belke A, Oeking A, Setzer R. Domestic demand, capacity constraints and exporting dynamics: Empirical evidence for vulnerable euro area countries[J]. Economic modelling, 2015, 48: 315 – 325.

[27]Belloc M. Information for sale in the European Union[J]. Journal of Economic Behavior & Organization, 2015, 120: 130 – 144.

[28]Benjamin D J, Heffetz O, Kimball M S, et al. Can marginal rates of substitution be inferred from happiness data? Evidence from residency choices[J]. The American economic review, 2014, 104(11): 3498 – 3528.

[29]Bergh A, Nilsson T. Is globalization reducing absolute poverty? [J]. World Development, 2014, 62: 42 – 61.

[30]Berument M H, Dincer N N, Mustafaoglu Z. External income shocks and Turkish exports: A sectoral analysis[J]. Economic Modelling, 2014, 37: 476 – 484.

[31]Beverelli C, Neumueller S, Teh R. Export diversification effects of the wto trade facilitation agreement[J]. World Development, 2015, 76: 293 – 310.

[32]Biais B, Hombert J, Weill P O. Equilibrium pricing and trading volume under preference uncertainty [J]. The Review of Economic Studies, 2014, 81(4):

1401 – 1437.

[33]Boateng A,Hua X,Nisar S,et al. Examining the determinants of inward FDI：Evidence from Norway[J]. Economic Modelling,2015,47:118 – 127.

[34] Bodenstein T,Kemmerling A. A Paradox of Redistribution in International Aid? The Determinants of Poverty-Oriented Development Assistance[J]. World Development,2015,76:359 – 369.

[35]Bøler E A,Moxnes A,Ulltveit – Moe K H. R&d,international sourcing,and the joint impact on firm performance[J]. The American Economic Review,2015,105(12):3704 – 3739.

[36]Bouras H,Raggad B. Foreign Direct Investment and Exports:Complementarity or Substitutability An Empirical Investigation[J]. International Journal of Economics and Financial Issues,2015,5(4).

[37]Bouvatier V. Heterogeneous bank regulatory standards and the cross-border supply of financial services[J]. Economic modelling,2014,40:342 – 354.

[38]Brandt L,Ma D,Rawski T G. From divergence to convergence:reevaluating the history behind China's economic boom[J]. Journal of Economic Literature,2014,52(1):45 – 123.

[39]Bräutigam D,Tang X. "Going Global in Groups":Structural Transformation and China's Special Economic Zones Overseas[J]. World Development,2014,63:78 – 91.

[40] Brockmeier M,Bektasoglu B. Model structure or data aggregation level:Which leads to greater bias of results? [J]. Economic Modelling,2014,38:238 – 245.

[41]Buigut S. The Effect of Zimbabwe's Multi-Currency Arrangement on Bilateral Trade:Myth versus Reality[J]. International Journal of Economics and Financial Issues,2015,5(3).

[42]Caglayan M,Demir F. Firm productivity,exchange rate movements,sources of finance,and export orientation[J]. World Development,2014,54:204 – 219.

[43]Caliendo L,Parro F. Estimates of the Trade and Welfare Effects of NAFTA[J]. The Review of Economic Studies,2015,82(1):1 – 44.

[44]Caron J,Fally T,Markusen J R. International trade puzzles:A solution linking production and preferences[J]. The Quarterly Journal of Economics,2014,129(3):1501 – 1552.

[45]Castañeda J G. NAFTA's Mixed Record:The View From Mexico[J]. Foreign Aff. ,2014,93:134.

[46]Chakraborty T. Trade Liberalization in a Traditional Society:Implications for Relative Female Survival[J]. World Development,2015,74:158 – 170.

[47]Chaney T. The network structure of international trade[J]. The American economic review,2014,104(11):3600 – 3634.

[48]Chang S C. The effects of trade liberalization on environmental degradation [J]. Quality & Quantity,2015,49(1):235 – 253.

[49]Chang T,Tsai C F. Globalization and inflation nexus:further evidence based on bootstrap panel causality[J]. Quality & Quantity,2015,49(2):867 – 877.

[50]Chari A,Henry P B. Learning from the doers:Developing country lessons for advanced economy growth [J]. The American Economic Review, 2014, 104 (5): 260 – 265.

[51]Charoenrat T,Harvie C. The efficiency of SMEs in Thai manufacturing:A stochastic frontier analysis[J]. Economic Modelling,2014,43:372 – 393.

[52]Chasovsky V I,Katrovsky A P. The territorial and sectoral trends in the industry of the Eurasian Economic Union[J]. International Journal of Economics and Financial Issues,2015,5(2S).

[53]Chen F,Wang Y. Integration risk in cross-border M&A based on internal and external resource:empirical evidence from China[J]. Quality & Quantity,2014:1 – 15.

[54]Chen F,Xu Y. Democratization in the host country and institutional risk of cross-border M&A:an empirical study on Chinese listed enterprises [J]. Quality & Quantity,2014,48(2):1013 – 1025.

[55]Chen F,Zhong F,Chen Y. Outward foreign direct investment and sovereign risks in developing host country[J]. Economic Modelling,2014,41:166 – 172.

[56]Cheong J,Kwak D W,Tang K K. Heterogeneous effects of preferential trade agreements:How does partner similarity matter? [J]. World Development,2015,66: 222 – 236.

[57]Chung K J,Cárdenas-Barrón L E,Ting P S. An inventory model with non-instantaneous receipt and exponentially deteriorating items for an integrated three layer supply chain system under two levels of trade credit[J]. International Journal of Production Economics,2014,155:310 – 317.

[58] Cleeve E A, Debrah Y, Yiheyis Z. Human capital and FDI inflow: An assessment of the African Case[J]. World Development, 2015, 74: 1 – 14.

[59] Coban S. Does the financial development spur export performance? Evidence from Turkish firm-level data[J]. International Journal of Economics and Financial Issues, 2015, 5(2).

[60] Commendatore P, Kubin I, Petraglia C, et al. Regional integration, international liberalisation and the dynamics of industrial agglomeration[J]. Journal of Economic Dynamics and Control, 2014, 48: 265 – 287.

[61] Contessi S. Multinational firms? entry and productivity: Some aggregate implications of firm-level heterogeneity[J]. Journal of Economic Dynamics and Control, 2015, 61: 61 – 80.

[62] Córcoles D, Díaz-Mora C, Gandoy R. Product sophistication: A tie that binds partners in international trade[J]. Economic Modelling, 2014, 44: S33 – S41.

[63] Corruption and Foreign Direct Investment in East Asia and South Asia: An Econometric Study

[64] Costinot A, Donaldson D, Vogel J, et al. Comparative advantage and optimal trade policy[J]. The Quarterly Journal of Economics, 2015, 130(2): 659 – 702.

[65] Dangol R, Bahl M, Karpak B. Timing cooperative relationships with sequential capability development process to reduce capability development trade-offs[J]. International Journal of Production Economics, 2015, 169: 179 – 189.

[66] Dinar Z. Transboundary pollution, R&D spillovers, absorptive capacity and international trade[R]. Economics Discussion Papers, 2013.

[67] Dix-Carneiro R, Kovak B K. Trade liberalization and the skill premium: A local labor markets approach [J]. The American Economic Review, 2015, 105 (5): 551 – 557.

[68] Dong Q, Bárcena – Ruiz J C. Does investment in capacity encourage FDI? [J]. Economic Modelling, 2015, 51: 58 – 64.

[69] Dreher A, Mikosch H, Voigt S. Membership has its Privileges – The Effect of Membership in International Organizations on FDI[J]. World Development, 2015, 66: 346 – 358.

[70] Du L, Harrison A, Jefferson G. FDI spillovers and industrial policy: The role of tariffs and tax holidays[J]. World Development, 2014, 64: 366 – 383.

[71] Dubois P, Griffith R, Nevo A. Do prices and attributes explain international differences in food purchases? [J]. The American Economic Review, 2014, 104 (3): 832 – 867.

[72] Dudin M N, Vasil N, Sekerin V D, et al. Provision of global economic and energy security in the context of the development of the Arctic resource base by industrialized countries [J]. International Journal of Economics and Financial Issues, 2015, 5 (3S).

[73] Dye C Y, Yang C T, Kung F C. A note on "Seller's optimal credit period and cycle time in a supply chain for deteriorating items with maximum lifetime" [J]. European Journal of Operational Research, 2014, 239 (3): 868 – 871.

[74] Edmond C, Midrigan V, Xu D Y. Competition, markups, and the gains from international trade [J]. The American Economic Review, 2015, 105 (10): 3183 – 3221.

[75] Egger P H, Merlo V, Wamser G. Unobserved tax avoidance and the tax elasticity of FDI [J]. Journal of Economic Behavior & Organization, 2014, 108: 1 – 18.

[76] Elliott R J R, Zhou Y. Co-location and spatial wage spillovers in China: The role of foreign ownership and trade [J]. World Development, 2015, 66: 629 – 644.

[77] Erzurumlu Y O, Gozgor G. Co-movement of foreign direct and portfolio investments in Central and Eastern Europe [J]. International Journal of Economics and Financial Issues, 2014, 4 (3): 457.

[78] Faber B. Trade integration, market size, and industrialization: evidence from China's National Trunk Highway System [J]. Review of Economic Studies, 2014, 81 (3): 1046 – 1070.

[79] Fajgelbaum P, Grossman G M, Helpman E. A Linder hypothesis for foreign direct investment [J]. The Review of Economic Studies, 2014, 82 (1): 83 – 121.

[80] Fan L, Wilson W W, Dahl B. Risk analysis in port competition for containerized imports [J]. European Journal of Operational Research, 2015, 245 (3): 743 – 753.

[81] Fan Y, Ren S, Cai H, et al. The state's role and position in international trade: A complex network perspective [J]. Economic Modelling, 2014, 39: 71 – 81.

[82] Fatima A, Waheed A. Economic uncertainty and growth performance: a macroeconomic modeling analysis for Pakistan [J]. Quality & Quantity, 2014, 48 (3): 1361 – 1387.

[83] Feenstra R C, Romalis J. International prices and endogenous quality [J]. The

Quarterly Journal of Economics,2014,129(2):477－527.

[84]Feenstra R C,Romalis J. International prices and endogenous quality[J]. The Quarterly Journal of Economics,2014,129(2):477－527.

[85]Friesen L,Earl P E. Multipart tariffs and bounded rationality:An experimental analysis of mobile phone plan choices[J]. Journal of Economic Behavior & Organization,2015,116:239－253.

[86]Froman M. The strategic logic of trade:new rules of the road for the global market[J]. Foreign Aff. ,2014,93:111.

[87]Gereffi G. Global value chains in a post－Washington Consensus world[J]. Review of International Political Economy,2014,21(1):9－37.

[88]Ghosh A,Saha S. Price competition,technology licensing and strategic trade policy[J]. Economic Modelling,2015,46:91－99.

[89]Girma S,Gong Y,Görg H,et al. Investment liberalisation,technology take-off and export markets entry:Does foreign ownership structure matter? [J]. Journal of Economic Behavior & Organization,2015,116:254－269.

[90]Gnanendran K,Iacocca K. The point of purchase decision in a supply chain with value-added reselling[J]. International Journal of Production Research,2015,53(22):6689－6700.

[91]Goos M,Manning A,Salomons A. Explaining job polarization:Routine-biased technological change and offshoring[J]. The American Economic Review,2014,104(8):2509－2526.

[92]Gopinath G,Neiman B. Trade adjustment and productivity in large crises [J]. The American Economic Review,2014,104(3):793－831.

[93]Gordon N,Pardo S. The European Union and Israel's occupation:Using technical customs rules as instruments of foreign policy[J]. The Middle East Journal,2015,69(1):74－90.

[94]Gouidar A,Nouira R. The Impact of Misalignment on FDI in the Developing Countries [J]. International Journal of Economics and Financial Issues, 2014, 4(4):784.

[95]Gozgor G. Aggregated and disaggregated import demand in China:An empirical study[J]. Economic Modelling,2014,43:1－8.

[96]Grossman G M,Helpman E. Globalization and growth[J]. The American E-

conomic Review,2015,105(5):100 – 104.

[97]Guesmi K,Fattoum S. Return and volatility transmission between oil prices and oil-exporting and oil-importing countries[J]. Economic Modelling, 2014, 38: 305 – 310.

[98]Gui-Diby S L,Renard M F. Foreign direct investment inflows and the industrialization of African countries[J]. World Development,2015,74:43 – 57.

[99]Güney T. Environmental sustainability and pressure groups[J]. Quality & Quantity,2015,49(6):2331 – 2344.

[100]Gur N. Financial Integration, Financial Dependence and Employment Growth[J]. International Journal of Economics and Financial Issues,2015,5(2).

[101]Gurgul H,Lach. Globalization and economic growth:Evidence from two decades of transition in CEE[J]. Economic Modelling,2014,36:99 – 107.

[102]Guris S,Sacildi I S,Genc E G. Determining the Effects of the Factors on FDI in Global Crisis Period[J]. International Journal of Economics and Financial Issues,2015,5(1):1.

[103]Haan J,Sturm J E. Income Inequality,Capitalism and Ethno – Linguistic Fractionalization[C]//SSES Annual Congress 2015. 2015.

[104]Handel B,Hendel I,Whinston M D. Equilibria in health exchanges:Adverse selection versus reclassification risk[J]. Econometrica,2015,83(4):1261 – 1313.

[105]Harris L J. Overseas Chinese Remittance Firms,the Limits of State Sovereignty,and Transnational Capitalism in East and Southeast Asia,1850s – 1930s[J]. The Journal of Asian Studies,2015,74(1):129 – 151.

[106]Hasani A,Zegordi S H,Nikbakhsh E. Robust closed-loop global supply chain network design under uncertainty:the case of the medical device industry[J]. International Journal of Production Research,2015,53(5):1596 – 1624.

[107]Hassanain K. Special drawing right and currency risk management[J]. International Journal of Economics and Financial Issues,2015,5(3).

[108]Hayaloglu P. The Impact of Developments in the Logistics Sector on Economic Growth:The Case of OECD Countries[J]. International Journal of Economics and Financial Issues,2015,5(2):523 – 530.

[109]He Q,Sun M. Does fiscal decentralization promote the inflow of FDI in China?[J]. Economic Modelling,2014,43:361 – 371.

[110] Head K, Mayer T, Thoenig M. Welfare and trade without pareto[J]. The American Economic Review, 2014, 104(5):310 - 316.

[111] Herwartz H, Walle Y M. Determinants of the link between financial and economic development: Evidence from a functional coefficient model[J]. Economic Modelling, 2014, 37:417 - 427.

[112] Hills C A. NAFTA's economic upsides: The view from the United States[J]. Foreign Aff., 2014, 93:122.

[113] Hlatshwayo S, Spence M. Demand and defective growth patterns: The role of the tradable and non-tradable sectors in an open economy[J]. The American Economic Review, 2014, 104(5):272 - 277.

[114] Hochberg F P. Protecting America's Competitive Advantage[J]. Foreign Aff., 2015, 94:59.

[115] Hooy C W, Siong - Hook L, Tze - Haw C. The impact of the Renminbi real exchange rate on ASEAN disaggregated exports to China[J]. Economic Modelling, 2015, 47:253 - 259.

[116] Hove S, Mama A T, Tchana F T. Monetary policy and commodity terms of trade shocks in emerging market economies[J]. Economic Modelling, 2015, 49:53 - 71.

[117] Hsu J, Tiao Y E. Patent rights protection and foreign direct investment in Asian countries[J]. Economic Modelling, 2015, 44:1 - 6.

[118] Hu A. Embracing China's "New Normal". Why the Economy Is Still on Track[J]. Foreign Affairs, 2015, 94(3):8 - 12.

[119] Hummels D, Jørgensen R, Munch J, et al. The wage effects of offshoring: Evidence from Danish matched worker-firm data[J]. The American Economic Review, 2014, 104(6):1597 - 1629.

[120] Hye Q M A, Lau W Y, Tourres M A. Does economic liberalization promote economic growth in Pakistan? An empirical analysis[J]. Quality & Quantity, 2014, 48(4):2097 - 2119.

[121] Iamsiraroj S, Ulubaşoglu M A. Foreign direct investment and economic growth: A real relationship or wishful thinking? [J]. Economic Modelling, 2015, 51:200 - 213.

[122] Inglesi - Lotz R, Chang T, Gupta R. Causality between research output and

economic growth in BRICS[J]. Quality & Quantity,2015,49(1):167 - 176.

[123]Ivanov D,Sokolov B,Dolgui A. The Ripple effect in supply chains:trade-off 'efficiency-flexibility-resilience' in disruption management[J]. International Journal of Production Research,2014,52(7):2154 - 2172.

[124]Iwasaki I,Tokunaga M. Macroeconomic impacts of FDI in transition econo- mies:a meta-analysis[J]. World Development,2014,61:53 - 69.

[125]Iyer R,Schoar A. Ex Post(In)Efficient Negotiation and Breakdown of Trade [J]. The American Economic Review,2015,105(5):291 - 294.

[126]Jacobson T,Schedvin E. Trade credit and the propagation of corporate fail- ure:an empirical analysis[J]. Econometrica,2015,83(4):1315 - 1371.

[127]Jean S,Mulder N,Ramos M P. A general equilibrium,ex-post evaluation of the EU-Chile Free Trade Agreement[J]. Economic Modelling,2014,41:33 - 45.

[128]Kalyoncu H,Kaplan M. Analyzing the sustainability of current account in ASEAN countries:Test of intertemporal borrowing constraints[J]. International Journal of Economics and Financial Issues,2014,4(3):564.

[129]Karam F,Zaki C. Trade volume and economic growth in the MENA region: Goods or services? [J]. Economic Modelling,2015,45:22 - 37.

[130]Katircioglu S,Fethi S,Caner H. Testing the higher education-led growth hy- pothesis in a small island:an empirical investigation from a new version of the Solow growth model[J]. Quality & Quantity,2014:1 - 16.

[131]Kaya A,Vereshchagina G. Partnerships versus corporations:Moral hazard, sorting,and ownership structure[J]. The American Economic Review,2014,104(1): 291 - 307.

[132]Ke S. Domestic market integration and regional economic growth—China's recent experience from 1995 - 2011[J]. World Development,2015,66:588 - 597.

[133]Khan M A,Khan M Z,Zaman K,et al. The evolving role of agricultural technology indicators and economic growth in rural poverty:has the ideas machine bro- ken down? [J]. Quality & Quantity,2014,48(4):2007 - 2022.

[134]Kilic C,Bayar Y,Arica F. Effects of currency unions on foreign direct in- vestment inflows:the European economic and monetary union case[J]. International Journal of Economics and Financial Issues,2014,4(1):8.

[135] King C. The Decline of International Studies [J]. Foreign Aff. ,2015,

94：88.

[136] Kolpakova T V, Kuchinskaya T N. China's" New Regionalism" as a Mechanism to Strengthen the Influence of China in the Global Integration Processes：An Example of Eurasian Economic Union[J]. International Journal of Economics and Financial Issues,2015,5(2S).

[137] Konstantakis K N, Michaelides P G, Tsionas E G, et al. System estimation of GVAR with two dominants and network theory：Evidence for BRICs[J]. Economic Modelling,2015,51：604 – 616.

[138] Koopman R, Wang Z, Wei S J. Tracing value-added and double counting in gross exports[J]. The American Economic Review,2014,104(2)：459 – 494.

[139] Kosack S, Tobin J L. Which Countries' Citizens Are Better Off With Trade? [J]. World Development,2015,76：95 – 113.

[140] Krishna P, Senses M Z. International trade and labour income risk in the us [J]. Review of Economic Studies,2014,81(1)：186 – 218.

[141] Kumar R R. Exploring the nexus between capital inflows and growth in Latin America and the Caribbean：a study of clusters led by Brazil and Mexico[J]. Quality & Quantity,2014,48(5)：2537 – 2552.

[142] Kurtovic S, Talovic S. Liberalization of Trade With The EU and Its Impact on The Reduction in CEFTA 2006 Trade Balance Deficit[J]. International Journal of Economics and Financial Issues,2015,5(2).

[143] Li C, Whalley J. China's potential future growth and gains from trade policy bargaining：Some numerical simulation results [J]. Economic Modelling, 2014, 37：65 – 78.

[144] Long C, Yang J, Zhang J. Institutional impact of foreign direct investment in China[J]. World Development,2015,66：31 – 48.

[145] Macchiavello R, Morjaria A. The value of relationships：evidence from a supply shock to Kenyan rose exports[J]. The American Economic Review,2015,105(9)：2911 – 2945.

[146] Malki M, Thompson H. Morocco and the US Free Trade Agreement：A specific factors model with unemployment and energy imports[J]. Economic Modelling, 2014,40：269 – 274.

[147] Manzenreiter W. Playing by Unfair Rules? Asia's Positioning within Global

Sports Production Networks[J]. The Journal of Asian Studies,2014,73(2):313 – 325.

[148]Martí J M C,Tancrez J S,Seifert R W. Carbon footprint and responsiveness trade-offs in supply chain network design[J]. International Journal of Production Economics,2015,166:129 – 142.

[149]Matsui K. Gray-market trade with product information service in global supply chains[J]. International Journal of Production Economics,2014,147:351 – 361.

[150]Mayer T, Melitz M J, Ottaviano G I P. Market size, competition, and the product mix of exporters [J]. The American Economic Review, 2014, 104 (2): 495 – 536.

[151]Melitz M J,Redding S J. New trade models,new welfare implications[J]. The American Economic Review,2015,105(3):1105 – 1146.

[152]Melo O,Engler A,Nahuehual L,et al. Do sanitary,phytosanitary,and quality-related standards affect international trade? Evidence from Chilean fruit exports[J]. World Development,2014,54:350 – 359.

[153]Meng S. Modeling the impact of exchange rates using a multicurrency framework[J]. Economic Modelling,2015,49:223 – 231.

[154]Menyah K, Nazlioglu S, Wolde – Rufael Y. Financial development, trade openness and economic growth in African countries:New insights from a panel causality approach[J]. Economic Modelling,2014,37:386 – 394.

[155]Merlevede B,Schoors K,Spatareanu M. FDI spillovers and time since foreign entry[J]. World Development,2014,56:108 – 126.

[156]Milani F,Park S H. The effects of globalization on macroeconomic dynamics in a trade-dependent economy:The case of Korea[J]. Economic Modelling,2015,48:292 – 305.

[157]Miltenburg J. Changes in manufacturing facility – ,network – ,and strategy-types at the Michelin North America Company from 1950 to 2014 [J]. International Journal of Production Research,2015,53(10):3175 – 3191.

[158]Mirza T,Narayanan B,van Leeuwen N. Impact of Chinese growth and trade on labor in developed countries[J]. Economic Modelling,2014,38:522 – 532.

[159]Mrázová M,Neary J P. Together at last:trade costs,demand structure,and welfare[J]. The American Economic Review,2014,104(5):298 – 303.

[160]Murat M. Out of sight,not out of mind. Education networks and international

trade[J]. World Development,2014,58:53 – 66.

[161]Nadarajah S,Chan S,Afuecheta E. Extreme value analysis for emerging African markets[J]. Quality & Quantity,2014,48(3):1347 – 1360.

[162]Namini J E. The short and long-run impact of globalization if firms differ in factor input ratios[J]. Journal of Economic Dynamics and Control,2014,38:37 – 64.

[163]Naranpanawa A,Arora R. Does trade liberalization promote regional disparities? Evidence from a multiregional CGE model of India[J]. World Development, 2014,64:339 – 349.

[164]Ni W,Shu J. Trade-off between service time and carbon emissions for safety stock placement in multi-echelon supply chains[J]. International Journal of Production Research,2015,53(22):6701 – 6718.

[165]Nieminen M. Trade imbalances within the euro area and with respect to the rest of the world[J]. Economic Modelling,2015,48:306 – 314.

[166]Nocco A,Ottaviano G I P,Salto M. Monopolistic competition and optimum product selection[J]. The American Economic Review,2014,104(5):304 – 309.

[167]Nordhaus W. Climate clubs:Overcoming free-riding in international climate policy[J]. The American Economic Review,2015,105(4):1339 – 1370.

[168]Omri A,Nguyen D K,Rault C. Causal interactions between CO_2 emissions, FDI,and economic growth:Evidence from dynamic simultaneous-equation models[J]. Economic Modelling,2014,42:382 – 389.

[169]Orji A,Anthony-Orji O I,Mba P N. Financial Liberalization and Output Growth in Nigeria:Empirical Evidence from Credit Channel[J]. International Journal of Economics and Financial Issues,2015,5(1).

[170]Osborn D R,Vehbi T. Growth in China and the US:Effects on a small commodity exporter economy[J]. Economic Modelling,2015,45:268 – 277.

[171]Osigwe A C,Uzonwanne M C. Causal Relationship among Foreign Reserves, Exchange Rate and Foreign Direct Investment:Evidence From Nigeria[J]. International Journal of Economics and Financial Issues,2015,5(4).

[172]Ossa R. Trade wars and trade talks with data[J]. The American Economic Review,2014,104(12):4104 – 4146.

[173]Paravisini D,Rappoport V,Schnabl P,et al. Dissecting the effect of credit supply on trade:Evidence from matched credit-export data[J]. The Review of Econom-

ic Studies,2014,82(1):333 – 359.

[174] Pascual-Ezama D, Fosgaard T R, Cardenas J C, et al. Context-dependent cheating:Experimental evidence from 16 countries[J]. Journal of Economic Behavior & Organization,2015,116:379 – 386.

[175] Patrick S. The Unruled World:The Case for Good Enough Global Governance[J]. Foreign Aff.,2014,93:58.

[176] Phillips O R, Nagler A M, Menkhaus D J, et al. Trading partner choice and bargaining culture in negotiations[J]. Journal of Economic Behavior & Organization, 2014,105:178 – 190.

[177] Polat A, Shahbaz M, Rehman I U, et al. Revisiting linkages between financial development,trade openness and economic growth in South Africa:fresh evidence from combined cointegration test[J]. Quality & Quantity,2015,49(2):785 – 803.

[178] Priebe J, Rudolf R. Does the Chinese Diaspora Speed Up Growth in Host Countries? [J]. World Development,2015,76:249 – 262.

[179] Puga D, Trefler D. International trade and institutional change:Medieval Venice's response to globalization[J]. The Quarterly Journal of Economics,2014,129 (2):753 – 821.

[180] Rafindadi A A, Yusof Z. Are the periods of currency collapse an impediment to entrepreneurship and entrepreneurial haven? evidence from regional comparison[J]. International Journal of Economics and Financial Issues,2014,4(4):886.

[181] Ramli N A, Munisamy S. Eco-efficiency in greenhouse emissions among manufacturing industries:A range adjusted measure[J]. Economic Modelling,2015,47: 219 – 227.

[182] Ramondo N, Rodríguez-Clare A, Tintelnot F. Multinational production:Data and stylized facts[J]. The American Economic Review,2015,105(5):530 – 536.

[183] Raouf R, Hafid H. Relocation and Inequalities between Skilled and Unskilled in Northern Countries:Simulation Using a CGE Model[J]. International Journal of Economics and Financial Issues,2014,4(4):758.

[184] Raza S A, Jawaid S T. Foreign capital inflows,economic growth and stock market capitalization in Asian countries:an ARDL bound testing approach[J]. Quality & Quantity,2014:1 – 11.

[185] Rousseau K, Gautier D, Wardell D A. Coping with the upheavals of global-

ization in the shea value chain: The maintenance and relevance of upstream shea nut supply chain organization in western Burkina Faso[J]. World Development,2015,66: 413 – 427.

[186] Rubio M. Restoring America's Strength: My Vision for US Foreign Policy [J]. Foreign Aff. ,2015,94:108.

[187] Ruhl K J. How Well is US Intrafirm Trade Measured? [J]. The American Economic Review,2015,105(5):524 – 529.

[188] Saifudin A M,Zainuddin N,Bahaudin A Y,et al. Enriching students' experience in logistics and transportation through simulation[J]. International Journal of Economics and Financial Issues,2015,5(1S).

[189] Sánchez M V,Cicowiez M. Trade-offs and payoffs of investing in human development[J]. World Development,2014,62:14 – 29.

[190] Sbia R,Shahbaz M,Hamdi H. A contribution of foreign direct investment, clean energy,trade openness,carbon emissions and economic growth to energy demand in UAE[J]. Economic Modelling,2014,36:191 – 197.

[191] Shavandi H,Valizadeh Khaki S,Khedmati M. Parallel importation and price competition in a duopoly supply chain [J]. International Journal of Production Research,2015,53(10):3104 – 3119.

[192] Singh P J,Wiengarten F,Nand A A,et al. Beyond the trade-off and cumulative capabilities models:alternative models of operations strategy[J]. International Journal of Production Research,2015,53(13):4001 – 4020.

[193] Solarin S A,Eric O O. Impact of Economic Globalization on Human Capital: Evidence from Nigerian Economy[J]. International Journal of Economics and Financial Issues,2015,5(3).

[194] Soysal M,Bloemhof – Ruwaard J M,Van der Vorst J. Modelling food logistics networks with emission considerations: The case of an international beef supply chain[J]. International Journal of Production Economics,2014,152:57 – 70.

[195] Stirbat L,Record R,Nghardsaysone K. The experience of survival:Determinants of export survival in Lao PDR[J]. World Development,2015,76:82 – 94.

[196] Suresh K G, Aswal N. Determinants of India's Manufactured Exports to South and North:A Gravity Model Analysis[J]. International Journal of Economics and Financial Issues,2014,4(1):144.

[197]Tang C F,Lai Y W,Ozturk I. How stable is the export-led growth hypothesis? Evidence from Asia's Four Little Dragons[J]. Economic Modelling,2015,44: 229 – 235.

[198]Tang C F,Yip C Y,Ozturk I. The determinants of foreign direct investment in Malaysia:A case for electrical and electronic industry[J]. Economic Modelling, 2014,43:287 – 292.

[199]Tastan S,Ozekicioglu H. Development of European Union and China Bilateral Trade After The 2008 Financial Crisis:A Cluster Analysis[J]. International Journal of Economics and Financial Issues,2014,4(2):336.

[200]Teker S,Tuzla H,Pala A. Foreign Direct Investments:Asian and European Transition Economies[J]. International Journal of Economics and Financial Issues, 2014,4(1):71.

[201]Terzi S,Trezzini A,Moroni L. A PLS path model to investigate the relations between institutions and human development[J]. Quality & Quantity,2014,48(3): 1271 – 1290.

[202]The role of customer integration in extended producer responsibility:A study of Chinese export manufacturers

[203]Ting P S. Comments on the EOQ model for deteriorating items with conditional trade credit linked to order quantity in the supply chain management[J]. European Journal of Operational Research,2015,246(1):108 – 118.

[204]Tretter A,Giannopoulou G,Baer M,et al. Minimising Access Conflicts on Shared Multi-Bank Memory[J]. ACM Transactions on Embedded Computing Systems (TECS),2017,16(5s):135.

[205]Tsao Y C,Lu J C,An N,et al. Retailer shelf-space management with trade allowance:A Stackelberg game between retailer and manufacturers[J]. International Journal of Production Economics,2014,148:133 – 144.

[206]Tuinstra J,Wegener M,Westerhoff F. Positive welfare effects of trade barriers in a dynamic partial equilibrium model[J]. Journal of Economic Dynamics and Control,2014,48:246 – 264.

[207]Vanhnalat B,Phonvisay A,Sengsourivong B. Assessment the Effect of Free Trade Agreements on Exports of Lao PDR[J]. International Journal of Economics and Financial Issues,2015,5(2).

[208] Vespignani J L. International transmission of monetary shocks to the Euro area: Evidence from the US, Japan and China[J]. Economic Modelling, 2015, 44: 131 – 141.

[209] von Massow M, Canbolat M. A strategic decision framework for a value added supply chain [J]. International journal of production research, 2014, 52 (7): 1940 – 1955.

[210] Wahiba N F, El Weriemmi M. The relationship between economic growth and income inequality[J]. International Journal of Economics and Financial Issues, 2014, 4(1): 135.

[211] Wang M, Wong M C S, Granato J. International comovement of economic fluctuations: A spatial analysis[J]. World Development, 2015, 67: 186 – 201.

[212] Wilson M. NAFTA's Unfinished Business: The View from Canada[J]. Foreign Aff. , 2014, 93: 128.

[213] Wubs – Mrozewicz J. Cities of Commerce: The Institutional Foundations of International Trade in the Low Countries, 1250 – 1650, by Oscar Gelderblom[J]. 2015.

[214] Zhang C, Guo B, Wang J. The different impacts of home countries characteristics in FDI on Chinese spillover effects: based on one-stage SFA[J]. Economic Modelling, 2014, 38: 572 – 580.

[215] Zhang J, Cui Z, Zu L. The evolution of free trade networks[J]. Journal of Economic Dynamics and Control, 2014, 38: 72 – 86.

[216] Zhang Q, Dong M, Luo J, et al. Supply chain coordination with trade credit and quantity discount incorporating default risk[J]. International Journal of Production Economics, 2014, 153: 352 – 360.

[217] Zhou J, Latorre M C. How FDI influences the triangular trade pattern among China, East Asia and the US? A CGE analysis of the sector of Electronics in China [J]. Economic Modelling, 2014, 44: S77 – S88.

[218] Zorzini M, Stevenson M, Hendry L C. Coordinating offshored operations in emerging economies: A contingency-based study[J]. International Journal of Production Economics, 2014, 153: 323 – 339.